THE
ISRAELI
CONNECTION

THE
ISRAELI
CONNECTION

WHO ISRAEL ARMS
AND WHY

BENJAMIN
BEIT-HALLAHMI

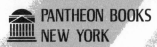

PANTHEON BOOKS
NEW YORK

All rights reserved under International and Pan-American Copyright
Conventions. Published in the United States by Pantheon Books, a division of
Random House, Inc., New York, and simultaneously in Canada by Random
House of Canada Limited, Toronto.

Library of Congress Cataloging-in-Publication Data

Beit-Hallahmi, Benjamin.
    The Israeli connection.

    Bibliography: p.
    Includes index.
    1. Israel—Military relations—Developing countries.
2. Developing countries—Military relations—Israel.
3. Munitions—Israel.   4. Israel—Military policy.
I. Title.
UA853.I8B385   1987   355′.032′095694   87-60154
ISBN 0-394-55922-3

Book design by The Sarabande Press

First American Edition

Manufactured in the United States of America

Contents

Contents

Acknowledgments

The completion of a book is customarily the occasion for a profusion of thanks and expressions of indebtedness to all those without whom the book could not have been produced. In this particular case it is no exaggeration or protestation. Indeed, this book could not have been written without the friendship, trust, support, and help—in many and varied ways—that came from numerous individuals and institutions.

The actual writing of this book took place while I was in residence at Stony Point Center, in Stony Point, New York. The Center was to me more than a home. It provided unlimited love and comfort, while making very few demands. In doing my research, I was fortunate to have access to the staff and collections of the University of Haifa library, the Elmer Holmes Bobst Library at New York University, and the Lehman Library at Columbia University. A grant from the American Middle East Peace Research Institute (AMEPRI) covered expenses related to researching and writing the book.

I would like to name below those individuals who not only supported me and helped me in my work, but made the whole project worthwhile. Many of them never realized how much help they provided. The idea for the book, incidentally, came from one of them: Mehdi Abhari, Florence Anson, Hanni Amit-Kochavi, Eqbal Ahmad, Yossi Amitai, Geoffrey Aronson, Margaret Brown, Deonne Barkley, Noam Chomsky, Erik Cohen, Margaret Flory, John S. Friedman, Angela Gelliam, Maxim Ghilan, Joseph C. Gerson, Yerach Gover, Stanley B. Greenberg, Arie Grumet, Nubar Hovsepian, Paul A. Hopkins, Edward Huenemann, Edna H. Hunt, Bill Johnston, Benjamin Joseph, Alex Massis, Seymour Melman, Kathy Meyer, Val Moghadam, James Palm, Louise Palm, James Peck, Victor Perera, Don Peretz, Roger Rosen, Cheryl Rubenberg, Edward W. Said, Milton

Acknowledgments

Schwebel, Paul Seto, Selma Seto, Talia Shay, Allan Salomonow, Stuart Schaar, Israel Shahak, Margaret O. Thomas, Madeleine Tress, Gordon Webster, Don Will, and Andrew Weir.

While the friendship and support offered by these individuals has been vital and indispensable to the completion of my work, I alone am responsible for what I have written, and all remaining faults in this book are mine.

Prologue:
Vorster in
Jerusalem, 1976

The journey that led me to the writing of this book started more than ten years ago, one night in April of 1976. I was sitting in my apartment in Haifa, watching the evening news on Israeli television. There were no particularly noteworthy events that day, and viewers were treated to a series of segments from here and there showing a variety of fairly routine happenings. I don't remember any of the others, but there was one segment I immediately responded to, and that became, to me at least, an important event. In it Balthazar Johannes (John) Vorster, the prime minister of the Republic of South Africa, was shown on the first day of his official visit in Israel. And what Israeli television broadcast to its viewers that night were images of Mr. Vorster as he visited Yad Vashem, the Holocaust memorial in Jerusalem.

A visit to Yad Vashem is the opening ritual of every state visit to Israel—usually the first stop en route from the airport to a hotel in Jerusalem. The aim of this ritual is to express Israel's relation to the Holocaust, to present the country as the haven for survivors and as the answer to the insecurity of Jewish existence in the Diaspora. A second aim is to induce the appropriate feelings of guilt in the visitor. So, when John Vorster was taken to the Yad Vashem memorial hall, he was being treated just like any other visitor.

What struck me as I watched Vorster on television was the surreal nature of the scene. The tactlessness of the Israeli Foreign Office, which had invited a known Nazi collaborator to a memorial to the victims of Nazism, and then subjected him to a lecture on the Nazis, was astounding. It was obvious that Vorster could have given a better lecture himself, but his reaction was proper and diplomatic. He listened patiently and nodded in all the right places, and then signed his name in the visitors' book.

What was the purpose of showing this on television? Why was that scene chosen to illustrate the first day of the Vorster visit? Why not something else? I started thinking, and I could not escape the conclusion that this bizarre incident was telling me something about Israel. It wasn't just its insensitivity. It was a wild sense of staging that turned the strange into the familiar. The scene was indeed strange, but its truth was haunting. And then I got the message: Vorster in the Holocaust memorial! What an image of Israel! Maybe it was the true image of Israel, staged for our benefit by a director of rare comic genius. Here was an old Nazi sympathizer showing more tact than his hosts, and at the same time exposing them to ridicule and criticism. Even if the manifold meanings of this work of art were lost on most of the viewers, no real film director searching for an anti-Israeli scene could have come up with a better one than this.

For most Israelis, the Vorster visit was just another state visit by a foreign leader. It did not draw much attention. Most Israelis did not even remember his name, and did not see anything unusual, much less surreal, in the scene: Vorster was just another visiting dignitary being treated to the usual routine. He was described by most of the Israeli press as a deeply religious man on a personal pilgrimage to the Holy Land, as well as a sincere friend of Israel. Both characterizations might have been true, but they hardly gave readers a well-rounded picture of John Vorster as a political leader. It took a letter to the editor of *Haaretz*, Israel's *New York Times*, to inform the public that Vorster had been a Nazi collaborator who, according to Israeli law, should have been arrested and put on trial the minute he set foot on Israeli soil. Instead, he landed at the Tel-Aviv airport, the red carpet was rolled out, and Israel's prime minister, Yitzhak Rabin, greeted him with a warm hug. There were plenty of welcoming articles in the Israeli press. The only exceptions to the chorus were two of Israel's distinguished radical journalists, Yuri Avneri and Amnon Kapeliouk.

As I watched the passing shadows on the television screen, I felt I had stumbled upon a deeply symbolic image expressive of the nature of the State of Israel. Some may find this an unjustified exaggeration or a groundless accusation: the scene by itself, some would say, might have been mere coincidence. But was it, really? Was this surreal image only a fleeting cloud in the blue skies of Zionist history, or was it bone of its bone, flesh of its flesh? Was it an aberration, a detour from the main road, or was it a symptom of something deeper and more significant?

I decided I had to decipher the message hidden in this image, and I promised myself that I would get to the bottom of the Israel–South Africa connection. I started reading up on it and collecting every bit of information I could get my hands on. In December of 1976, I submitted to *New Outlook,* the Israeli peace-movement monthly, an article on the Israel–South Africa alliance, the first fruits of my work. The editors, representing the best in progressive Zionism, were not completely ready to accept my assessment of the situation and edited the article, toning down its language. The article was then subjected to military censorship, which eliminated all references to military and nuclear matters. It finally appeared in a much-muted form in the April-May 1977 issue.

As time passed, my files on the Israel–South Africa alliance kept growing, with press clippings and reports. In the late 1970s, another part of the world caught the media's attention: in July of 1979, the evening news one Friday night showed Sandinista rebels, in their advance toward Managua, uncovering brand-new Israeli rifles, sent from Israel to Anastasio Somoza in his last days. One of the Sandinistas expressed his amazement, as he opened a box of the rifles, that Israel would support Somoza. I started another file, this one on Central America; soon it, too, bulged with clippings and booklets. My growing collection of files covering Israeli involvements all over the globe, from Manila to Managua, forced me to realize that I was indeed exploring a global strategy, and that understanding it would require a more extensive effort.

The extent of Israeli activities in the Third World is baffling and disquieting to both friends and foes of Israel. Looking at the whole picture, and trying to discern an underlying pattern, both may wonder what its strategy really is. Mention any trouble spot in the Third World over the past ten years, and, inevitably, you will find smiling Israeli officers and shiny Israeli weapons on the news pages. The images have become familiar: the Uzi submachine gun or the Galil assault rifle, with Israeli officers named Uzi and Galil, or Golan, for good measure. We have seen them in South Africa, Iran, Nicaragua, El Salvador, Guatemala, Haiti, Namibia, Taiwan, Indonesia, the Philippines, Chile, Bolivia, and many other places. From Manila to San Salvador, from Seoul to Tegucigalpa, from Walvis Bay to Guatemala City, from Taipei to Port-au-Prince, Israeli civilians and military men have been helping, in their own words, in "the defense of the West."

In the chapters that follow, I will present many facts about Israeli involvement in the Third World, and then offer an analysis of how that involvement is related to the history of Zionism and of the State of Israel. Most of the facts are beyond dispute. What is in dispute is their meaning, and the correct way to interpret them. My aim is to answer the following questions: Is there a coherent strategy, a coherent policy, a coherent worldview, that explains these disparate activities? And, if there is one, what is its essence?

We are concerned here with the actions of the State of Israel on a global scale. To determine whether what Israel has been doing in the Third World (beyond the boundaries of the Middle East) is a temporary aberration or a basic policy, we have to look at it methodically, observing how it changes over time and how it may be related to other events, policies, and beliefs. Only then will we be able to pass judgment. The aim of writing history is to discover shapes, patterns, and designs in the flux of human events. We discover connections, and then we realize we face whole themes, repeated time and again, as in a symphony. But it is always a difficult and dangerous task. For if we are searching for one red thread that runs through all of Israel's global actions, we will not find it. The world is too complex for simple explanations.

So let me state quite clearly what this book is not. It is not a presentation of a conspiracy theory or of the One Theory That Will Explain Everything. If there is such a theory, it certainly cannot explain much. There are exceptions to every rule; more importantly, human behavior is filled with inconsistencies, errors, and oversights. Many decisions are made on the basis of such errors and misconceptions. Nevertheless, we may find themes and relationships that will explain much of what is going on.

This book is also not an encyclopedia of all Israeli activities in the Third World, and not just because such an encyclopedia is an impossible undertaking. We have enough facts to go on, and the ones presented here have all been checked and doublechecked, but they serve merely as illustrations.

There are several levels of Israeli activities vis-à-vis the rest of the world that have to be looked at in order to assess Israeli ideology and foreign policy. First, there is the official diplomatic level, which includes diplomatic contacts and statements made in the context of state-to-state dialogue or at the United Nations. Second, there is the area of military cooperation, ranging from arms sales to military training in the host country to military advisers in the client country. This is an area that is usually kept covert by the Israeli government. Third, there are secret operations aimed at gaining influence and intelligence conducted by the Mossad, the Israeli equivalent of the U.S. Central Intelligence Agency. And fourth, there are private activities that may be connected with all three of the above.

One of our problems in presenting the facts and analyzing them stems from the reality of modern power politics, in which much of what goes on, and much of what is important, comes under the heading of covert operations, and is thus kept hidden from our searching eyes. In writing this book, I had no access to the classified files of various governments. I naturally feel hampered by this, but the amount of information available from open sources is so huge that my objective was nonetheless attainable.

To understand recent Israeli involvement in the Third World we need to go back to events of the 1950s and 1960s, and, in many cases, even before that. In trying to identify patterns, we can learn much about the Israeli *modus operandi* from the history of such cases as Somoza in Nicaragua, the shah in Iran, Idi Amin in Uganda, and the relations with Portugal and its African colonies. From Israeli actions in Lebanon, Iran, Sudan, Morocco, and other places, we can formulate some ideas about its present activities.

What the past teaches us is quite clear. First, there is a pattern of serious and deep Israeli involvement in supporting certain regimes in the Third World. Second, most of the details of these involvements are not known while they take place, so that reliance on open sources will inevitably lead us to underestimate the extent of these involvements. Consequently, present Israeli activities are probably much wider and deeper than we have been told in public forums or the media. For example, what was known of Israel's involvement with the shah's regime in Iran was, at the time, hardly anything compared to what we know today.

On November 1, 1986, a little-known Beirut weekly published the preliminary details of what was to become Irangate, then Contragate. The Iran-contra affair seems like a clear vindication of the thesis presented in this book, but my aim is to go further than that. The media have provided a constant bombardment of disclosures, most of them tangential to the substantial iceberg lying below the exposed tip. This book deals with what does not get published most of the time: the patterns and the continuities. It will serve as a useful guide to what will be published in the future, as Israel's world war goes on, and more stories unfold.

Some of the things you are about to read may sound fantastic, but, as we have already seen, some of the most obvious facts in this story *are* fantastic enough. Whenever you are in doubt about anything you read in this book, remember Vorster in the Holocaust memorial.

THE
ISRAELI
CONNECTION

1

Fighting Radicalization in the Middle East and Beyond

o understand contemporary Israeli behavior, we have to go back to the 1950s. The decade opened with the triumph of Zionism, a triumph so great it seemed like a prophecy fulfilled. Theodor Herzl, the founder of political Zionism, was a visionary and prophet. Most Israelis know Herzl's words by heart: in 1897, following the first Zionist Congress, he said, "It may take five years or fifty years, but the Jewish state is a fact now." And indeed, on November 29, 1947, the United Nations General Assembly passed Resolution 181(II), which called for the partition of Palestine and the creation of a Jewish state. The Jewish state became a fact of life during the 1948 war, in which the Jewish community of Palestine defeated the Arabs of Palestine and of neighboring countries, and established the State of Israel.

The achievement of Jewish sovereignty in Palestine seems even today like a miracle. On January 1, 1948, there were over 600,000 Jews in Palestine—and twice as many Arabs. On January 1, 1950, the new state of Israel had only about 150,000 Arab inhabitants. The biggest problem of Zionism had been solved, and the Arab majority in Palestine became a minority almost overnight. The 1948 war was not only a total defeat for the Palestinians, but for the whole Arab world. The Arabs were left humiliated and dazed, still waiting for the new Saladin, who would unite them to match the might of the new Crusaders.

The leaders of Israel looked at the world in 1950 with a reasonable and justified amount of confidence. The army that had fought and won the 1948 war was demobilized. The surrounding Arab countries had signed cease-fire agreements with Israel, one by one, and thus recognized the new state *de facto*. Most of the Palestinians were powerless refugees, and thus posed no threat. The United States, France, West Germany, and Britain were Israel's major benefactors in the 1950s, and other European countries were sympathetic. Decolonization of the Third World was still in an early, uncertain stage. An Israeli observer remembers the 1950s as a time of "ultimately different strategic conditions. On the global level there was an American superiority over the Soviet Union. On the regional level, under the Western umbrella, Israel had a strategic advantage over the Arabs" (Kesse, 1983, p. 8).* Nevertheless, there were problems for Israel on the horizon.

The 1950s presented Israel with a novel and serious challenge. The Arab regimes Israeli leaders had dealt with earlier were feudal, reactionary, and corrupt. Israel prevailed over them militarily and diplomatically. Following the Arab defeat in 1948, however, those regimes began to disappear one by one, as a shock wave of radicalization started changing the face of the Arab world. King Abdullah ibn Hussein of Jordan was assassinated in 1950. Egypt, in many ways the most important Arab state, was experiencing a revolution, starting in 1952. Syria was radicalized, and then Iraq. This changing Arab world represented a new and serious threat, requiring new strategies. The new Arab world, following the lead of Nasser's Egypt, divorced itself

*References are listed alphabetically at the back of the book.

from the European powers and began to form alliances within the Third World as well as with the Second World of the Soviet bloc. As decolonization of the old European empires began, the Arabs found acceptance, quite naturally, among the emerging new nations, as shown at the Bandung Conference of nonaligned nations in April 1955. The developing alliances between Arabs and the rest of the Third World were a clear threat to Israel, as were the alliances between Arab countries and the Soviet Union.

David Ben-Gurion, Israel's founding father, said in January 1957, "From the point of view of our existence and security, the friendship of one European country is more valuable than the views of all the people of Asia" (Medzini, 1976, p. 75). And of Moshe Dayan, one observer wrote, "According to him the Jewish people has a mission, especially its Israeli branch. In this part of the world, it has to be a rock, an extension of the West, against which the waves of Nasser's Arab nationalism will be broken" (Schweitzer, 1958, p. 3).

Such attitudes were characteristic of Israel's leaders in the 1950s. In Ben-Gurion's plan for a Middle East "settlement," presented at the Sèvres Conference between the leaders of France and Israel in October 1956, he argues that "Jordan has no right to exist and should be divided. East of the Jordan River, it will become part of Iraq, and Arab [Palestinian] refugees will be settled there. The West Bank will be annexed to Israel, as an autonomous region. Lebanon will get rid of its Moslem regions to assure stability based on the Christian part. Britain will hold sway over Iraq, including the East Bank, and the southern Arabian Peninsula. France—over Lebanon, perhaps Syria, with close ties to Israel. The Suez Canal will be internationalized, and the Red Sea straits will be under Israeli control" (Dayan, 1976, p. 255). Ben-Gurion's new Middle East was but an old, colonized one, with Israel in alliance with Britain and France. Ben-Gurion simply could not imagine a Middle East without colonialism, because he thought such a region would be too dangerous for Israel's survival. In his mind, the region would have to be recolonized, and Israel would help with the job.

It was clear to Israeli leaders from the early 1950s on that any radical movement aimed at furthering the progress of decolonization in the Third World, and within the Middle East specifically, was a threat, and Israel had to act accordingly. It is in this light that we should consider Israel's actions toward Egypt after the 1952 revolution and toward independence movements in North Africa throughout the decade. Two telling events from the 1950s are the surrealistic 1954 Cairo "mishap" and the 1956 Suez War.

The prospect of British evacuation of Egypt, which meant complete Egyptian independence, was viewed with alarm by the leaders of Israel. On July 16, 1954, the defense minister, Pinhas Lavon, held a meeting at his home to discuss "the meaning of the British evacuation of Suez." Mr. Lavon presented the idea of "operating against British objectives in Egypt," and later that month, amateurish sabotage acts were carried out against Egyptian and American targets there. The goal of these actions, according to the head of the Mossad at the time, was "to undermine the confidence of the West in the existing regime by creating public disorder," creating a crisis that would prevent the British evacuation from taking place (Harel, 1982, p. 126). The group that was to cause the crisis by its sabotage was a cell of Egyptian Jews, under the control of Israeli military intelligence. At the end of July 1954 it was ordered to plant bombs in U.S. and British installations in Cairo and Alexandria. The members of the cell were young amateurs, and their operators made every possible mistake known to the readers of spy books; they botched the job miserably. All the members were arrested. The Israeli government officially described the arrests and the ensuing trial as "blood libel." One Israeli agent committed suicide, two Egyptian Jews were hanged, and the others were sentenced to prison terms.

The Israeli commitment to opposing decolonization in the Middle East in the 1950s culminated in the invasion of Egypt in October 1956—a joint operation of France, Britain, and Israel in an attempt to destroy the radical Nasser regime. Egypt's nationalizing the Suez Canal had been its final declaration of true independence, and it brought about an attempt by the regional colonial powers to reverse the process. Israel was a willing partner in this scheme.

There is a clear connection between the Israeli "mishap" of 1954 and the Suez War of 1956. The same perceptions, the same goals, and the same failures can be observed in both cases. Stopping decolonization, even at the last moment, seems to have been the guiding aim. In Israel the 1956 Suez War was hailed as a "preemptive war" (though it also gave rise to a wave of yearnings for imperial status—Ben-

Gurion himself spoke of "the Third Kingdom of Israel," and vowed never to return Sinai to Egypt). The reality of the war was different, however, and in retrospect can be seen simply as an attempt by the declining colonial powers to regain their domination, with the help of their Middle East ally.

FRANCE AND ISRAEL
IN THE 1950s

The alliance between Israel and France in the 1950s can serve as a model for Israel's interventions in the Third World in the 1980s. It was created as France's colonial empire disintegrated: France's defeat in Vietnam was followed by rebellions in its North African colonies, where the Arab natives were claiming their rights to complete independence. A community of interests between Israel and France made an alliance natural. Israeli leaders saw the prospect of more independent countries in the Arab world as a direct threat. Both France and Israel were committed to stopping decolonization in North Africa and the Middle East, and thus an "eternal friendship," in the words of Shimon Peres, was formed.

France quickly became Israel's main arms supplier and then Israel's fighting partner in the 1956 Suez War. "French military circles, convinced that the Suez Canal was strategically vital, from 1954 on had their eyes on Israel, which was located not only atop the Red Sea, and so on line with Djibouti, but on the other side of the canal." The military alliance between Israel and France was most intimate, but it was more favored by the French defense establishment than by the civilian government. The defense establishment "developed the *guerre revolutionnaire* school of thought—the official doctrine of the French army and the pattern of action for Algeria which had grown out of the defeat in Indochina. They could see developments in the Middle East as a Communist phenomenon, assume that Arab nationalism was Communist subversion in another guise, and believe that the Algerian war, the Suez invasion, and support for Israel were integral to a global crusade against Communism." Most of the French generals "were particularly in tune with Israel's philosophy of political behavior and active military defense. More important, the military were the first . . . to regard the military establishment of Israel as a

7

future ally, an instrument for remote control in the area" (Crosbie, 1974, p. 18).

Against the Arabs of the Middle East and North Africa, fighting for their independence, Israel and France presented a united front of European domination. "According to General Maurice Challe, the Israelis were 'consummate artists' at dealing with the Arabs. General Challe hoped, moreover, to use the Israeli [kibbutz] as a model for his pacification program in Algeria" (p. 107). The French colonialists felt they could learn a lesson or two from the Israelis.

Many of the military men who supported the French-Israeli alliance most avidly were "survivors of Dienbienphu who had also been involved in the Suez invasion and the North African campaigns" (p. 119). These old colonial warriors had come to see Israel as their natural ally. Explaining the enthusiastic support of the French Defense Ministry for Israel, as opposed to the lukewarm attitude of the Foreign Ministry, Shimon Peres said in 1956, "The Defence Ministry sees in Israel 1.6 million people, and it sees 1.6 million Frenchmen in Algeria" (Golan, 1982, p. 43).

THE "PERIPHERY STRATEGY": FIGHTING ARAB ENCIRCLEMENT

In the 1950s, Israeli leaders formulated a geopolitical survival strategy to deal with the emerging Arab decolonization around them. The "periphery" plan was based on the idea that Israel should create alliances with the non-Arab nations on the periphery of the Arab Middle East, countries such as Turkey, Ethiopia (see chapter 3), and Iran, in order to outflank the bordering Arab states. Over the years, the strategy has called for ties with the Phalangists in Lebanon, royalists in Yemen, rebels in Southern Sudan (see chapter 3), and Kurds in Iraq. It has called for encouraging non-Arab and non-Moslem minorities in the Middle East—among them the Lebanese Maronites, the Druze, and the Kurds—to seek political independence in cooperation with Israel. These facts have become the basis of Israel's geostrategy in the Middle East.

Iran

Iran was the great hope of the periphery strategy, a hope realized and utilized to an impressive extent. The success of the strategy in Iran, however, became known only after the alliance itself had collapsed under the pressures of Islamic fundamentalism. Still, Israel was second only to the United States in its involvement and influence in Iran, and in some areas, such as domestic intelligence, Israeli involvement was even greater. Describing the events of 1979, one observer wrote: "It was an extraordinary revolution on all counts, and its success caused the United States and Israel their worst strategic defeat in the past thirty years" (Segev, 1981, p. 43). But even Khomeini's rise to power and the internal changes in Iran did not completely discourage those in Israel who still dream of a revival of this grand alliance, as we shall see.

Israeli contacts with Iran started in 1948, but did not reach a level of real closeness until the late 1960s (Bialer, 1985). However, 1957 saw the cementing of contacts between the two countries that later developed into an "unwritten pact" (Bar-Zohar, 1977). In September 1957, there was a meeting in Paris between the Iranian deputy prime minister, General Tymor Bakhtiar, and the Israeli ambassador to Paris, Yaakov Tzur. Also present at the meeting was Yaakov Karoz, Mossad station chief in Paris, who later coordinated all contacts with Iran. In October, there was a meeting in Rome between Bakhtiar and Karoz, and in December, Karoz visited Teheran. In 1958, an Israeli "trade mission" was opened in Teheran, and this remained the official cover for the Israeli operation for years to come.

The year 1958 saw a surge of radicalism in the Arab world and a time of reversals for Israel. The unification of Syria and Egypt in February, and the revolution in Iraq, followed by an Iraq-Jordan federation, caused much anxiety in Israel. David Ben-Gurion wrote a personal message to Mohammed Reza Pahlavi proposing a closer alliance, in view of the threat to the "Free World" (Segev, 1981). In December 1958, the Iranian government decided to reactivate its diplomatic mission in Tel-Aviv, which had lain dormant since 1951. (Officially, the new mission was only an interests section in the Swiss embassy.) At the same time, the Israeli diplomatic mission in Teheran was expanded.

9

The Israeli Connection

Despite the fact that Iran and Israel never established official diplomatic relations, the existence of an Israeli embassy in Teheran was well known. One political scientist painted a picture of extensive cooperation between the two countries, as Iran "supplies much of Israel's oil needs despite the Arab boycott. Israel is presently training more than 1500 rural cooperative workers and it has helped Iranian tourism and agricultural development. In another area, although not generally known, Iran maintains a close military liaison with Israel's army staff. . . . The magnitude of the Iran-Israel program remains generally secret" (Bayne, 1965, p. 247). In December of 1961 there was a secret visit to Teheran by David Ben-Gurion on his way to an official visit in Burma. In June 1966, on the way back from a visit to Africa, Israeli prime minister Levi Eshkol stopped in Teheran and met with Iranian prime minister Amir Abbas Hoveida. After the 1967 war, Iran and Israel cooperated on developing a new pipeline from Eilat to the Mediterranean, which was completed in December 1969, enabling Iran to bypass the closed Suez Canal. Golda Meir, as prime minister, visited Teheran in May 1972 at the invitation of the shah. It is said that the shah was the originator of the idea of a peace settlement between Egypt and Israel, and tried to mediate between Anwar al-Sadat and Golda Meir (Segev, 1981).

The growing significance of the Iran-Israel alliance to Israel is underscored by the number of visits made by Israeli leaders to the shah's palace in the 1970s. According to Uri Lubrani, who was then Israeli ambassador to Iran, between 1974 and 1979 there were three visits by Yitzhak Rabin (prime minister, 1974–1977), two by Yigal Allon (foreign minister, 1974–1977), three by Moshe Dayan (foreign minister, 1977–1979), one by Shimon Peres (defense minister, 1974–1977), and one by Menahem Begin (prime minister, 1977–1983). The man who hosted all these visits was Nematollah Nasiri, deputy prime minister and head of SAVAK, the Iranian secret police (Lubrani, 1980). And all the visits had the explicit approval of the shah. In addition, Abbas Ali Khalatbari, Iran's foreign minister, visited Israel in 1977 as the guest of Yigal Allon.

One reason the shah decided to move toward contacts with Israel as early as 1949 was reportedly his recognition that American Jews could help improve his fortunes with the U.S. Congress (Segev, 1981). The legendary Israel lobby in Washington has attracted the attention of many Third World regimes, and the shah, having his troubles with U.S. public opinion, was no different than other rulers who see Israel as omnipotent on the domestic political scene in the United States.

While the shah and his officials believed that Israel could sway public opinion in the United States, it was Uri Lubrani who suggested to them in 1976 that they organize a public-relations campaign there. The idea for the proposed campaign was handled by Shlomo Argov, then deputy director-general of the Israeli Foreign Ministry. He mobilized the services of Daniel Yankelovitch, the well-known New York public-relations expert, but it does not seem that the campaign had much of an effect.

Military cooperation between Iran and Israel throughout the period was extensive, and included both arms sales and training of Iranian officers in ground warfare, intelligence, counterintelligence, and air warfare (Rivlin and Fomerand, 1976). From 1954 on, SAVAK got guidance and training from the CIA and Turkey, as well as Israel (Ledeen and Lewis, 1982). A permanent representative of the Israeli Defense Force was sent to Teheran in 1955, later officially becoming a military attaché. It is reported that "innumerable Iranians, including many in a position to know, told me that the Israelis oversee SAVAK techniques" (Sale, 1977, p. A7).

In January 1963 there was an official and public visit to Teheran by Israel's chief-of-staff, Zvi Tzur, a clear indication of the growing importance of the alliance and of the increasing role of military cooperation in it. Israel offered the Iranian army help and advice when it was fighting dissident tribesmen in southern Iran in 1963 (Reppa, 1974). In 1964, Iran bought a large quantity of Uzi submachine guns. (When Saudi King Faisal visited Iran in 1965, the parading Iranian soldiers were equipped with the Israeli Uzis. The Uzi has since become the standard issue for the Revolutionary Guard under Khomeini.)

One Israeli-Iranian project that indicates the intimacy of the alliance was to develop a long-range missile capable of carrying nuclear warheads. The missile was the product of Israeli research and development, starting in the late 1950s. In the spring of 1977, Israeli Defense Minister Shimon Peres signed a secret agreement in Teheran for the development of a more advanced missile. Iran was to finance it through the delivery of $1 billion worth of oil to Israel, and would also provide a special airport, an assembly plant, and the site for a long-range test. The project was halted by the end of the shah's reign; its details were revealed when the new Iranian regime published documents found in the Israeli embassy building in Teheran (Bailey, 1986; Sciolino, 1986a). These secret documents also revealed that Israel had tried to interest the Iranians in the Lavi project, the ambitious plan to produce a state-of-the-art jet fighter by the 1990s.

Trade relations between Israel and Iran were also extensive. In 1973, Israeli exports to Iran amounted to $33 million, in 1974 to $63 million, and in 1977 to $195 million. By 1978, Israeli exports, including military equipment, amounted to $225 million, 7 percent of total Israeli exports. Most leading Israeli corporations had profitable business deals with the Iranian government, gaining numerous contracts for construction and supply. El Al, the national airline, started flying to Teheran once a week in 1960, and had at least one flight a day in the 1970s. El Al also operated, starting in 1962, the Tel-Aviv–Teheran–Nairobi–Johannesburg route, which "brought much benefit to the four countries involved" (Segev, 1981, p. 94).

The end of the shah's regime did not come as a complete surprise to Israel, but Israeli leaders were hoping for its survival even when it seemed beyond hope. On June 13, 1978, Ambassador Lubrani submitted a memorandum to Prime Minister Begin in which he stated that the shah's regime was on the verge of collapse and could be expected to come to an end within two to three years. According to some reports, Ariel Sharon advocated an Israeli military intervention in order to prevent the downfall of the shah. In September of that year Lubrani was replaced by Joseph Hermelin, former (1964–1974) director of SHABAK (Israel's internal security service) and future ambassador to Pretoria. The Israeli government was hoping, as late as January 1979, for a military takeover in Iran, so Hermelin and a group of twenty embassy officials stayed on in Teheran until February 18, 1979, when they were evacuated together with the last eight hundred Americans (Segev, 1984). Huge political demonstrations took place in Teheran in February 1979, and "in the eyes of the demonstrators there was a connection between the United States and Israel and the shah, and so these two countries became the most hated in Iran" (Segev, 1981, p. 64).

The Iran-Iraq war, which started in September 1980 with an

Iraqi attack, has been a source of increased business for arms merchants all over the world. At last count, there were twenty-nine arms suppliers to Iran, including Israel, Libya, North Korea, South Korea, South Africa, Syria, China, and Taiwan, and twenty-one to Iraq. In fact, most of the countries in the world that export arms are involved directly or indirectly, including the United States and the Soviet Union, and many of the sellers have crossed normal political boundaries in order to make a profit from the continuing misery in the region.

A BBC *Panorama* program shown on Israeli state television on February 8, 1982, included interviews with David Kimche, director-general of the Foreign Ministry (and former deputy Mossad chief), former ambassador Lubrani, and General Yaakov Nimrodi, former military attaché to Teheran. Kimche spoke about the need to supply equipment to the Iranian military, as well as the need to keep the Iranian military strong. Lubrani went further, and recommended a military coup against the Khomeini government: Teheran could be taken by a hundred tanks, with "only" ten thousand dead. He made it clear that Israel was eager for a coup without delay, as opposed to the United States, which was slow in reaching a decision (Schiff, 1982).

Defense Minister Ariel Sharon, during a visit to the United States in May 1982, was the first to disclose that Israel had sold military equipment to the Khomeini regime, valued at $27 million. In a news conference in Paris on September 28, 1983, Sharon said that Israel was selling arms to Iran with the consent of the United States. Israeli ambassador to the United States (and later defense minister) Moshe Arens said in October 1982 that Israeli arms supplies to Iran were taking place in coordination with the highest levels of the U.S. government. The logic behind these supplies, according to Arens, was to keep channels to the Iranian military open, with the ultimate aim of bringing down the Khomeini regime (Frenkel, 1983b). During an appearance at a synagogue in Bridgeport, Connecticut, in May 1984, Sharon said again that Israeli arms supplies to Iran were made with the knowledge of the U.S. government (Reuters, 1984). He explained that Israel wished Iran to win against Iraq, which is an Arab enemy state.

In July 1981, Israel agreed to sell Iran significant quantities of ammunition totaling $135.8 million. The contract was signed by Yaakov Nimrodi, who has been active as an arms salesman since his retirement from government service in 1968 (Eytan, 1983a). Another contract, signed in January 1983, was worth $21 million (Eytan, 1983b). Later in 1983, the Israeli Defense Ministry planned a huge arms deal to sell five hundred M-48 tanks. The deal was ultimately aborted because of U.S. objections. One journalist even claimed that Israeli arms were shipped to Iran by way of Syria, and that Israel was a major source of crucial spare parts for Iran's F-4 Phantom jets, the mainstay of its air force (Kestin, 1984).

For eighteen months, between the summer of 1985 and October 1986, there were contacts and arms deals, between the United States and the Islamic Republic of Iran. In this affair Israel had a major role, as the source of ideas, connections, and arms. When the American involvement became known, it led to a major political crisis in the United States, and to additional disclosures about other joint American-Israeli operations. Actually, as shown above, the United States was involved in all earlier Israeli contacts, without exception. The prime minister's office in Jerusalem stated on May 30, 1982, "This topic [of contacts with Iran] was discussed with American leaders at the highest levels, and actions were carried out with their knowledge" (Sharon, 1986, p. 13).

The Iran-contra affair grew out of earlier Israeli deals with Iran and the continuing contact since 1979, maintained with American knowledge and approval. Israel had the connections with Iran, and the intelligence. The Israelis came up with the idea of encouraging "moderate elements"—that is, the military. They have been proposing such moves ever since the 1979 revolution. The Iran-contra affair was just another episode in the Israeli connection with the Islamic Republic of Iran. This connection continues, unaffected by developments in Washington and media disclosures. As of 1987, shipments of artillery shells, spare parts, and other military equipment continued to leave Israel every week, bound for Iran.

Yitzhak Shamir's explanations for Israel's contacts with Iran, as expressed during his February 1987 visit to the United States, were honest and straightforward. Israel was indeed interested in a strategic alliance with Iran, despite its distance from the current regime. The strategy has three points:

14

1. Israel should keep its traditional contacts with the Iranian military.
2. A continuing war between Iraq, an Arab enemy state, and Iran, a potential enemy under the current regime, is to Israel's strategic advantage. Involved elsewhere, Iraq has been counted out of any military Arab coalition against Israel. (It should also be noted that Iraq has moved closer to the United States and has moderated its position regarding Israel since the war began.)
3. The war has caused further rifts in the Arab world, with Syria and Libya supporting Iran, while all other Arab countries support Iraq.

According to one Israeli expert, there are forces in Israel that are interested in strengthening not only Iran but all radical forces in the Middle East, because that will prevent any peace settlement, which would be likely only if moderate forces—Jordan and Egypt—tied to Iraq get stronger. Thus, these right-wing groups in Israel are pushing for more arms deliveries to Iran (Hirschfeld, 1985).

According to one respected American journalist, Israel was still hoping for a strategic alliance with Turkey and Iran even as Khomeini consolidated his power (Shipler, 1982). The long-range reasons for Israel's support for Iran are clear: "Arab hostility will continue, while the common interests of Teheran and Jerusalem will be recognized. Now Israel needs to keep a foothold in Iran, so that cooperation can be renewed when ideological-religious obstacles are removed, since the latter are more ephemeral than centuries-old national considerations" (Salpeter, 1984, p. 13). After expressing a "quiet sympathy" for Iran because (like Israel) it was isolated and persecuted by the whole world, another observer writes, "Iran destabilizes the Arab camp and neutralizes one of the strongest and most venomous of our potential enemies, Iraq. In this respect there is a payoff to an Israeli policy formulated in saner days; Khomeini's Iran is a hidden Israeli ally, just as Pahlavi's Iran was, though in a less hidden manner. There is truth in the laws of geopolitics: whoever rules Teheran becomes, willy-nilly, an ally of whoever rules Jerusalem. The rule has proven its validity since the days of Cyrus. . . . There are those who ask whether it would not be desirable to prepare the ground for a renewal of overt (or semi-overt) ties, in preparation for the day when the nuisance known as Khomeini disappears. . . . Israel and Iran need each other. That is the way it has been and that is the way it will be" (Schweitzer, 1984, p. 7).

Turkey

Turkey was an ideal component of Ben-Gurion's periphery strategy, being non-Arab (though predominantly Moslem, like Iran) and pro-Western, as well as having a significant military potential. Turkey offered Israel *de facto* recognition in March 1949, but there were no special contacts until the late 1950s. Official diplomatic representation between Turkey and Israel has always been at the *chargé d'affaires* level. In 1958, there was a secret visit to Turkey by Golda Meir, then Israel's foreign minister. On August 29, 1958, a secret agreement was reached between prime ministers David Ben-Gurion and Adnan Menderes, calling for collaboration between Israel and Turkey against Middle East radicalism and "Soviet influence" (Segev, 1981). After the military coup in May 1960, however, relations between the two countries grew more distant. In an attempt to revive the alliance, prime ministers Levi Eshkol and Ismet Inonu met in Paris in July 1964 (Crosbie, 1974).

Israel has helped Turkey in technical training for intelligence and security services (CIA, 1979). The Mossad has had a station in Turkey since the 1950s, and following the Trident agreement of 1958, the Israeli intelligence services have provided training for the Turkish secret services. In 1974, there were rumors of Israeli aid in the Turkish invasion of Cyprus. Since 1975, the Turkish air force has been acquiring Israeli-made Shafrir air-to-air missiles. Ground-force equipment purchased from Israel includes Hetz antitank shells, Uzi submachine guns, and ammunition.

During the 1970s, when internal unrest in Turkey almost grew to civil war, Israel had reason to worry. Two political forces in particular caused its concern: right-wing Islamic groups hoping to push Turkey closer to the Arab camp, and radical left-wing groups agitating for closer ties to the radical Third World. The events of these years, when scores of right-wing and left-wing militants were killed every month, were followed closely by the Mossad.

Since the military coup of 1980 there have been various indications of renewed secret contacts between Israel and the Turkish regime. There have also been public contacts. Four members of the Turkish parliament visited Israel in September of 1984 and met with Foreign Minister Yitzhak Shamir (Siegel, 1984). On April 4, 1985, Turkey's foreign minister, Vahit Halefoglu, met in Washington with Israeli ambassador Meir Rosenne. On that occasion, Israeli sources reported that the Turks, impressed by Israel's clout in Washington, wanted to use it to obtain more U.S. aid (*Israeli Foreign Affairs,* 1985b).

There is one well-publicized aspect of the unpublicized contacts between Israel and Turkey: the Israeli government forbids any mention of the Turkish genocide of Armenians in 1915 in any government-controlled media or government-sponsored activities. It does not allow the showing of television programs dealing with the events of 1915, and has taken actions against any mention of the Armenian cause. Israeli schoolchildren never hear about the Armenian holocaust, and the Israeli Foreign Ministry makes every effort to prevent any public or scholarly event that mentions what happened in 1915. In 1982, even the International Conference on the Holocaust and Genocide was a target of Foreign Ministry displeasure and pressure, because the Armenian genocide was also scheduled to be discussed.

Civil Wars in Yemen and Oman

The logic of Israeli intervention in inter-Arab conflicts is quite clear: it prevents Arab unity and stability, and channels Arab energies into internal rivalries, making sure that an Arab coalition against Israel does not develop. Any inter-Arab fighting, whether between states or within states, is judged to be to Israel's advantage. At the same time, Israel is committed to the stability and survival of conservative Arab regimes—as long as they oppose radical ones. Two cases where Israel has taken sides in Arab civil wars are those of North Yemen and Oman.

During the civil war in North Yemen between royalists and republicans (1962–1970), Egypt supported the republicans, while Israel, Iran, and Saudi Arabia supported the royalists with war matériel and training. The Israeli involvement in the Yemeni civil war was even coordinated with the United States (Zak, 1980). At the time, this now-forgotten conflict was seen as a test of Egypt's radical influence. For Israel, having Egyptian forces bogged down in Yemen was an obvious strategic plus (Halliday, 1979; Reppa, 1974).

Israel's current interest and activities in the region stem from two concerns. One is the strategic issue of the Bab al-Mandab straits—the opening to the Red Sea from the Indian Ocean, controlled by a headland shared by both Yemens—which must be kept open to Israeli shipping. The second is concern about the regimes in North and South Yemen. The one in the north is acceptable to Israel, and must, as far as it is concerned, be kept in power. The one in the south is hostile, and, from Israel's point of view, must be removed.

Israel's readiness to intervene in Arab civil wars has paid off handsomely in Oman. Sultan Qaboos ibn Said, who came into power in 1970, is its absolute ruler. There are no political parties or elected officials of any kind; Oman simply belongs to Qaboos. In the years after he came to power, Qaboos battled a radical guerrilla movement in the southern province of Dhofar with the help of Iran, Britain, and Israel. His efforts to defeat the Popular Front for the Liberation of Oman were successful, and the friendship between this absolute ruler and Israel has since been one of the best-kept secrets of the Middle East. The alliance stems from their common interests and perceptions of the world. Qaboos, like Israel, is seriously concerned about radical movements in the Middle East, and finds Israel, the United States, and Britain sympathetic and supportive.

The Kurdish Rebellion

The Kurds are a Middle East minority split between five countries: Iraq, Iran, Turkey, Syria, and the Soviet Union. Iraq has the largest and most distinct population. The Kurds' language, culture, and history are different from those of the Arab and non-Arab groups that surround them; their fate as a national minority is one of the tragedies of the Middle East. In Turkey, where they are officially known as "mountain Turks," their separate identity is violently suppressed. They have had the greatest success in achieving recognition in Iraq, but their dream of a separate Kurdish state has been anathema to Iraqi regimes, as it has been to other Middle East governments.

Being a non-Arab minority, the Kurds have always attracted Israeli attention. The simmering Kurdish rebellion in Iraq, an avowed enemy, has been of great interest to Israel, and the initial opportunity to intervene on behalf of the rebels came as a result of the developing alliance with Iran in the 1950s.

Mossad support for the Kurds began in 1958 (Weir and Bloch, 1981). Large-scale aid, in the form of arms, ammunition, and Israeli military advisers, began in 1963 (Segev, 1981), and was channeled through Iran. In August 1965, the first training course for Kurdish officers, run by Israeli instructors, was held in the Kurdistan mountains. Meetings with Kurdish leaders were held in Teheran by Levi Eshkol (in June 1966) and by others. One report states that the Kurds aided the Israeli war effort in June 1967 by mounting an offensive against the Iraqis, which kept the latter from offering aid to other Arab armies (Morris, 1980). In return, after the 1967 war the Kurds were supplied with Soviet equipment captured from the armies of Egypt and Syria. Israel also aided the Kurds with money, to the tune of $500,000 a month, and Mula Mustafa Barazani, their leader, visited Israel in September 1967 and again in September 1973 (Segev, 1981).

The Kurdish rebellion, initially an Israeli-Iranian project, later became an Israeli-Iranian-American project. In 1972, the United States joined the Iranian effort on behalf of the Kurds, and several CIA liaison officers were stationed in Barazani's headquarters (Segev, 1981).

The Kurdish rebellion ended on March 6, 1975, when Iran reached an agreement with Iraq and called off its support for the Kurds (a decision made by the shah and Secretary of State Henry Kissinger). Thus ended the Barazani revolt. The Israeli effort on behalf of the Kurds was totally dependent on access to the rebels through Iran, and so came to an end when Iran and Iraq reached their accord (Halliday, 1979).

Lebanon

Israel's relations with the Maronite Christians of Lebanon, including the designs for a Maronite state, are part of its periphery strategy. The dream of an alliance with the Maronites first appeared in Zionist writings as early as the 1920s. Vladimir Jabotinsky expressed the hope

19

for a Christian Lebanon allied with Zionism in the 1930s. David Ben-Gurion's diary of May 24, 1948, contains a reference to a "Christian state" in Lebanon whose southern border would be the Litani River, just north of Tyre. A June 11, 1948, entry mentions that Israel's war goals included a "Christian" revolt in Lebanon. This dream of a Maronite Lebanon allied with Israel was so prevalent that it was even expressed by the Zionist-Marxist Mordecai Bentov before the Israeli cabinet in December of 1948 (Ben-Gurion, 1984).

Pierre Gemayel, a Lebanese pharmacist who studied in Europe, founded his own version of a fascist party, the Lebanese Phalanges, in 1936. The social base of the party was a small group of wealthy Maronite families whose money often came from the illegal trade in drugs. This party of Maronite Lebanese came to prominence in the 1940s through its military organization and financial resources, and employed the classic fascist slogan, "God, Fatherland, and Family." Israel made contact with the Phalangists during the 1948 war, and in 1951 it contributed money to the Phalangist election campaign. The amount of money given was only $3,000, and the Phalangists did not achieve much success, but from these meager beginnings a close military alliance was to grow in the 1970s.

The diaries of Moshe Sharett, Israel's prime minister from 1953 to 1955, show that the question of a Maronite state in Lebanon, or in place of Lebanon, was often discussed by Israeli leaders in the 1950s. In a February 27, 1954, letter to Sharett, David Ben-Gurion proposed that the creation of a Maronite state should be one of the major objectives of Israeli foreign policy, if not the most important one, and suggested spending money and using covert means and agents to that end. Moshe Dayan, the chief of staff of the Israeli Defense Force, suggested on May 16, 1955, that Israel should find or buy a Lebanese officer, even a mere major, to declare himself a savior of the Maronites. Then Israel could invade Lebanon, create a Christian regime allied with Israel, and annex the territory south of the Litani River. Sharett wrote on June 17, 1955, that Israel had been in touch with one group in Lebanon, and that it should attempt contacts with the Lebanese military (Sharett, 1978).

Dayan's dream, in a much modified version, became a reality in 1976 with the creation of the South Lebanon Army, a puppet organization initially headed by a Lebanese major named Saad Haddad.

From 1976 on, hundreds of Phalangist fighters were trained in Israel alongside Israeli paratroopers. Between 1975 and 1977 Israel spent $150 million on military supplies for the Phalangist militia, but it seems likely that the United States paid the bill.

LOOKING BACK

One Israeli observer states that what Israel achieved in the 1950s and early 1960s was "the stabilization of the Middle East. Israel prevented the radical Arab states from taking over the conservative ones; prevented the survival of the United Arab Republic [the union of Egypt and Syria]; prevented Nasser from taking over Saudi Arabia; was responsible for Hussein in Jordan remaining in power; and stopped Syria and Iraq from invading Jordan" (Kesse, 1983, p. 5). Israeli leaders today probably look back on the good old days of the 1950s and early 1960s with some nostalgia.

2

A Dream of Asia

While the Middle East seemed more and more like a cage for the Israeli lion in the 1950s, the world beyond it echoed with the sounds of limitless possibilities. The Middle East was becoming radical and menacing, and Gamal Abdul Nasser seemed more and more like a potential Saladin, but East Asia beckoned from a distance as an unknown and promising territory. Israel dreamed of newly independent Third World countries far removed from the Middle East that would not share Arab hostility to it; it was a dream of a fresh start, another chance.

It was in East Asia in the 1950s that Israel made its first attempts to win friends in the Third World beyond the Middle East. Its policy was based on two assumptions (which were later tested in Africa as well). The first held that at least some of the Third World leadership was not familiar with the history of the Arab-Israeli conflict, and was, therefore, less likely to identify with the Arabs. The second held that Israel has something to offer Third World countries in terms of ways to accelerate development. Like the periphery strategy, this offensive aimed at outflanking the Arab world and preventing the formation of a Third World coalition that would include the Arabs (Rivkin, 1959).

The image that Israel tried to project to the unknown and unknowing Third World in the 1950s and 1960s was that of a new nation, an underdeveloped nation, making great strides in agriculture through social experimentation ("making the desert bloom"). The kibbutz, a successful socialist commune that represents the way of life of 3 percent of Israelis, was the image projected as if it were the norm in Israeli society. Socialism was presented as the dominant Israeli ideology, though even the term itself was removed from the platform of the Mapai Party (today's Labor Party) in 1955. An attempt was made to present David Ben-Gurion as another founding father of an emerging nation, just like Gandhi or Nkrumah, and Israel as just another decolonized country. What was always omitted from this image was the reality of Zionism's original sin of colonialism: Israel had been created through the dispossession of a native population. The Israeli strategy initially worked in some cases. Many Third World leaders in the 1950s and 1960s had little knowledge of, or interest in, the Middle East situation. The most significant examples of Israel's involvement in Asia have been with Burma in the late 1950s and early 1960s, Singapore since the early 1960s, Taiwan since the early 1960s, South Korea, the Philippines under Marcos, and Sri Lanka and China, both in the 1980s.

India

A leader of the Third World long before its formal independence in 1948, India has been a pioneer in developing a Third World stand on Zionism and Israel. It was Mohandas Gandhi, the founding father of modern India, who set forth the country's basic attitude. In the late 1930s, he diagnosed the conflict in Palestine between Arabs and Jews, quite correctly, as one between settlers and natives, and stated unequivocally that Palestine belonged to its Arab natives. Their rights took precedence over any other claims. Gandhi wrote: "The cry for the national home for the Jews does not have much appeal to me. The sanction for it is sought in the Bible and the tenacity with which the Jews have hankered after a return to Palestine. Why should they not, like other peoples of the earth, make that country their home where they are born and where they earn their livelihood? Palestine belongs to the Arabs in the same sense that England belongs to the English or France to the French. It is wrong and inhuman to impose the Jews on the Arabs. What is going on in Palestine today cannot be justified by any moral code of conduct" (Mendes-Flohr, 1983, p. 108).

From Israel's point of view, Gandhi's judgment showed just how difficult it would be to make Zionism acceptable to Third World leaders. In the West, Zionism has always appealed to the history of Jewish victimization, and to the Bible, as justifications for its political program. In India, both arguments were irrelevant. Gandhi did not experience either the reality of European anti-Semitism or the Christian tradition of respect for Biblical authority. He merely looked at what was happening in Palestine, and saw natives and settlers. Claims about persecution in Europe or appeals to ancient mythology could not change his perception of colonialism, pure and simple. (Martin Buber, the famous Zionist philosopher, tried to change Gandhi's mind in a famous letter expounding on the special ties between Jews and Palestine. Gandhi probably never received the letter, and it is doubtful whether it would have affected him if he had [Mendes-Flohr, 1983].) This basic Gandhian view has dominated Indian policy toward Israel ever since.

India granted *de facto* recognition to Israel in 1950 (Eytan, 1958), and an Israeli consulate operated in Bombay between 1952 and 1982, but beyond that India has been consistent in its criticism of Zionism and Israel. In every Third World conference, going back to the Bandung Conference in 1955, India has been among those countries that shaped the consensus on the Middle East. The 1956 invasion of Egypt by France, Britain, and Israel has often been cited by Indians as evidence of Israel's colonialist nature.

There have been Israeli attempts to offer military aid to India, and there were secret contacts by the military over the years, but India does not need Israeli military technology: it has developed its own arms industry, being the only noncommunist country in the world allowed to manufacture Soviet military equipment, including jet fighters. The "most populous democracy" in the world, as it is often described in the United States, remains impenetrable to Israeli advances. Recent Israeli ties with Sri Lanka, where Israel is on the same side as Pakistan, and with China, have increased India's hostility.

Burma

Diplomatic relations between Israel and Burma were established in 1953, and in August 1954, a Burmese military mission visited Israel. Prime Minister U Nu visited Israel in 1955, and it was the high point of an alliance that ended seven years later. In 1954, Burma purchased British-made World War II Spitfires from Israel, and was assisted by Israeli flight instructors and technical experts. There was also a significant program of civilian cooperation, mainly in agriculture (Cashman, 1984; Rivkin, 1959). The development of these ties with Burma in the early 1950s was a major diplomatic success, as extensive as it was unexpected. It was really Israel's first breakthrough in relations with the Third World, serving as a model for later efforts in other countries.

The alliance with Burma was for Israel a dream come true in that it had managed to reach beyond the Arab encirclement and gain acceptance in an important part of the Third World. The visit to Burma by Israel's head of state, President Yitzhak Ben-Zvi, in October 1959 symbolized this diplomatic achievement. And in December 1961, it was David Ben-Gurion himself who traveled to Burma, on what some have described as a "pilgrimage" to meet U Nu, learn more about Buddhism, and celebrate a friendship that was about to end. U Nu, the visionary prime minister who favored contacts with Israel, was overthrown in 1962 by a military coup led by General Ne Win, and for all practical purposes, Israel's relations with Burma came to an end. Ne Win initiated what he called "the Burmese Way to Socialism," which meant cutting off most outside contacts and adhering to a strict nonalignment policy. Since 1975, contacts have been renewed with the United States, West Germany, Australia, Japan, and China. But although Israel still maintains an embassy in Rangoon, the relations between the two countries are formal and limited.

Singapore

Long a British colony, Singapore was granted limited self-rule in 1959, and won complete independence in August 1965. The People's Action Party has been in control since 1959, most of that time under Prime Minister Lee Kuan Yew. Over the years, Singapore has established a reputation for prosperity, efficiency, and authoritarian government.

The regime in Singapore is among the most conservative in Asia, and its ties with Israel date back to the early 1960s. An Israeli military mission was stationed in Singapore between the end of 1965 and May of 1974. The high point of the Israeli presence there was 1969, when forty-five Israeli advisers were on active duty (Chee, 1985). In 1969, fifty used French-made AMX-13 tanks were delivered, and in 1972, thirty-six Israeli Gabriel missiles. Singapore now produces arms under license from Israel (Quinn-Judge, 1982).

According to the CIA (1979), Singapore is the location of the main Mossad station in Asia. The Israeli presence has excited some unwanted attention: a package containing a bomb was delivered to the Israeli embassy in Singapore in 1976, and the building was the target of another bombing attempt on March 17, 1985 (Reuters, 1985).

General Efraim Poran, former military adviser to Prime Minister Begin, served as a defense adviser to the Singapore government (Kartin, 1984a). (We will see that he has been involved in other military and civilian deals in Haiti and Ciskei as well.)

Taiwan

Taiwan, whose official name is the Republic of China, is the last remnant of the Kuomintang regime that once ruled mainland China under Generalissimo Chiang Kai-shek. In 1949, the Kuomintang leadership, headed by the Chiang family, fled to Taiwan. The Chiangs still rule the island despite resentment from native islanders, who make up 80 percent of the population.

Taiwan is the classic outcast state, existing on the margin of history and trying to cope with the reality of growing isolation and decreasing legitimacy. While its political support base is diminishing constantly, its short-term situation is still quite impressive. Although Taiwan had the support of the United States between 1949 and 1972, its leaders, well aware of their precarious legitimacy, prepared for their uncertain future. Because of the relatively benevolent attitude of the People's Republic of China, and because of its own behavior, Taiwan does not attract much overt hostility in the Third World. More often than not, it is ignored or pitied, since its eventual demise seems so certain. But meanwhile, Taiwan shows the possibilities of survival under extremely difficult conditions and growing isolation.

Taiwan moved closer to Israel as the United States was moving away from it (Butterfield, 1977), although there were earlier contacts. The Israeli Defense Ministry now operates a permanent mission in Taipei, charged with military cooperation. Taiwan is considered one of Israel's most important partners in the development of military technology (Fishman, 1985b). Taiwan has been receiving weapons technology from Israel in its attempt to become self-sufficient in arming itself (Aronson, 1985). The results of these joint activities include thirty Dvora missile boats (known locally as Tsu-chiangs), Gabriel missiles produced in Taiwan under license, Shafrir air-to-air missiles, artillery guns and mortars (including a 127mm multiple rocket launcher), Galil rifles and Uzi submachine guns, electronic equipment, and ammunition. But the cooperation goes beyond conventional weaponry: it has been reported that Israel has transferred to Taiwan both nuclear technology and chemical-warfare technology (Frenkel, 1983b), and a CIA report states that Israel has provided intelligence training to the Taiwanese secret services (CIA, 1979).

Israel reportedly asked the United States for permission to sell Kfir jets to Taiwan in 1981 (Miller, 1981). According to the *Christian Science Monitor,* Israel acts as a U.S. proxy in supplying arms to Taiwan, since U.S. strategic interests and its global conception of a bipolar struggle dictate support for Taiwan, while open military aid is out of the question (Yemma, 1982).

South Korea

Over the past forty years South Korea has become a symbol for Americans and Koreans alike of the struggle against communism. The ideology of successive dictatorial regimes, from Syngman Rhee to Chun Doo Hwan, has been amazingly unoriginal: the same anticommunism, mixed with strong support for religion and free enterprise, can be found today in South Korea, Chile, and Paraguay. South Korea is widely regarded in the Third World as an American proxy, with a regime that fits the image. It tries to overcome these legitimacy problems by vigorous diplomatic efforts, some of which have been very successful. Nevertheless, South Korea's military rulers, being totally dependent on the United States, feel quite insecure.

Like Taiwan, South Korea is a regional power tied to Israel

through military contacts (Klieman, 1984). Like other isolated nations, it is intent upon achieving self-sufficiency in conventional weapons. Enjoying remarkable economic growth, it has made a major effort to develop its own arms industry, and manufactures its own version of the U.S. M-16 rifle. Nevertheless, the South Korean army has purchased a large number of Galil rifles from Israel.

There has also been cooperation between the two governments in civilian fields: Israel has hosted Korean trainees in medicine and agriculture at Israeli universities. But the cooperation has its limits—in the fall of 1985, the finance minister, Yitzhak Modai, and the governor of the Bank of Israel, Moshe Mandelbaum, visited South Korea to ask for economic aid. There was little indication Seoul was willing to sink money into the bottomless pit of Israel's economy—it was content to leave that job to the United States.

South Korea is involved in various international right-wing ventures under the aegis of the Unification Church, headed by the ubiquitous Sun Yung Moon. The "Moonies" have surfaced time and again —from Central America to Washington—as supporters and instigators of aid to various right-wing campaigns. Congressional investigations of the Unification Church have led to the conclusion that it is operated as an arm of the South Korean government, specifically linked to the Korean CIA (Reid, 1977).

The Philippines

A collection of four thousand islands with 50 million people, the Philippines possesses the unique distinction of having been an official U.S. colony between 1898 and 1946. U.S. corporations and a small local oligarchy have found the country extremely profitable. Ferdinand Marcos, with the blessing of the United States, became president in 1965. In 1972, barred from continuing as president for a third term, he declared martial law. His regime was one of several in the Third World where the country is not just run by an oligarchy, but is virtually owned by a single family and its associates—similar to Iran under the shah, and Zaire under Mobutu (see chapter 3). Through a variety of government agencies, government corporations, and private corporations, the Marcos family and its friends controlled most of the wealth produced by the Filipino people as well as all the financial aid coming from the United States.

Israel has had an active embassy in Manila, but relations between the two countries have not attracted much attention until recently, when the need of Marcos and Company for trustworthy friends became more apparent. As a result, before their fall, Ferdinand and Imelda Marcos were described as "tied to Israel with a thousand and one overt and covert strings" (*Haolam Hazeh,* 1986, p. 8). On the occasion of a well-publicized visit to the Israeli trade mission in New York City in November 1981, Mrs. Marcos spoke about a Filipino-Israeli alliance, and gave interviews to Israeli journalists filled with praise for Israel (Golan, 1981). One Israeli official was quoted as saying, "She believes, apparently, that we have excellent ties in the business world here and we influence U.S. Jews, who in turn influence the mass media and other institutions" (Hadar, 1981, p. 13). In early 1982 there was a less-publicized visit to Manila by Israel's economic planning minister, Yaakov Meridor. His entourage included Israeli singers, who entertained the guests at a reception for Mrs. Marcos with songs in three languages about the greatness of the First Lady (*Haolam Hazeh,* 1982a).

During negotiations in Washington between Israeli leaders and the Reagan administration in November 1983, Israel requested permission for the Philippines to use American military credits to buy Israeli arms, a proposal rejected by the United States. Israel officially offered the Marcos regime aid in counterinsurgency operations (Quinn-Judge, 1982).

According to eyewitnesses, Israeli mercenaries were visible in the Philippines at least as early as 1980. Ferdinand Marcos's life was protected by Israeli bodyguards who had served in elite Israeli commando units. The wealthy friends of the president also enjoyed such services, and only they could afford it (Egozi, 1985). Several of Marcos's friends headed their own private armies. The best known among them was Eduardo Conjuangco, Jr., the former president of United Coconut Oil Mills (Unicom) and a close friend of Marcos, probably the country's second wealthiest man after the ex-president. He also ran the largest private army in the Philippines, reportedly trained by Israelis (Quinn-Judge, 1985). Reports in 1985 claimed that four hundred Filipino trainees graduated from a basic training course run by Israeli mercenaries on the island of Palawan; the project's chief sponsor was the same Conjuangco. It is safe to assume that these mercenaries, like other Israelis in the Philippines, operated with the full knowledge and approval of the Israeli embassy in Manila.

Most "private" Israeli involvements in the Philippines have been channeled through a company known as Tamuz Control Systems, a Tel-Aviv corporation founded by Israeli generals who, though retired from active duty, are still in the reserves. Tamuz offers Third World regimes assistance in solving their security problems, and has been especially active in the Philippines. One Israeli journalist reported that General Dov Tamari recruited members of the elite units of the Israel Defense Force, offering them lucrative one-year contracts in the Philippines (Baram, 1983). When Assaf Hefetz, a bright young police officer, former commander of a police antiterror unit, and former paratroop officer, was suspended from his duties for leaking internal police information to journalists, a job was waiting for him—working for an Israeli consulting firm in the Philippines charged with defending the Marcos regime. For personal reasons, Hefetz decided to stay in Israel, and was eventually returned to active police duty, where he earned promotions and further distinction (*Haolam Hazeh,* 1984a).

The nature of private Israeli activity in the Philippines was illuminated by an incident reported in the Israeli press in 1984. According to published reports, two former officials in the police antiterrorism unit who work for an unnamed private organization (which turned out to be Tamuz) used classified documents that had been made available to them through their service in the unit (they reportedly made unauthorized copies of training manuals used at the special police antiterror school). Despite the apparent seriousness of their using classified material (including methods for imposing curfews, conducting searches, etc.), the matter did not become a legal issue. The reason, as given by two reporters, was as follows: "The company is headed by former generals and the transfer of material to Third World countries is coordinated with senior defense officials" (Handwerker and Levy, 1984, p. 2). Another reporter stated the case more plainly: "The offense is only technical, because, as is known, the company is directed by former generals, who are in constant contact with SHABAK and the Mossad" (Bachar, 1984, p. 7). These reports make clear that, in this case at least, private enterprise was coordinated with secret intelligence services, and that those secret services supported what was being done. The matter of Israeli training of private armies in the Philippines was raised in the Knesset by Matityahu Peled on July 30, 1985. On September 2, 1985, Deputy Foreign Minister Roni Milo gave the government's reply, denying any official Israeli involvement.

Since coming into power in early 1986, the Aquino regime has managed to show its reservations about Israel's connections to the Marcos era by playing a tight diplomatic game. When Israel's President Haim Herzog was scheduled to make an official trip to Asia and Oceania in November 1986, Manila was announced as one of the planned stops. This was arranged through the good offices of Congressman Stephen Solarz, who had to put pressure on the Manila government. But the visit was still unpalatable to too many Filipinos, so that at the last minute President Corazón Aquino canceled it, through an elegant diplomatic excuse. The memories of earlier Israeli visits, of another kind, are still too fresh.

Indonesia

The fifth-largest country on earth, Indonesia gained its independence from the Dutch under the leadership of Ahmad Sukarno, who was declared a dangerous leftist by the United States in the 1950s. There followed a number of U.S.-sponsored attempts to depose him, and in 1965 he was ousted by General Suharto, who immediately charted a right-wing course for the country. Since then, the riches of Indonesia have been owned by a small circle of generals and their families (Kwitny, 1984b). Not surprisingly, it has enjoyed a positive image in the U.S. media for a long time—since 1965, to be exact—never mind that the Suharto regime is credited with killing 600,000 of its opponents in the 1960s, according to Amnesty International. Large-scale corruption, of the kind practiced by Marcos, Duvalier, and their ilk, is also one of the hallmarks of the regime. According to recent estimates, Suharto and his friends have accumulated between $2 billion and $3 billion while in power (Koeppel, 1986).

The invasion of East Timor illustrates the *modus operandi* of the regime. East Timor used to be a Portuguese colony, and its culture and religion are different from that of the majority of Indonesians. Following the Portuguese revolution of 1974 it became independent. In 1975, following official visits to Jakarta by Secretary of State Henry Kissinger and President Gerald Ford, which served to highlight Suharto's close ties to the United States, Indonesia invaded East Timor (Cantarow, 1979). The U.S. media and political establishment, supposedly sensitive to human-rights violations and oppressive regimes, completely ignored the invasion and the mass slaughter of Timorese who opposed the Indonesian army. When President Reagan visited there in 1986, he spoke of freedom, friendship, and cooperation; in earnest of these ideals, the United States has supported Suharto since 1976 with grants of $2 billion and loans of $4 billion.

While Indonesia is officially and constitutionally a secular state, it is also the world's most populous (150 million) Islamic nation. Officially, it is also a country with a hostile attitude toward Israel. Unofficially, however, things are different. According to the CIA (1979), the Mossad has a station in Jakarta operating under a commercial cover. A British journalist reported that Israel has had "major military contracts" with Indonesia (Coone, 1980). And an Israeli journalist stated that Israeli arms were used in the war Indonesia waged against the people of East Timor (Baram, 1982b).

In 1979, the United States arranged the sale of fourteen Skyhawk planes from Israel to Indonesia (Klich, 1982a). An American journalist reported at the time that "the U.S. government is fronting an arms deal in which Israel, without being publicly identified as the source, is selling Indonesia used warplanes obtained from the United States. Pentagon officials confirmed yesterday that Israel is shipping Indonesia sixteen A4 fighters, bought for $25.8 million in the first such third-country sale of U.S. warplanes" (Wilson, 1979, p. A10). In 1983, another squadron was said to be in the process of delivery (Melman, 1983b).

Afghanistan

The CIA has invested more than $500 million in helping the Afghan Moslem rebels, an effort that has been aided by China, Saudi Arabia, Egypt, and Israel (Lathem, 1983). American sources were quoted as saying that Israel, Saudi Arabia, and China were supporting the anti-

Soviet forces in Afghanistan to the tune of $100 million a year (Barel, 1984). Israel may not be the major financial contributor, but it can supply Soviet-made weapons it has captured in the Middle East; these are then delivered to the rebel forces, which can claim to have captured them in Afghanistan itself. Some Soviet-made weapons coming from Israel were said to be delivered to Afghanistan by way of Saudi Arabia, which has close relations with the *mujahedeen*. If true, this is another example of Israeli collaboration with conservative Arab regimes.

Thailand

Thailand, with much natural and human beauty, has been ruled since 1976 by the military, and has always had close relations with the United States and Israel. Following the 1976 military coup, a Thai military delegation visited Israel; twenty thousand Galil rifles and five thousand Uzi submachine guns were delivered to Thailand in short order. The Mossad has an important and active station in Bangkok, and has had contacts with Thai secret services (CIA, 1979). There was an official visit to Thailand in 1984 by David Kimche, director-general of the Foreign Ministry. Deputy Foreign Minister Roni Milo visited Thailand in June 1985.

Israeli involvement with Thailand has led to two unusual incidents in the form of bombings directed at the Israeli embassy in Bangkok, the first in December 1983 and the second in August 1985. No damages or injuries were reported in either case. Since 1984, the presence of Israeli military advisers in Thailand has been reported, as have plans for a large-scale arms deal. Thai generals look up to their Israeli counterparts and see them as an example to be followed and emulated.

Sri Lanka

Ceylon gained its independence from Britain in 1948, and changed its name to Sri Lanka in 1972. In the 1950s, Israel developed both military and civilian aid programs in Ceylon. In 1959, Israel sold Ceylon two World War II British-made frigates that were considered too obsolete for the Israeli navy (Medzini, 1976). In the 1960s, agricultural advisers from Israel were successful and productive on the island, but in 1970, all diplomatic contacts were suspended by the Ceylon government, headed at the time by Sirimavo Bandaranaike, leader of the socialist Sri Lanka Freedom Party. After 1970, successive governments in Colombo adhered to the Third World consensus on Israel, periodically announcing their public support for the PLO, which began to operate an office there in 1976. The government headed by Junius Jayewardene since 1977, however, has had a marked right-wing bias and has deviated from the Third World consensus. This change in the government's orientation has been reflected in a radical shift of economic policies toward an Asian variant of "supply-side" free-market economics (Subasinghe, 1983).

There were few apparent problems between the Sinhalese majority and the Tamil minority until 1956, when Sinhalese was declared the only official language; friction grew. Subsequent nationalistic fervor and intolerance on the part of the Sinhalese majority has turned the Tamil minority struggle for civil rights in the 1970s into an armed insurrection in the 1980s. The serious violence started in 1977 as Tamils were organized to challenge Sinhalese domination. By 1983, a full-scale guerrilla war had broken out. The Sri Lankan government asked Britain and the United States for help; however, they did not want to be directly involved in an ethnic conflict. When the Sri Lankans asked the United States for counterinsurgency advisers, it refused again, but turned the matter over to the Israeli government.

Israel was the only country that did not hesitate. The decision was made by David Kimche, director-general of the Foreign Ministry and former Mossad deputy chief. An Associated Press correspondent reported that National Security Minister Lalith Athulathmudali said that the Sri Lankan army was being trained by SHABAK advisers in counterinsurgency activities (Graham, 1984). Athulathmudali also said, "Our men say that they never had such good training. Every state is entitled to the best it can get." As of August 1984, there were reportedly up to six domestic intelligence experts from Israel working with the government to develop a new intelligence network against the Tamils (Smolowe, 1984). Douglas Liyanage, secretary of the Sri Lanka State Ministry—who had been accused in 1961 of leading an abortive military coup, had barely escaped conviction, and had languished in political oblivion until 1979, when he joined the government—visited Israel in August 1984, publicly lauded relations with Israel, and met with Kimche (Eldar, 1984). Liyanage's visit and his statements caused an uproar in Sri Lanka, and on his return to Colombo he was forced to resign.

The conflict with the Tamils has led the Sri Lankan government to purchase armaments from the United States, Israel, South Africa, Britain, Italy, Pakistan, and China (Weisman, 1985; Crossette, 1985). Six patrol boats were ordered from Israel to control the sea lanes between India and Sri Lanka. The question of a deal between Israel and Sri Lanka for the sale of these boats was raised in the Knesset by Matityahu Peled, who on May 27, 1985, asked whether reports about the deal were true, and whether Israeli instructors would be sent to Sri Lanka. Defense Minister Yitzhak Rabin refused to answer the question, stating that it would be harmful to state security.

In return for its help, Israel was allowed to open an interests section in the American embassy in Colombo in the summer of 1984 —the first time the United States had acted in such a capacity for Israel. The official announcement in Colombo mentioned an Israeli-interests section not only in the U.S. embassy, but under "American auspices." The Israeli-interests section was headed by David Matnai, a specialist on Asian affairs who was identified by British sources as a Mossad agent. On June 28, 1984, a bomb was detonated near his room in a Colombo hotel, killing one woman. The renewed contacts between Israel and Sri Lanka also brought about expressions of opposition from Moslem groups, as well as from the left-wing Freedom Party, headed by Anura Bandaranaike, son of the leader who had broken off relations with Israel in August 1970 (Krivine, 1984).

The case of Sri Lanka is one example of Israeli involvement in the Third World that was instigated by the United States. Without the United States, Israel would never have gotten involved with aiding the Sri Lankan government in its struggle against the Tamil minority. The operation was run by the Mossad, while the actual men in the field were on loan from the SHABAK. An Israeli journalist provides us with the only public justification for this involvement: the Tamil insurgency is the result of Marxist incitement, and therefore it is clear that Israel should oppose it (Prister, 1985).

The matter of Israeli aid to the Sri Lanka government's suppression of the Tamils was raised in the Knesset by Matityahu Peled on

October 23, 1984. Prime Minister Shimon Peres answered the parliamentary question on January 22, 1985, denying any Israeli involvement. In the fall of 1985, there was a secret meeting between Sri Lankan president Junius Jayawardene and Prime Minister Shimon Peres, during a visit by the latter to Paris. After Peres told of the meeting during a Knesset debate, the Sri Lankan government decided to suspend further official contacts (Eldar, 1985). In any event, this renewal of contacts with an Asian country was not a complete success. The help received by the Sri Lankan government has not enabled it to subdue the insurgents. If anything, it seems that since Israel became involved in 1984, things have become bloodier and less hopeful. Sri Lanka has now earned the frightening nickname of the "Lebanon of South Asia."

China

The government of Israel, then just nineteen months old, was among the first to recognize the People's Republic of China, in January 1950. Israel was still on speaking terms with the Soviet Union, and nominally nonaligned. As the decade wore on, it was the Chinese who became interested in developing relations. By that time, however, Israel had clearly joined the U.S. camp. Chinese overtures seeking official diplomatic relations were rebuffed in 1954 and again in 1955; Israel clearly did not want to flout the wishes of the United States (Brecher, 1974). Since then, China has become a leader of the Third World and part of its consensus for Palestinian rights and against Israeli policies. Accordingly, there have been no formal relations. Covert contacts started only in the 1980s. One journalist described the relationship as that of "semisecret trade and cooperation, surfacing from time to time" (Schweitzer, 1985b, p. 5).

There have been scores of press reports since 1983 about military and economic contacts between Israel and China. In addition to stories about commercial deals in agriculture and construction, the reports about military contacts have attracted much attention. According to some, China has purchased equipment worth $3 billion. As with all stories about the insatiable Chinese market, the reality is a little less rosy for Israel's balance of payments. The Chinese were less interested in finished products and more in technological know-how that would enable them to achieve arms self-sufficiency. The drive to modernize their ground forces, and specifically the armored corps, utilized Israeli expertise in upgrading older weapons, especially Soviet-made tanks (with which Israeli experts have become quite familiar over the years), as well as how to use them in battle once they are modernized. According to one journalist, however, Israeli disclosures of contacts with China have caused the Chinese to change their minds on several commercial deals, and have caused a shroud of secrecy to fall again over the relations (Becker, 1985b).

In a prophetic statement made in 1969, Yigal Allon, then Israel's deputy prime minister, expressed regrets over the Israeli rebuff to China's approaches in 1955, saying, "Perhaps, when a positive change occurs in the relations between the USA and China, some sort of change will occur in the Chinese attitude toward us" (Brecher, 1972, p. 348). The recent Chinese readiness to turn to Israel is a reflection of Chinese "pragmatism" since the early 1980s, and the general political turn to the right in China. A *New York Times* report described it as "one more manifestation of China's new economic policy, which is aimed at achieving rapid industrial development by adopting Western methods and technology from any country willing to sell it" (Friedman, 1985a, p. 1). China has been ready to have *de facto* contacts with Israel, but, consistent with its position in the Third World, it cannot accord Israel formal legitimacy, which is what Israel very much needs. Open diplomatic relations with China would be the greatest achievement in the history of Israeli Third World diplomacy.

3

In and Out of Africa

srael's Asian drive continued over the fifties, until the Sinai
war of 1956. Subsequently, Africa became Israel's major
foreign-policy goal in the developing world . . . coinciding
with the creation of a large number of new states, aspiring
for rapid development and with no traditional positions on
the Middle East conflict" (Kaufman et al., 1979, p. 93).

In 1950, there were only four officially independent countries in
the whole of Africa. Africa was the most colonized continent,
thoroughly dominated by Europe, with the exception of Liberia and
Ethiopia. By 1962, the number of independent countries had grown
to thirty; by 1977, except for South Africa's control of Namibia, the
continent was totally independent, at least in name. Nowhere else was
decolonization so manifest and so recent. African decolonization
brought about Western concern and attempts at recolonization. Israel
became part of this Western reaction very early on.

ISRAEL
ENTERS AFRICA

Israel established relations with Ethiopia in 1956 and with Liberia in 1957. It established contacts with the newly independent countries of Africa as soon as independence was declared, and sometimes even earlier. This time Israel was seemingly on the side of (formal) decolonization. After Ghana became independent in 1957, more nations raised their own flags, and the Israeli flag was flown soon afterwards in the Congo, Nigeria, the Ivory Coast (all 1960); and Tanzania (1961). By 1967, Israel had diplomatic contacts with thirty-three out of the forty-one African states, the remaining eight being the six Arab nations of North Africa (Sudan, Egypt, Libya, Tunisia, Algeria, and Morocco), and the predominantly Moslem countries of Somalia and Mauritania.

In 1958, the International Institute for Development Cooperation and Labor Studies was founded in Tel-Aviv; since then, 14,500 have graduated from its training courses—half from Africa (40 percent were from Asia, the rest from Latin America). The Israeli involvement with black Africa in the early 1960s was undoubtedly the greatest triumph of Israeli diplomacy. Israel's diplomats had seemingly overcome the problem of its isolation in the world, as all of black Africa played host to thousands of Israeli representatives. There were also successes in South America and Asia, but Africa was clearly the greatest. The Israeli civilian-aid program in Africa, which accounted for only 0.5 percent of all the aid received by Africa in the 1960s, had a political impact that was clearly disproportionately large.

In the 1960s, Israel was involved in the training of the military in the Ivory Coast, the Central African Republic, Dahomey (Benin), Cameroon, Senegal, Togo, Tanzania, Uganda, Ethiopia, Nigeria, and Somalia—all pro-Western at the time. "If Israeli ambitions in Africa had been allowed to proceed without interruption, the logical result could have been a vast bloc of pro-Western, anti-Communist nations stretching from Israel in the north to South Africa. Such a grouping would have virtually guaranteed the security of the two most vulnerable nations at either end of the African continent and reduced the ability of the Soviet Union to expand its sphere of influence in the region" (Adams, 1984, p. 13).

According to the Africa Research Group (1969), Israel's activities on the continent were shaped and financed by the United States and other Western powers. Israel was a "third force" in Africa, between the West and the Communist block, but at the same time its activities were of benefit to the West (Rivkin, 1962). "Israel is not entirely free in the contest for the neutrals that makes Africa important," wrote one observer in 1965, "for it has chosen the Western camp, a decision which exacts its costs" (Bayne, 1965, p. 247). Logically, then, its operations should be financed by such countries as the United States and West Germany. And cooperation between Israel and West Germany in civilian aid to Third World countries has lasted into the 1980s: an agreement to continue such projects was announced during a visit to Israel in June 1985 by Jürgen Warnke, West German economic cooperation minister (Isacowitz, 1985b).

There was also some Israeli-French cooperation in the former French colonies in Africa (Crosbie, 1974). Israel had hoped for French financing of its programs, but financial support was limited to $160,000, enough to cover costs of some of its activities in the Ivory Coast (Crosbie, 1974; Laufer, 1967). On the other hand, it is quite clear that there was much French diplomatic support, without which Israel could not have operated in the countries of French-speaking Africa. A list of the countries hosting Israeli operations makes this clear: Cameroon, Central African Republic, Dahomey (Benin), Niger, Togo, Upper Volta (Burkina Faso), Senegal, Gabon, the Ivory Coast, and the Malagasy Republic (Madagascar). Crosbie writes: "Paris had been consulted before a diplomatic offensive in Africa was launched in 1957 by visits to that continent of Ambassador Yaakov Tzur and Foreign Minister Golda Meir" (1974, p. 102).

There was another, covert, side to Israeli contacts in Africa. A study of American covert operations in Africa suggests that Israel's effort at the time to overcome its isolation in the Third World was utilized by the CIA. Starting in 1960, the CIA paid Israel tens of millions of dollars; its aim was "to give the anti-communist West, through the highly effective good offices of Israel, competitive equality in political penetration of newly independent states in black Africa" (Dingeman, 1979, p. 92). This Israeli involvement gave a strong boost to CIA activities in Africa at the time.

The *Wall Street Journal* reported in 1977 that the CIA financed

Israeli "foreign aid" operations in Africa between 1964 and 1968. Checks for several hundred thousand dollars each were delivered to the Foreign Ministry in Jerusalem in the late 1960s. The money was then channeled to African recipients (Behr, 1977). The total paid by the CIA was estimated to be in the millions—perhaps as much as $80 million (Weir and Bloch, 1981). A top-secret White House document, dated May 23, 1967, reveals that the United States increased its allocation to Israel for operation in Africa by $5 million for 1967 (Wright, 1983). Israeli activities in Africa in the 1960s financed by the CIA "fulfilled expectations as a counterweight to Soviet-Chinese penetration. . . . The huge Israeli subsidies . . . were designed to finance Israeli 'penetration' of the politics, culture, economics and military organizations of black African states rapidly moving out of colonialism into independence. Against this undercover U.S.-Israeli operation was arrayed the power of the Soviet empire, as well as the tenacious but smaller efforts of the Chinese Communists." Israeli-U.S. covert operations in Africa were aimed at giving "the anti-Communist West, through the highly effective good offices of Israel, competitive equality in political penetration of newly independent states in black Africa" (Evans and Novak, 1977, p. A15). And in the 1970s, the CIA regularly paid millions of dollars "to finance an expansion of Mossad operations in Africa" (Levin, 1979, p. 23).

Israel's diplomatic decline in Africa was as dramatic as its earlier success. It started when Tanzania reduced the level of relations in 1965, followed by Congo Brazzaville in 1966. Five African countries broke off relations with Israel between 1967 and 1972, and the end of Israel's halcyon days in Africa came in 1973 (table 1). The massive termination of relations with Israel started in the summer of 1973, after the Organization of African Unity conference in May, so it was not just a result of the 1973 war and the Arab oil boycott. All but four ended relations in 1973, and one of those broke off in 1976.

The ties between African countries and Israel in the 1960s were increasingly out of step with budding Third World consciousness at the time. At the 1966 Tricontinental Solidarity Conference in Havana, a strong anti-Israeli resolution was passed, which, among other things, denounced Israeli technical assistance as a form of imperialism. A year later, the 1967 war was a turning point in the perception of Israel by the Third World, and especially by African countries. It changed

TABLE 1

BLACK AFRICA BREAKS OFF RELATIONS
WITH ISRAEL: THE PROCESS

Country	Date of Break-off	Date of Renewal	Unofficial Contact Since
Guinea	June 6, 1967		Interests section, 1983; closed 1986.
Uganda	March 30, 1972		
Chad	November 28, 1972		Visits, 1982, 1983
Congo Brazzaville	December 5, 1972		
Niger	December 10, 1972		
Mali	January 5, 1973		
Burundi	May 16, 1973		
Togo	September 21, 1973		Interests section, January 1982
Zaire	October 4, 1973	May 15, 1982	
Benin	October 6, 1973		
Rwanda	October 9, 1973		
Burkina Faso (Upper Volta)	October 11, 1973		
Cameroon	October 15, 1973	August 26, 1986	
Equatorial Guinea	October 15, 1973		
Tanzania	October 18, 1973		
Madagascar	October 20, 1973		
Central African Republic	October 21, 1973		Interests section
Ethiopia	October 23, 1973		Visits
Nigeria	October 23, 1973		
Gambia	October 26, 1973		
Zambia	October 26, 1973		
Ghana	October 28, 1973		
Senegal	October 30, 1973		Leaders met November 1976
Gabon	October 30, 1973		Visits, interests section, January 1982
Sierra Leone	October 30, 1973		
Kenya	November 1, 1973		Interests section
Liberia	November 2, 1973	August 15, 1983	
Ivory Coast	November 8, 1973	February 16, 1986	
Botswana	November 13, 1973		
Mauritius	May 1976		
Malawi	No break-off		
Lesotho	No break-off		
Swaziland	No break-off		

African views on the broader Arab-Israeli conflict and on the rights of the Palestinians. After the 1967 war, the Arabs scored more and more diplomatic successes in a variety of international forums, with more and more African countries, some considered extremely friendly to Israel, voting in the United Nations to condemn it time and again (Nyang, 1980). Later on, the 1973 war was seen as the result of continuing Israeli occupation, and the wish by an African state, Egypt, to unfreeze the situation.

Israel's downfall in Africa was tied to a growing disenchantment with Western aid and Western-style politics, to the ideology of African unity and the policies of the Organization of African Unity, and to the growth of Islamic and Arab influence in Africa. After five African nations broke off relations in 1972, Israeli diplomats were quoted as attributing the change to a "general radicalization of the African continent and growing disillusion with the West among many African leaders" (Smith, 1973, p. 3). The end of the Israeli-French alliance also reduced Israel's penetration of French-speaking Africa (Decalo, 1976). And Israel's alliance with South Africa and Rhodesia was yet another factor in the decline (Gitelson, 1976).

There were several aspects of Israel's overall policies on African questions that might have led to the eventual demise of the Israeli success story in Africa, among them the following:

1. The development of a Third World consciousness, and the identification with anticolonialist movements on the part of African nations.
2. The growing influence of Arab countries in international organizations, including the Organization of African Unity.
3. Growing awareness in Africa of the Palestinian movement.
4. Israel's alliance with South Africa, developing since the 1950s (see chapter 5).
5. Israel's aid to Portugal in the 1960s during the Portuguese effort to maintain colonial rule over Angola, Mozambique, and Guinea-Bissau.
6. Israel voted with the West on most questions at the United Nations. In 1959, it voted against elections in

Cameroon (whose independence movement was considered communist by France and the United States), against the Liberian resolution to grant independence to all African colonies, and against censure of France for its nuclear tests in the Sahara. In 1960, Israel abstained on the question of independence for Tanganyika, Rwanda, and Burundi; and in 1962, it voted against Algeria's membership in the United Nations.

Israel did vote for anti-apartheid resolutions at the United Nations between 1960 and 1965. But a proposed Israeli contribution to African liberation movements in 1971 turned out to be one of the greatest fiascos in the history of Israeli diplomacy in Africa. Israel offered $2,000—a sum that managed to offend the Africans because it was so small, and the South Africans because it was an indication of support for "terrorists." The offer was declined by the OAU, and the South Africans were delighted.

Only three African nations never broke off relations: Malawi, Lesotho, and Swaziland.

Algeria

In a unique version of colonialism, Algeria under French rule was officially a part of France. Since it was French territory, giving it independence and recognizing the rights of the natives was to most of the French, even left-wingers, inconceivable. Socialists and communists (François Mitterrand among them) loyally supported the French cause in the Algerian war. (France's claims to justify the denial of Algerian rights included some ideas used today to justify Zionism: many French intellectuals said that there was no such thing as Algerian nationality or identity, and that Arabs in Algeria had equal opportunities for advancement within the French system.)

The Algerian war of independence between 1954 and 1962 caused a major crisis in France, and brought about the end of the Fourth Republic and the rise of a presidential system under Charles de Gaulle. Israel, at the time a close ally of France (see chapter 1), played a role in the Algerian war. "Israeli intelligence services were well informed on events in Algeria even before 1953 and had begun to work very closely with the French services in 1954" (Crosbie, 1974, p. 107). During the war, "Israeli study missions were welcomed in Algeria, where they expressed particular interest in the French use of helicopters to fight the guerrillas." In January 1960, two Israeli generals, Yitzhak Rabin (later chief-of-staff and prime minister) and Haim Herzog (later U.N. ambassador and president of Israel) visited Algeria and witnessed the French paratroopers in action in the Kabil mountains (Eytan, 1986). In general, "Algeria was another arena for cooperative effort [between Israel and France] in the last years of the Fourth Republic" (Crosbie, 1974, p. 107).

During 1961 and 1962, there were numerous reports of Israeli support for the French OAS movement (Organisation de l'Armée Secrète) in Algeria, the ultra-rightist organization of French settlers that was trying to maintain French control over Algeria (Crosbie, 1974; Kenan, 1982). "When in 1961 the OAS was created, it was a natural development that Israel, as keen on *Algérie-Française* as the OAS themselves, should lock themselves into the organization" (Steven, 1980, p. 207).

A move made by the Algerian liberation movement toward Israel was rebuffed. In August of 1957, a representative of the FLN, the Algerian National Liberation Front, contacted the Israeli mission to the United Nations and asked for Israel's support in the General Assembly debate on the future of Algeria. A positive Israeli response could have been a historical breakthrough, but such a response was out of the question (*Haolam Hazeh,* 1957). When Algeria, finally independent, joined the United Nations, only Israel voted against its admission.

It is reported that the Mossad was wrong in its predictions on the outcome of the Algerian war of independence and on the significance of that outcome (Steven, 1980). If true, then we have here not just a policy of opposition to the rise of the Third World, but also a blindness to the reality of decolonization.

Morocco

An absolute monarchy, Morocco has been run since 1961 by King Hassan II. It is also the westernmost part of the Arab world—almost as close to the United States as it is to the eastern part. What is true geographically is just as accurate politically. But although Morocco has often enjoyed a positive image in the Western media, it is still an absolute monarchy, and a feudal monarchy in the twentieth century is bound to run into problems. To cope with its problems, Morocco has adopted an extremely conservative foreign policy, with alliances that put it firmly into an international conservative coalition, with such countries as South Africa, Saudi Arabia, and Taiwan.

The alliance between Israel and Morocco began in the early 1960s, against the background of growing radicalism in the Arab world. One by one, monarchies in the Arab world seemed to be disappearing from the scene. King Hassan of Morocco decided that the one power that would stop this process was Israel.

By 1965, Israel had set up Hassan's internal security system, including the personal guard unit to the king himself (Steven, 1980). By 1966, the cooperation between Morocco and Israel brought about a major international and internal crisis for Israel—the Ben-Barka affair, involving France, Morocco, and Israel. Mehdi Ben-Barka was a radical Moroccan intellectual living in exile and sentenced to death *in absentia* by the Hassan regime. General Mohammed Oufkir, the head of the Moroccan secret service, received orders from the king in early 1965 to eliminate Ben-Barka, and immediately sought the help of the Mossad. As it turned out, the Mossad, having been shadowing Moroccan exiles, could indeed help. The Mossad became involved in the kidnapping of Ben-Barka in Paris. He was later murdered in cold blood. Since the affair took place on French soil, and involved collaboration with right-wing elements in the French secret service, it led to a major political crisis, to a purge of the service by De Gaulle, and to a trial in which General Oufkir was sentenced *in absentia* for murder. In Israel it caused a major crisis within the ruling elite, though Israeli censorship did not allow any mention of the affair (it was only referred to vaguely as another "security mishap," similar to the one in Cairo in 1954 mentioned in chapter 1). Nonetheless, the Moroccan secret service has had close ties with the Mossad ever since.

It is widely known that meetings in Morocco between Israeli foreign minister Moshe Dayan and Egyptian delegates laid the groundwork for Sadat's visit to Jerusalem in 1977. Secret agreements between Israel and Morocco were signed in 1977 when Yitzhak Rabin was prime minister. Rabin himself visited Morocco in October 1976 and May 1977. A Moroccan delegation visited Israel in the same year (Zayad, 1984). Morocco has been helped by Israel since 1975 in its war against Polisario rebels, who are seeking independence for the Western Sahara region (Sachar, 1981). Israel sold Morocco some of its French-made AMX-13 tanks and armored personnel carriers (Segev, 1984).

Morocco's relationship with Israel has been very similar to Israel's with Iran under the shah. There is a basic similarity in the Moroccan and Iranian regimes, each headed by a monarch with extremely centralized powers. In Rabat, the Moroccan capital, Israel maintains a permanent mission—to all intents and purposes an embassy. It serves as headquarters for other contacts with the Arab world.

Given the close collaboration between the two countries, the summit meeting between Shimon Peres and King Hassan in July 1986 was totally predictable. The two leaders had much to gain in terms of domestic politics (in the case of Peres) and U.S. public opinion (in the case of Hassan). "King Hassan II of Morocco scored brownie points in Washington by receiving Israel's soon-to-be ex-premier, Shimon Peres. King Hassan is in line for improved U.S. subsidies for his gesture. [He] is in economic difficulties and could use more U.S. economic aid" (Harsch, 1986, p. 9). This is one cynical but realistic assessment of the Moroccan gesture. Israeli influence in Washington has been used since the 1970s in obtaining Congressional support for Morocco. Congressman Stephen Solarz has been persuaded by his Israeli friends to drop his reservations about King Hassan (Zak, 1986).

Sudan

The Sudan was a part of Israel's extended periphery strategy as early as the 1950s. In 1956, Israel developed contacts with the pro-Western Umma Moslem Party of Sudan (Bar-Zohar, 1977). The Umma Party, one of the two traditional leading parties in the Sudan (and winner of the 1986 elections), has always been nationalist, leaning away from close relations with Egypt. Israeli interests in supporting it were quite clear.

But Israel's most serious intervention in the Sudan took place in the 1960s, and was part and parcel of other Israeli involvements. It was the secret operation in support of separatists rebels in southern Sudan. "The Southern Sudanese, like the Kurds in the Middle East, are a minority ripe for manipulation by more powerful forces in the course of regional power politics" (Bloch and Fitzgerald, 1983, p. 159). The southerners, 6 million out of a population of 15 million, are black and mostly Christian, while the northerners are Arabs and Moslems. The south is much poorer. Since the 1960s, frictions between north and south have led more than once to open war. Israel was involved in the civil war in southern Sudan in the late 1960s. The southern rebel movement, Anyanya, was supported by an Israeli military mission, which supplied training and arms, the arms presumably captured during the 1967 war.

Israeli involvement in southern Sudan was in evidence as early as 1963 (Beshir, 1975), through contacts with Israeli embassies in Uganda, Ethiopia (Halliday and Molyneux, 1981), the Congo, and Chad. After 1969, the Israeli support took the form of arms, advisers, and training. There was an Israeli mission in Torit, and thirty Anyanya men were trained in Israel. The Israeli ambassador to Kampala, Uri Lubrani, was in charge of the Anyanya connections.

The mercenary Rolf Steiner, who fought with the Anyanya, testified in August 1971 before a military tribunal in Khartoum that Israel reached an agreement with Uganda in 1970 regarding the use of Ugandan territory to aid the Sudanese rebels (*Le Monde,* 1971a). Steiner also stated that Israel was the only effective source of aid to the rebels (*Le Monde,* 1971b). Others state that these covert operations were coordinated with the United States (Zak, 1980).

The Addis Ababa Agreement on Southern Sudan of 1972 ended the southern rebellion and the Israeli intervention. Between 1972 and 1985, during the regime of Gaafar al-Nimeiry, Israeli contacts with the Sudan were rather friendly, though mostly secretive. The end of the rebellion in southern Sudan led to closer relations. The Mossad has had a station in Khartoum since then. There have been extensive contacts between the Mossad and its Sudanese equivalent in the 1980s. Mossad activities in the Sudan have been coordinated with the CIA, as many sources indicate. In public, Nimeiry was one of the few Arab leaders to support the peace treaty between Egypt and Israel in 1979. The coup in Sudan on April 6, 1985, ended the cooperation between Nimeiry and the Israeli government. The new military regime headed by General Abdel Rahman Siwar al-Dahab has been cool toward the United States and has developed closer ties with Libya and Ethiopia.

Ghana

If Burma was the great Israeli success story in Asia, Ghana was the equivalent in Africa. But Israeli ties with Burma remained almost alone in Asia, while Ghana turned out to be a stepping stone to the rest of black Africa. The first Israeli ambassador in Africa was Ehud Avriel, stationed in Ghana in 1957, and widely believed to be a Mossad operative (Steven, 1980). Avriel was active in recruiting individuals for "special missions" all over Africa (Samet, 1986).

Cooperation with Ghana took many forms, marked by mutual enthusiasm and openness. There were commercial ventures, the best-known of which was the Black Star shipping company. Hundreds of Ghanian trainees went to Israel, and hundreds of Israeli experts came to Ghana. There was also military and intelligence cooperation: Ghana's air force was supplied with reconditioned military aircraft and training (Bayne, 1965), and intelligence training was given by the Mossad (CIA, 1979).

Israel was described as "Ghana's closest friend in the early years" (Thompson, 1969, p. 46). Nevertheless, Kwame Nkrumah always demonstrated some reservations about Israel. He started moving closer to Egypt, which he visited several times, while refusing to visit Israel (Thompson, 1969). While Israel established close ties with Ghana as early as 1957, and with the Ghanian leadership even before formal independence in 1956, the special relationship between the two countries was over by 1967. Formal relations ended on October 28, 1973.

Elements in the Ghanian secret service are said to have kept contacts with the Mossad even while their countries did not have diplomatic relations (*Africa Now,* 1983), but relations with Ghana have worsened since the coup led by Lieutenant Jerry Rawlings. The Ghanian government accused Israel of being involved in a planned coup attempt, together with the CIA and Liberia (Brittain, 1983). (Relations with the United States have deteriorated since then, with mutual accusations of spying, and an exchange of accused spies between the United States and Ghana in 1985.)

Ethiopia

Until 1974 a kingdom dating back to ancient times, Ethiopia fired the imaginations of many people outside of Africa, and served as a symbol of African dignity and independence. Emperor Haile Selassie (under his former name, Ras Tafari) became the god of a new religion, Rastafarianism, founded in the Western hemisphere as a religion of black people yearning for independence (Cashmore, 1979). Many blacks identified with predominantly Christian Ethiopia, and its former name, Abyssinia, is still part of the name of numerous churches in the United States. Europeans were also impressed by Haile Selassie, and following the 1936 invasion, he became a symbol of resistance to European fascism and colonialism.

Haile Selassie's regime, like Liberia's, represented the paradox of an independent black nation, never subjected to colonialism, being one of the most conservative and backward forces in Africa. As the face of Africa was changing, bringing more nations to independence, Haile Selassie was preoccupied with internal rebellions and became totally dependent on American and other Western support.

Friendly contacts between Ethiopia and Israel started in the 1950s, with civilian trade ties as early as 1952 (Bayne, 1965). Shortly after the 1956 Suez war, an Israeli representative visited Ethiopia for meetings with Haile Selassie and his senior aides. The meeting took place in coordination with France (Bar-Zohar, 1977). Ethiopia was part of Israel's triangular periphery strategy (along with Turkey and Iran; see chapter 1). The alliance with Ethiopia existed at the highest level (the emperor) starting in 1958, and was based on the joint interest of stopping radicalization and Pan-Arabism (Segev, 1981). This Israeli-Ethiopian alliance was successful until the 1970s (Hoagland, 1972a). The ideological basis for this alliance was the perception of the Israelis "as a brave people surrounded by hostile Muslim forces that seek to seize their historic homeland, a situation the Ethiopian Christians consider analogous to their own history in the midst of a threatening Muslim sea" (Kaplan et al., 1971, p. 320). A startling admission of Ethiopia's importance in Israel's strategic designs is contained in an interview given by Shimon Peres in June 1966 (Brecher, 1972, p. 343). In it Peres lists his eight goals for Israel's foreign policy; the first is "To build a 'second Egypt' in Africa, that is, to help convert Ethiopia's economic and military strength into a counterforce to Egypt, thereby giving Africans another focus."

The Ethiopian military under Haile Selassie was assisted by military missions from Britain, Sweden, Norway, India, Israel, and the United States (Kaplan et al., 1971). In the 1960s Israel proposed to the United States a joint military advisory group in Ethiopia, but this idea was turned down (Evans and Novak, 1977). However, Israeli activities in Ethiopia were reportedly coordinated with the United States: "Until the overthrow of Haile Selassie, the United States, Israel, and Ethiopia were more or less allied in a common fight against the Eritrean Liberation Front" (Schwab, 1979, p. 95). The Israeli military aid included training for commando units and counterinsurgency experts, as well as setting up communications for the Ethiopian military (Gitelson, 1976). "From 1962 onwards, Israeli advisers trained the Emergency Police, an elite counterinsurgency group of 3,100 men established to operate in Eritrea. The official number of Israeli advisers is stated to have been around forty" (Halliday and Molyneux, 1981, p. 232). Israeli advisers were attached to the Second Division in the Eritrea region in 1970–1971.

In 1962, the Israeli diplomatic mission to Ethiopia was upgraded from a consulate-general to an embassy. Between 1968 and 1971, Israel's ambassador to Ethiopia was Uri Lubrani (earlier ambassador to Uganda, and later posted to Iran). The ubiquitous Lubrani apparently tried to alert U.S. representatives to the growing weakness of Haile Selassie's regime, to no avail (Ledeen and Lewis, 1982). In 1978, Lubrani would repeat this performance in Iran.

There were many visits to Ethiopia by high Israeli officers, including a visit in August 1971 by the Israeli chief-of-staff, General Haim Bar-Lev. Arab sources reported in 1971 that Ethiopia gave Israel the right for its navy to use two islands in the Red Sea close to the crucial Bab al-Mandab straits. The islands were Haleb and Fatima, located just north of the French Territory of the Afars and Issas (later Djibouti [Reppa, 1974]). The importance of military contacts with Ethiopia was reflected in the fact that Israeli military attachés there included General Haim Ben-David, former military adviser to Prime Minister Ben-Gurion, and General Abraham Orly, future governor of all Israeli-occupied territories and future supplier of the Rhodesian security fence.

Ethiopia was a convenient way station for covert activities all over the Middle East and Africa, masked by commercial fronts. Thus, Incoda, a company that exported Ethiopian beef and was owned by Israelis, was used between 1955 and 1964 as a successful commercial front for intelligence activities. One of its directors says: "Incoda was a station for Israeli intelligence in Africa. We had a huge arms cache. It was there when we arrived. We just served as the cover. There was a military delegation, and they did their correspondence through us. With Israeli spies in Arab countries as well. We were only a cover in Mossad deals. When they had to send somebody to an Arab country, they did it through us. . . . We transmitted mail to spies in Arab countries in our ships" (Duek, 1986, p. 25).

One of the leading Israeli experts on Ethiopia described the situation in the early 1970s as follows: "The ambassador boasted with some justification that we were practically 'running the country.' . . . Israel offered a lot of help to the Ethiopian government in various fields, particularly in the area of maintaining internal security" (Schenker, 1985, p. 22). The Israeli contribution to "internal security" in Ethiopia took the form of training a highly efficient secret police. According to General Matityahu Peled, former member of the IDF general staff, the efficient Israeli advisers to the secret police in Addis Ababa saved Haile Selassie three times from coup attempts. But in 1974, they failed to save him from a revolution that changed the monarchy into a Marxist military regime.

Even after the fall of Haile Selassie, the contacts between Israel and Ethiopia continued. There were indications of an Israeli presence in Ethiopia as late as 1977, in the form of counterinsurgency advisers and shipments of spare parts for military equipment (Mann, 1977). The continuing ties with Israelis were explained by the common stance of the two countries against Islamic groups in the region. The relations with Israel were maintained by Colonel Mengistu Haile Mariam, possibly because of a desire to keep more options open, and possibly because of good personal and professional relations with Israeli officers and Israelis in general.

Whatever Israel has been doing for, and with, the Marxist government of Ethiopia has been coordinated with the United States (Lathem, 1983). According to the *Economist,* the United States has used Israel to "keep a channel to Ethiopia's Marxist leaders" (1977, p. 91). Even Mengistu joined the list of Third World leaders who want to use Israel's intercession, and asked Israel in 1977 for help in improving relations with the United States (Shipler, 1983). Prime Minister Menahem Begin then asked President Jimmy Carter in a personal meeting to change American policy toward Ethiopia; the Americans were totally surprised.

It is reported that in 1977, Israel agreed to supply arms to Ethiopia in return for letting Ethiopian Jews emigrate to Israel (Newman and Gouterman, 1985). But in 1978, the Israeli presence in Ethiopia was practically terminated, apparently because of a public statement by Moshe Dayan, then foreign minister, about the contacts with the Mengistu regime. Nevertheless, there have been reports of Israeli arms sales to Ethiopia even after that. According to one report, Israel sold Soviet-made weapons captured in Lebanon to Ethiopia at prices much lower than those charged by the Soviet Union—but still worth an estimated $20 million.

Relations between Israel and Ethiopia have another little-known aspect, reflecting the complicated history of the Middle East. Anybody who has ever visited the Church of the Holy Sepulchre in Jerusalem has seen a crazy quilt of numerous Christian denominations, each fighting for its own particular brand of eternal truth and its own bit of temporal turf. Disputes over both are the lifeblood of this holy place. Visitors are treated to the noisy spectacle of mass being celebrated simultaneously by all tenant groups, each trying to drown out the sounds of the others. One visible presence in the church is that of Ethiopian Orthodox priests, who live in an actual Ethiopian village built on the roof of an adjacent building, and have a chapel in the main structure. In 1971, the Ethiopians invaded an old and neglected part of the structure, thus increasing their real-estate holdings. The place used to belong to the Egyptian Coptic Church, and so started an international dispute. The Egyptian government takes the Coptic side, naturally. The Ethiopian government, despite its commitment to revolutionary Marxism, supports this Ethiopian conquest. The Israeli government, seeing this as an opportunity to improve relations with Ethiopia, has adopted a policy of lenient neutrality.

Zaire

A hairdresser on New York's fashionable East Side flies to Europe once a month at the invitation of one of his customers. The hairdresser, who can also invite several friends to join him on the trip, goes in style, as befits a hairdresser to the rich and powerful. He travels by Concorde, and can come back to his New York clientele after just a few hours in the Old World. The customer who pays for all this is Mobutu Sese Seko, president of Zaire, one of the most corrupt dictators in the world.

Zaire, which was known for almost a century as the Congo (or the Belgian Congo) can serve as the best example for the ravages and horrors of colonialism in Africa. It entered European history in 1885, when, in a show of what was known as European civilization, it was placed under the personal rule of King Leopold II of Belgium, who had sent Henry Morton Stanley to acquire for him unclaimed pieces of African territory. The Berlin Conference of 1885 sealed the division of Africa among European powers, and gave Leopold the Congo as his private property, aptly misnamed the Free State of the Congo. It was natural that the capital of the new state was named Leopoldville. The history of personal ownership of a whole country seems to be repeating itself in the Zaire of today, owned by Mobutu Sese Seko (formerly Joseph Désiré Mobutu) and his friends. The country is marked by an unusual wealth of natural resources (copper, cobalt, diamonds, zinc, tin, uranium, water power)—as well as an unusual, and unnatural, human poverty. Despite the riches extracted from its soil, the people of Zaire are among the poorest in Africa, and spend most of their lives in a state of semistarvation or worse (Kwitny, 1984b).

Mobutu was born in 1930, and received his education in the Congo and in Belgium. He served for seven years in the Belgian colonial army, and then had a career as a journalist. In 1960, after independence, he became the chief-of-staff, and in 1965, in a coup, he became president. On October 27, 1971, when the Congo became Zaire, he dropped his French names and became Sese Seko. The regime of Mobutu Sese Seko in Zaire can be described only as a murderous tyranny; what has been happening in this country is reminiscent of the nineteenth-century practices of King Leopold. The people of Zaire starve and enjoy a per-capita income of less than $80 annually, while Mobutu siphons billions to his Swiss bank accounts. The list of real estate owned by the dictator all over Africa and Europe takes at least five pages, excluding his commercial holdings. Amnesty International regularly singles out Mobutu as one of the most oppressive rulers in Africa, while the United States regards him, not too surprisingly, as a friendly champion of Western values (Kwitny, 1984a). As a result of the systematic pillage of the country's assets by the dictator and his friends, Mobutu's personal fortune is estimated at $4 billion, while the real average income of the Zairian people is now 10 percent of what it was in 1960 (Young and Turner, 1985). The horror of Zaire, a century after "Heart of Darkness," has recently been described thus: "Malnutrition kills more than one-third of Zaire's citizens and leaves countless others with permanent brain damage, usually suffered in youth. The 25 to 28 million people of Zaire, half of them children, are literally starving to death in their mud huts" (Kwitny, 1984b, p. 101).

When we look at the record carefully, we discover that Israel has played a continuous role for twenty-five years in keeping Zaire under Western control and under Mobutu's. Israeli involvement dates back to the early 1960s, when Zaire was still the newly independent Congo. Diplomatic relations between the two countries were first established in 1962, and in December 1963, President Joseph Kasavubu visited Israel. Israel started by training Congolese paratroopers (Dodenhoff, 1969). "First, early in 1963, Israeli officers were dispatched to the Congo. . . . In August 1963 and again in November, Congolese units totaling about 250 men came to Israel. The first group was joined by the then Army Commander, General Joseph Mobutu . . . , who along with his soldiers won his parachute wings in Israel. At the end of their course, 45 of the soldiers stayed on for advanced training" (Laufer, 1967, p. 171).

In 1964, Israel delivered the first tanks, ten obsolete M-4 Sherman models. As of 1969, the Democratic Republic of the Congo had enjoyed "technical assistance and military training" from France, West Germany, Italy, Denmark, Canada, and Israel. Taiwan offered a technical-assistance program (McDonald et al., 1971). A parachute-training center was operated with the help of Israeli instructors. In 1969, Israeli advisers started training the First Paracommando Battalion, an elite unit in Mobutu's army. When an agreement on military cooperation was signed between the two countries on September 8, 1971, the foreign minister of the Congo said that it was only a formalization of activities that had gone on over the previous eight years, and credited Israel with training the elite of the Congolese army. The Israeli involvement in the Congo in the 1960s has been described as "one of the best dividends from this CIA investment" of financing Israeli activities in Africa (Evans and Novak, 1977, p. A15), and it was fully coordinated with U.S. covert operations.

Mobutu announced the breaking off of Zaire's diplomatic relations with Israel on October 4, 1973, during a speech to the U.N. General Assembly. The reason given was solidarity with Egypt, whose land had been occupied by Israel. This was only two days before Egypt started the 1973 war to change that situation. But during the years 1973–1982, with no formal diplomatic relations, there were still many secret contacts; a resident agent of the Mossad was very active in Zaire, as a close associate of Mobutu. Still, Mobutu was now receiving Arab (as well as U.S.) aid, and was not ready for any public contacts. Israel renewed its efforts to court him in the late 1970s. Defense Minister Ezer Weizman visited Zaire in December 1979, offering military aid (Klich, 1982a). There was a secret visit by David Kimche on May 20, 1981 (Eytan, 1982). In November 1981 another defense minister, Ariel Sharon, visited secretly, and an agreement was reached for Israel to train the special Presidential Brigade. An Israeli-interests section in the Canadian embassy in Kinshasa was opened in January 1982, and full diplomatic relations were reinstated on May 15, 1982.

On May 21, 1982, the Israeli embassy reopened in Kinshasa, staffed initially by members of the Israeli-interests section. According to *Haolam Hazeh* (1982b), Mobutu was paid $10 million for the renewal of relations; such a payment would not be out of line, given what we know about him. In January 1983, during an official four-day visit by Sharon, an agreement was reached to increase the Presidential Brigade from 3,000 to 7,500 soldiers, under Israeli supervision, and for the training of the Kamanyola Brigade in Shaba province (formerly Katanga) by Israel. During this visit Mobutu declared: "We have recognized the PLO since 1975 as the main representative of the Palestinian people. Israel knows about it and I do not see any contradiction between our recognition of the PLO and our friendships for Israel" (quoted by Kfir, 1983a, p. 7).

The new Israeli ambassador in Kinshasa was Michael Michael, formerly Israeli ambassador to Pretoria, and a former director of the Foreign Ministry's intelligence unit (Segev, 1983). Mobutu indicated his wishes for Israel to act on his behalf to induce U.S. Jews to invest in Zaire. President Haim Herzog, during his official visit to Zaire in 1984, had "practical ideas about encouraging Jews from all over the world to invest in Zaire" (Becker, 1984, p. 8; Segal, 1984). Most of these grandiose plans have never materialized. Another consequence of Israeli efforts was the recruitment of Kenneth Bialkin, chairman of the President's Conference of American Jewish Leaders, to represent Mobutu in the United States (Segal, 1984). In September 1984 Shamir met with Mobutu, who expressed his great disappointment with the rate of investment in Zaire by American Jews; he had expected Israel to do more.

The official visit by Mobutu Sese Seko to Israel in May 1985 was a celebration of the alliance between the two countries. Three official agreements were signed, covering aviation, investments, and technical aid. Mobutu was ceremoniously welcomed by President Haim Herzog, with twenty-one-gun salutes and a flyover of Israeli air force jets. Amidst all the good feelings, he stunned his Israeli hosts by expressing his support for the idea of a Palestinian state—even Mobutu felt that he could not stray from the Third World consensus. Civilian aid to Zaire, since 1981, has focused on developing agricultural production in two farms, which have become extremely prosperous, thanks to Israeli experts. They happen to be owned by Mobutu Sese Seko, so the aid is rather personal. On February 16, 1986, Israel ratified a new agreement for technological cooperation with Zaire.

Ideas about the inordinate power of Israel, and the Jews, in the world system, and especially in the United States, seemed to have played a major role in Mobutu's decision to renew formal relations with Israel. A Western diplomat in Zaire is quoted as saying, "President Mobutu has not read *The Protocols of the Elders of Zion,* but if you ask what motivated him to renew the relations with Israel, it was his belief in the great power of the Jews to influence governments and the press, essentially in the United States" (Salpeter, 1982, p. 7). Mobutu's decision to renew relations with Israel came at a low point in the history of his regime, when Zaire, as a state, was defaulting on its loans, and the U.S. Congress canceled all aid because of Mobutu's corruption. According to *Haolam Hazeh,* Mobutu had two requests for Israel—to train his secret police, and to improve his image in the United States. The first request could be easily met, because many Israeli SHABAK experts, who used to work with the SAVAK in Iran, were looking for something to do in 1982. The second would be harder. "Mobutu is convinced that American Jews control the mass media and the banks, and so can change his image and obtain new loans for him" (1982b, p. 10).

While Israeli and Jewish influence is not as powerful as Mobutu imagined, Israel has tried to use its influence in the United States to help him. The names of two Jewish U.S. congressmen, Howard Wolpe and Stephen Solarz, came up during Foreign Minister Yitzhak Shamir's visit to Zaire in December 1982. Shamir told reporters that "there have been discussions with Solarz" about Zaire and that "Solarz takes Israeli interests into consideration" (Karny, 1982b, p. 2). Congressman Wolpe had been under pressure from Israel to increase U.S. aid to Zaire (Becker, 1985a). Wolpe, who chairs a special subcommittee on Africa, visits Israel regularly. Several Jewish U.S. congressmen were reportedly involved in helping Mobutu obtain loans from the International Monetary Fund (Allon, 1984).

The Israeli Foreign Ministry spokesman, Avi Pazner, responding to the refusal of congressmen Wolpe and Solarz to join the Israeli public-relations campaign on behalf of Mobutu, said, "Their personal opinions are their business, and they are entitled to them. We demand no right to interfere in their reasoning. We have something to tell them, and not only them. We intend to act on behalf of Zaire in American public opinion, not only on the individual level" (Karny, 1982b, p. 2). Israel took the matter of changing Mobutu's image in the United States seriously. A visit by an American Jewish delegation to Zaire in 1982 was the first shot in a public-relations campaign coordinated by a firm run by the Israeli Zeev First, who had been involved in the Likud election campaign in 1981 (Karny, 1982a).

Representative Clarence Long, head of the House Appropria-
tions Subcommittee on Foreign Operations, received a request from
Israel on behalf of Zaire (Evans and Novak, 1983). Mobutu ended up
winning $20 million in military aid, with some of the money going to
Israel. Israel's support for Zaire, like Israeli support in other similar
cases, was welcomed by the Reagan administration (Barak, 1983a).
What better connection for a Third World pariah? In August 1983,
the same Subcommittee on African Affairs that refused to grant aid
to Zaire a year earlier changed its mind and granted most of Mobutu's
wishes.

Zaire has accepted military aid, including advisers, from the
People's Republic of China, from Belgium, France, Egypt, Morocco,
and the United States. However, since 1983 Israel has become Zaire's
prime military supplier. Mobutu was supported by fifteen hundred
Moroccan troops, as well as small numbers of French and Belgian
paratroopers, between 1978 and 1982. After 1982, Israel has been seen
as taking over the main support role. Even before Sharon's visit in
1981, a military delegation was sent to Kinshasa; its head, Colonel
Yonadav Navon, was appointed officially as military adviser to
Mobutu. A five-man military team arrived in Kinshasa in March 1982
to retrain Mobutu's bodyguards. On October 25, 1982, General
Mobutu met with an Israeli military delegation headed by two generals, Abraham Tamir and Ehud Barak, to discuss details of the
military-aid program. There were four elements in the military-aid
plan for Zaire, as developed by Israeli teams visiting in 1981–1982:

1. Training and expanding the Special Presidential Brigade
   (BSP).
2. Training and expanding the Kamanyola Brigade into a
   division.
3. Developing artillery units.
4. Training Mobutu's bodyguards and domestic intelligence
   services.

The Presidential Brigade of the Zairian army, stationed around the
presidential palace in Kinshasa, is the main guarantee for the survival
of the regime and of Mobutu personally. Most of its members have
been trained in Israel; and hundreds sport Israeli paratroopers' wings.

59

Not all the plans for military cooperation announced during the Sharon visit have been carried out, for a variety of reasons. The visit was followed by misunderstandings and frictions. Mobutu claimed that Sharon promised him the retraining and expansion of the Kamanyola Brigade into a division, with all expenses covered by Israel. This was denied by the Israeli government, which was ready to supply only instructors. The dispute was settled in June 1983, with Mobutu agreeing to foot the bill (Kfir, 1983b).

In 1983, the Zairian defense minister, Rear Admiral Laponda Wa Botende, visited Israel to work out details of military-aid programs. Under the military agreements, Israel agreed to take on a five-year reorganization of the Zairian Army. In addition to training and expanding existing units, Israel agreed to set up a new artillery battalion. The Zairian national security service has also received Israeli aid. In 1984 there were twenty Israeli military advisers in Zaire (Allon, 1984). Israel supplied Zaire with Uzi submachine guns, AK-47 rifles (captured in Lebanon), and Galil rifles. A new infantry brigade, number 14, joined the Zairian army in January 1986, after being trained for a year by Israeli advisers. During the ceremonial commissioning of the new unit, General David Rosh, head of the Israeli military mission, announced that Israel was ready to assume any duties assigned by the Zairian government (*Maariv,* 1986).

The renewed military contacts with Israel paid another dividend. Two months after the Sharon visit, a U.S. Defense Department delegation visited Zaire to meet with Mobutu and discuss "the security of African nations" (Reuters, 1983). The strengthened ties between Zaire and Israel in 1982 and 1983 were the result of a plan that included South Africa (Hall, 1983). Zaire under Mobutu enjoys close and friendly relations with South Africa, including visits by South African leaders. Relations with South Korea are good, and Mobutu paid an official visit to Seoul in 1982. Morocco and Saudi Arabia have also supported the Mobutu regime. According to reliable sources, most of the money from Saudi Arabia, like other funds in Zaire, ended up in Mobutu's numerous bank accounts.

Behind the story of Israel's continuing contacts with Zaire since 1963 lies the amazing personal history of a Mossad agent. Meir Meyouhas, born in Cairo in 1926, has been Mobutu's right-hand man since 1963; he enabled Israel to continue with an unofficial presence and much influence in Zaire between 1973 and 1982, when there were no diplomatic relations. Meyouhas went to Palestine in 1945, as a Zionist, and after 1948 was sent back by Israeli intelligence to Egypt. In 1954 he was arrested, together with other members of the intelligence network, in the famous "Cairo mishap" (see chapter 1). Convicted, he spent five years in prison, and was released in 1960. One would expect a man who had just been released from prison to take a break from risky activities, but in 1961 Meyouhas was already in Zaire, becoming Mobutu's best friend and business partner. He has remained in that capacity ever since, though he maintains a home in Israel as well. In 1982 he was appointed Israel's honorary consul in Kinshasa. According to Israelis in Kinshasa, "Meyouhas is our strong man in Zaire." He is active in all Zairian-Israeli affairs, and is in a position to influence Mobutu. He arranged the three visits by Sharon (two of them secret) and the official visit by Shamir. Being Mobutu's business partner, he is also quite wealthy (Allon, 1984; Steven, 1980). Meyouhas goes along on Mobutu's official visits abroad. During Mobutu's visit to the United States in 1983, Meyouhas was among those arranging the contacts between Mobutu and "leaders of the Jewish community, who were put into action to mobilize loans and credits from the International Monetary Fund, and investments by Jewish magnates" (Allon, 1984, p. 7). Meyouhas was mentioned in connection with the renewal of diplomatic relations between Cameroon and Israel in 1986. At the age of sixty, he shows no signs of slowing down, and will surely be remembered as one of Israel's most effective emissaries ever.

Uganda

Israel assumed full responsibility for the development of the Ugandan armed forces in 1966. Between 1964 and 1971, Israel sold Uganda twenty-six training and transport planes; in the same period, Uganda received seven MIG fighters from the Eastern bloc. In 1970, Israel also sold Uganda twelve obsolete World War II M-4 Sherman tanks (some were in action in Uganda as late as 1986, in units of the National Resistance Army.)

The Israeli advisers in Uganda were especially close to Colonel Idi Amin, who in January 1971 carried out a coup against President

Milton Obote, who had been moving to the left in his politics. Idi Amin moved to the right. The overthrow was supported by the Mossad, the CIA, and the British MI6 (Weir and Bloch, 1981); Colonel Baruch Bar-Lev, commander of the Israeli military delegation in Uganda, was instrumental in the coup (Golan, 1982). The rationale: "The Israelis . . . were disturbed by Obote's growing anti-zionism. . . . Amin, they thought, would be a useful puppet and come to rely on a large Israeli military presence for his survival" (Bloch and Fitzgerald, 1983, p. 162).

The honeymoon was short-lived; Idi Amin kept the Israeli advisers until April 1972, when all of them were asked to leave. At that point Amin was moving closer to Libya. He ruled Uganda for eight years—years of a repulsive, cruel tyranny. Later on he found refuge in the Arab world, and at last report was living in Saudi Arabia.

After Amin's departure, there came five years of chaos under former President Obote, and then another bloody dictatorship under Tito Okello. A new age, with some promises of peace and something resembling normal life, dawned on Uganda on January 27, 1986, with the victory of the National Resistance Army, a popular guerrilla movement led by Yoweri Museveni. The 1971 coup in Uganda, which the Israelis involved would like to forget, was the beginning of a long period of madness and bloodshed that still has not ended.

Zimbabwe (Rhodesia)

The story of white Rhodesia, from the unilateral declaration of independence from Britain in 1965 to black majority rule of the nation renamed Zimbabwe in 1980, sounds today like a rehearsal for the battle over apartheid in South Africa. Rhodesia was the next to last domino in Africa, and its struggle was watched closely by those in similar situations and with similar interests. When white Rhodesia was struggling to survive, the United States was there to help, with U.S. oil companies—Mobil, Texaco, and Standard Oil of California—shipping oil with impunity, and with U.S. mercenaries active on the side of Ian Smith. The U.S. government did nothing to stop the involvement of American citizens (Kwitny, 1984b). Israel was there as well, in the person of both individual citizens and official delegates.

On December 16, 1966, the United Nations Security Council

imposed mandatory sanctions against Rhodesia. Israel went on record as supporting them, but in practice there was a significant alliance between Israel and Rhodesia. Israel was clearly committed to the survival of the white regime in Rhodesia, and helped it in substantial ways. A quantity of Uzi submachine guns was sold to Rhodesia in 1977. In addition, Rhodesia won the right to produce its own Uzis, named Ruzis in this version. The Ruzi became standard in the Rhodesian armed forces and police, and was also sold to (white) citizens for $100 (*Bamahane,* 1977). In 1978, a shipment of eleven Bell 205 helicopters reached Rhodesia, through a scheme that evaded official embargoes on exports to that country. The helicopters, manufactured in the United States, were sold to the Israeli air force. The Israeli government, acting through private Israeli and U.S. companies, sold them to Rhodesia, and shipped them via South Africa. The Smith government used them in counterinsurgency operations (Mullen, 1979).

In the Rhodesian counterinsurgency campaign, "There was close study of Israeli techniques, particularly in terms of external operations" (Beckett, 1985, p. 176). One example of the inspiration provided by Israel to the Rhodesians: "It was a crib from the Israelis and the general idea was for a huge mine belt to be laid and buckled tight around our hostile borders, fitted where practicable with elements of an early warning system designed to detect and warn of any attempted or actual breachings" (Daly, 1982, p. 144). An Israeli corporation, owned by Reserve General Abraham Orly, built the five-hundred-mile "belt" along the border with Mozambique and Zambia.

In May 1976, a Rhodesian delegation visited Israel to recruit mercenaries for the Rhodesian army. They succeeded in gaining a few. As a result of private initiative, or private readiness, there were Israeli mercenaries in the Rhodesian army (*Haolam Hazeh,* 1978), at least one of whom was killed in action.

The end of Rhodesia and the beginning of Zimbabwe on April 18, 1980, was a bad day for Israel—another gamble that ended in total loss.

Angola and Mozambique

Though Israel was busy establishing ties with newly independent African nations in the 1960s, it did not support all forms of decolonization. When it came to Portugal's colonies, Israel was on the side of continuing European rule.

In the 1960s, Portugal, the poorest country in Western Europe and one of its two dictatorships, still held the last colonial empire in Africa—Mozambique, Angola, Guinea-Bissau, Cape Verde, São Tomé, and Príncipe. The spirit of decolonization had not bypassed Portugal's colonies, though, and rebellions started in the 1960s. In these rebellions Portugal found an ally in Israel. Liberation movements in Mozambique and Angola were fighting against a Portuguese army equipped by Israel. The ubiquitous Uzi was manufactured in Portugal under Israeli license, and was used heavily in the African colonies. The Israeli role in helping Portugal was marginal, compared to those of the United States, Great Britain, and other Western countries. At the same time it should be considered as part of the overall Western effort.

Israeli involvement in Angola has to be seen in the context of Israel's relations with pre-1974 fascist Portugal, with the United States, and with South Africa. Besides supporting Portugal in its colonial wars, Israel became more directly involved in Angola, thanks to the CIA. By now Israel has been a partner in two CIA operations in Angola —one during the war of 1975–1976, which started with the South African invasion; and the continuing operation of supporting the UNITA (National Union for the Total Independence of Angola) under Jonas Savimbi since 1976. Holden Roberto, the leader of the FNLA (National Front for the Liberation of Angola) visited Israel in the 1960s. Israeli support for the FNLA was in evidence between 1963 and 1969, the exact time when Roberto was enjoying direct CIA support (Marcum, 1978). Members of the group were trained in Israel. Israel's presence in Zaire has enabled it to transfer arms to the FNLA in Angola in the mid-1970s and to UNITA forces in the 1980s (*Africa Now,* 1983).

A Western observer has expressed the view that the renewed alliance between Israel and Zaire might have strategic consequences for Angola, benefiting South Africa and the United States: "The extra pressure of knowing the Israelis are next door could hasten a deal with Savimbi, then the removal of the Cubans. This, in turn, could lead to a settlement in Namibia—strictly on the terms the Americans and South Africans have long been seeking" (Hall, 1983, p. 5).

UNITA, to all intents and purposes, is a branch of the South African government and of the South African Defense Force. Israeli aid to UNITA is coordinated through the SADF, and is part of the South African war effort. UNITA has received arms captured by Israel from the PLO in Lebanon. As in other cases, the use of captured arms enables Israel, and the recipients, to hide their origins; it can be claimed that the arms were captured locally. During a visit to the United States in 1986, Jonas Savimbi reported that he was supported by several Arab countries, and even by France under Socialist president François Mitterrand. The Arab countries he mentioned are apparently Saudi Arabia, Morocco, and Egypt (Ottaway, 1986). This demonstrates once again that Israelis and Arabs can work together when they are on the same side of an issue.

When Mozambique became independent, Israel joined those who were trying to regain it as a colony. The main instrument of South Africa in its war against independent Mozambique is the MNR movement, which is another African "contra" organization, totally created from the outside. The MNR (Mozambique National Resistance) was started by Rhodesia, when there was still a Rhodesia. Since Rhodesia became Zimbabwe, the MNR has been supported by South Africa and Israel (Bloch, 1985). Israel's support for the MNR is really part of the Israeli alliance with South Africa (see chapter 5). There have also been reports of financial support by Saudi Arabia.

The Mozambique army has repeatedly claimed that the MNR forces are trained by Israelis and supplied by South Africa (AFP, 1984), supporting the claim with captured documents. The MNR forces have also gotten captured Soviet-made weapons from Israel. Two Israelis have been arrested in Mozambique since 1978 on suspicion of being connected with the MNR guerrillas. The first, Miron Marcus, was released in 1981, as part of a spy exchange. The second, Amikam Afrati, was arrested in 1982 and released in February 1983 (Karny, 1983a).

Kenya

Because of its pro-Western policies, Kenya has always enjoyed a good image in the Western press. Jomo Kenyatta, the grand old man who led his country to independence in 1964, became a corrupt ruler afterwards, "parceling out [Kenya's] dwindling resources among his family" (Kwitny, 1984b, p. 126) and favoring his own Kikuyu tribe. Daniel Arap Moi, a non-Kikuyu who became president upon the death of Kenyatta in 1978, created a more favorable impression, but turned out to be almost as repressive. The regime in Kenya, under Kenyatta and later under Moi, has been noted for its unusual ability to enrich officeholders. The Kenyatta family has amassed great fortunes, and President Moi is considered one of the wealthiest individuals in Africa (Girandet, 1986).

The CIA has been involved in Kenyan politics, offering regular payments to national leaders such as Tom Mboya and to Kenyatta himself (Kwitny, 1984b), and Nairobi has become a base for various Western intelligence services, including the Israeli one. The extent of Mossad contacts in Kenya became clear during the Entebbe raid of July 1976. That operation could not have been carried out without Kenyan support and involvement. Israeli planes were allowed to land in Nairobi, and a rear base for the operation was established there.

Extremely friendly relations between Israel and Kenya have continued through the 1980s. While Kenya's relations with Israel have been well known, the government has rejected Israeli requests for formal diplomatic relations. The more radical groups in Kenya are opposed to ties with Israel, which has become identified all over the continent with South Africa.

There have been many secret visits by Israeli officials, though; some have become public knowledge. In March 1981, two Israeli representatives paid a secret visit to Nairobi: Rahamim Timor, director of the Division on International Cooperation in the Foreign Ministry, and David Kimche, Mossad regional chief for Africa. In

December 1982, on his way back from Kinshasa, Foreign Minister Yitzhak Shamir paid a brief visit. At the Nairobi airport, at night, he met with President Moi, who asked Israel for help with his personal security (*Jeune Afrique*, 1982).

The lack of formal relations has not stopped Kenya from purchasing Israeli weapons. In 1978 it bought two missile boats and forty-eight Gabriel missiles for them (Segev, 1984); they were delivered in 1979 and 1982. It has also brought nonlethal military equipment, such as field kitchens, uniforms, and personal gear (Kartin, 1984b).

The issue of the unofficial close contacts with Israel does come up on occasion, revealing divided opinion in the government regarding any public display of support for Israel. Such an occasion was the visit to Nairobi in May 1983 of the Israeli dance troupe Bat Dor, which stopped in Kenya following appearances in Zaire. Contemporary ballet became a political issue, with the more conservative elements in government supporting the visit. The ballet performances went on without any problems.

Chad

A desert land with a very few oases, Chad is the poorest of the poor countries in the world, with a per-capita income below $80 a year and infant mortality at 16 percent. It is saved from media oblivion by an ongoing civil war, which has crept into the headlines time and again since 1980. The regime of the first president, François Tombalbaye, ended with his assassination in 1975, and since then the political situation has been deteriorating, and the inhabitants getting fewer and poorer. There are many historical and cultural divisions in the population, mainly between northern Moslems and southern Bantu. One of the strange things about this civil war is that the leaders of the two warring parties are both northern Moslems, Goukouni Oueddi and Hissen Habré. The first is more radical, supported by Libya. The second—which controls the capital—is more conservative, supported by the United States, France, and Israel (Israel had relations with the Tombalbaye regime until they were broken off on November 30, 1972).

The civil war in Chad heated up in 1982, and then Israel became involved. Israel, together with the CIA, has supported Habré's forces, supplying them with Soviet-made weapons (Lathem, 1983). There have been persistent reports, from a variety of sources, about Israeli military advisers in Chad during 1983. According to *AfricAsia* (1984), President Mobutu of Zaire was instrumental in arranging aid for Habré in the form of new Israeli advisers charged with developing a paratrooper battalion. Troops loyal to Habré were trained in Zaire by Zairian troops, who in turn had been trained by Israel.

Rebel forces in Chad claimed in August 1983 that Israeli instructors arrived in Chad together with twenty-five hundred Zairian soldiers, supporting the Habré government forces (*Yediot Aharonot,* 1983b). According to French sources, Israel had twelve military advisers in Chad during the fighting in 1983–1984, but they were removed in early 1984, lest they be captured by the rebels (Golan, 1984). Ariel Sharon first paid a visit to Chad in January 1983, just before leaving the Defense Ministry. His visit symbolized Israel's readiness to become more involved there.

Ivory Coast

The Ivory Coast, considered the most prosperous country in black Africa, has been ruled since gaining its independence from France in 1960 by Félix Houphouët-Boigny, who has become known as an authoritarian, pro-Western ruler. Houphouët-Boigny, a physician turned politician, served in the French National Assembly and was even a minister in the French government in the 1950s. On October 28, 1985, he was elected to a sixth term as president—not through an election, but by a referendum with 99 percent approval, and a 98 percent voting rate. Houphouët-Boigny is one of the most pro-Western of African leaders, protected by a permanent French garrison in Abidjan. The regime in the Ivory Coast is reminiscent of other African regimes where one leader has been in power since independence and his relatives and friends, not to mention himself, seem to benefit financially. Houphouët-Boigny himself was unusually candid when he admitted having "billions" in Swiss banks (Karny, 1983c). While the Ivory Coast has often been described as an African economic miracle, there are indications that this success is fading (Hoche, 1984).

Houphouët-Boigny has been among the few African leaders

ready to have public contacts with both Israel and South Africa. This consistent behavior has mede him into the epitome of the African right-wing leader. He has hosted Prime Minister Vorster of South Africa in Abidjan, and has had numerous meetings with Israeli leaders even after the Ivory Coast, despite its friendliness and conservatism, joined other African countries and cut off relations with Israel on November 8, 1973.

Even without formal relations, however, the Houphouët-Boigny regime was extremely friendly to Israel. A Mossad station in Abidjan controls Israeli activities in Western Africa. There has been an Israeli-interests section at the Belgian embassy in Abidjan since 1973. Houphouët-Boigny met with Prime Minister Yitzhak Rabin on February 4, 1977 (Shepherd, 1977). There was a secret visit by Ariel Sharon in November 1981. Secret talks between Houphouët-Boigny and Foreign Minister Yitzhak Shamir were reported in 1983 (Eliason, 1983).

On December 18, 1985, the leaders of the Ivory Coast and Israel met in Geneva and announced the resumption of full diplomatic ties —the culmination of a long, arduous campaign to court Houphouët-Boigny into a formal and open relationship.

Liberia

Liberia remains one of a group of African countries closely allied with the United States. "American ties to Liberia reach back to its founding by freed American slaves in 1847. Today, Liberia is the only nation in West Africa where the United States has landing and refueling rights for military planes on a 24-hour notice. A Voice of America radio transmitter and a satellite relay station used by American fleets in the eastern Atlantic are also based in Liberia" (Wills, 1985, p. A8). U.S. financial assistance to Liberia has grown sixfold since the military takeover in 1980.

Israel had contacts with Liberia since the 1950s (Avriel, 1976). President William Tubman, who was in office from 1944 until his death in 1971, visited Israel in the 1960s. He described the two nations as being very similar, with Liberia being the "Black Zion." Not everybody in Israel took this as a compliment, given the corruption of the Tubman regime.

During the years in which Israel did not have diplomatic relations with Liberia (1973–1984), it enjoyed the services of a liaison man, Charles Rosenbaum, who had developed extensive contacts with Liberian leaders, including the military. A secret visit by Ariel Sharon in November 1981 signaled a new beginning in relations; a Liberian delegation then visited Israel, also secretly. Liberia finally renewed diplomatic relations on August 14, 1983, and a week later President Samuel Doe visited Israel. A cooperation agreement between Liberia and Israel was signed on August 26, during this visit. Doe expressed his support to his Israeli hosts, though in accordance with Third World consensus, he supports Palestinian rights as well. The regime of President Samuel Doe has enjoyed Israeli aid in what is officially called "internal security."

Israeli president Haim Herzog was awarded an honorary doctorate in law by the University of Monrovia during a visit in January 1984. On October 21, 1984, the defense minister of Liberia, General Gray Alison, arrived in Israel for an official visit. He met with Prime Minister Peres, Foreign Minister Shamir, and Defense Minister Rabin.

Liberia, like Zaire, is relatively isolated. Improving its tarnished image in the United States and gaining the support of U.S. Jewish organizations were among the objectives that led Liberia to renew diplomatic relations (Bloch, 1985). As in many other cases, Third World regimes feel, and with reason, that they can benefit from Israel's coattails in Washington. Israel's President Haim Herzog declared during a visit to Liberia that Israel would act among world Jews in order to improve Liberia's economy (Becker, 1984). President Herzog did not specify the nature of actions expected from "world Jews," but the largest Jewish community in the world is in the United States. Some observers have seen the Israeli presence in Liberia as an extension of U.S. interests, and suggested that it was the influence of the Reagan administration that led to the renewed relations with Israel.

Central African Republic

The relations of Israel with the Central African Republic were closest when it was the Central African Empire (1976–1979), under the murderous, demented regime of Emperor Bokassa, who had first ruled as Marshal after a year-end coup in 1965. The imperial army was trained and armed by Israel, and Bokassa's closest adviser was a retired Israeli general, Shmuel Gonen. After Bokassa was overthrown, there was a secret visit by Ezer Weizman to the restored republic in December 1979 (Klich, 1982a). In the summer of 1981, agreement was reached to restore diplomatic relations, but this was prevented by another coup, this one overthrowing President David Dacko. However, a visit in November 1981 by Defense Minister Ariel Sharon resulted in a secret military agreement and the opening of an Israeli-interests section in January 1982. According to Evans and Novak (1983), Israel has tried to use its influence in Washington to obtain more favorable treatment for the Central African Republic.

Lesotho and Swaziland

Completely surrounded by South Africa, Lesotho and Swaziland will have only a semblance of independence as long as the apartheid regime exists. The relations between Israel and these countries are simply a reflection of the Israeli alliance with South Africa, and not much more (Weisfelder, 1982). Swaziland is among the most conservative of African countries. It is officially still a monarchy, and it is closely tied to South Africa. In the words of an Israeli journalist, there is "an alliance of interests between the ruling class of Swaziland and South African capitalism" (Sagir, 1986, p. 9). Prime Minister Maphevu Dlamini of Swaziland paid an official visit to Israel in December 1978. A delegation from Swaziland, including the foreign minister, the defense minister, labor minister, and other officials, and headed by Prince Mkhatshwa Dlamini, visited Israel in September 1984, and met with President Herzog, Prime Minister Shamir, and other government officials. Plans for economic cooperation were announced on that occasion, but it is doubtful whether any have materialized.

Malawi

It isn't surprising to find that Malawi, one of the least radical African states, which has always had relations with South Africa, has also had close relations with Israel. Israel has offered Malawi a variety of civilian-aid programs. Several European countries and Taiwan have also been involved in Malawi.

President Hastings Banda of Malawi has become known as South Africa's best friend on the continent. Banda, known to those under his rule as Ngwazi (Savior), is the prototypical conservative African leader. In power since 1964, he has been a ruthless despot who owns most of the businesses in his country. He has hosted South African leaders on numerous visits to his country. Lilongwe, his capital, has boasted a South African embassy since 1967. There have been reports of MNR guerrillas from Mozambique being trained in Malawi by Israeli and South African officers.

ISRAEL AND AFRICA SINCE 1973

Israel's contacts in Africa were always with pro-Western countries, and it is with such countries that contacts have been maintained, even without official diplomatic relations. There is a clear correlation between a country's closeness to the West and its readiness to have relations with Israel. In addition to such countries as the Ivory Coast and Kenya, which have always had right-wing policies and have always had contacts with Israel, several African countries have become ready to deal with Israel following a change of direction from left-wing to right-wing (Guinea and Cameroon are cases in point). After the public and official break in diplomatic relations, only a minority of African countries—those known best for their ties with the United States and France—have maintained informal contacts with Israel. Those African countries that have had the closest relations with Israel since the 1960s and that have kept the relations going unofficially after 1973 have also been ready to maintain formal and informal contacts with South Africa. These include Malawi, Mauritius, the Ivory Coast, Kenya, Lesotho, and Swaziland.

Israel's successes in Africa since 1973 have been in securing relations with regimes that are either right-wing, isolated, or both, such as Zaire, the Ivory Coast, and Liberia. In several African countries, we can observe a pattern in which, without formal relations, an Israeli agent manages to get very close to the head of state, becoming known as the president's personal adviser, his right-hand man, or his best friend. Such patterns were in evidence in Senegal, Zaire, Liberia, the Ivory Coast, and other places. The Mossad agent performing this assignment is typically charming, intelligent, and highly knowledgeable—some have written excellent scholarly analyses of African problems. They have used business or journalistic covers quite effectively. They have also shown persistence and devotion—some have been in the field since the 1950s or early 1960s. First and foremost among them has been David Kimche, most recently the director-general of the Israeli Foreign Ministry.

Israel's attempts to regain a foothold in Africa started almost as soon as African nations broke off relations in the 1970s. In a long series of secret meetings, Israeli leaders have tried to persuade African leaders to reopen public contacts. The campaign has led to some results. Since 1980, there has been a general improvement in relations between Israel and black Africa, though only three countries have renewed formal relations. There were only eight black African countries with which Israel had no contact at all as of August 1983: Angola, Mozambique, Tanzania, Madagascar, Benin, Mali, the Congo (Brazzaville), and Uganda (Shipler, 1983).

As of 1987, Israel had embassies in seven black African countries: Malawi, Swaziland, and Lesotho (which did not break off relations with Israel when the rest of Africa did), and Zaire, Liberia, Cameroon, and the Ivory Coast (which renewed contacts in the 1980s). In addition, Israel has interests sections, which amount to unofficial diplomatic representation, in Kenya, Guinea, Togo, Central African Republic, and Gabon.

For several African nations, the pattern of relations with Israel has become one of *de facto* contacts and support, without formal diplomatic recognition. While secret contacts with several countries are very much in evidence (Central African Republic, Kenya) and economic contacts continue, the often-predicted public recognition has remained elusive. Formal recognition may be only a gesture, but such symbols are the stuff of diplomacy. These nations still do not wish to deviate from the consensus on the rights of natives in both South Africa and the Middle East. Africa since 1960 has seen a process of relative radicalization and the rise of Third World solidarity, which have caused growing hostility to Israel and the decline of Israel's diplomatic fortunes in the continent. Moves back toward Israel have often been motivated by an African country's desire to improve its standing with the U.S. Congress and the American public or by the wish to blackmail Arab countries into increasing their aid.

As of 1987, Israel has succeeded in keeping its ties to conservative regimes in Africa, some of which also have close ties to South Africa. There can be little doubt that South Africa and Israel follow a coordinated strategy toward the rest of Africa. The joint effort was described as "Israel's joining such black African conservatives as Mr. Houphouët-Boigny in trying to forge a non-Communist, pro-Western alliance based partly on South African funding" (Morris, 1977, p. 4). The African countries that have relations with Israel, formal or informal, also have contacts with South Africa. The same leaders that will host South African leaders, such as Mobutu and Houphouët-Boigny, are ready to host Israeli ministers. One of the lesser-known cases in point is Somalia. In December 1984, the leader of Somalia, President Mohamed Siad Barre, met with the foreign minister of South Africa, R. F. Botha, and discussed arms sales and landing rights for South African Airways. In February 1985, another Somali leader, Abdel Rahman Abdi Hussein—the president's son-in-law—paid a two-week secret visit to Jerusalem to discuss military cooperation. The resulting agreement covered a comprehensive program of "counterinsurgency," such as training security personnel. South Africa served as the intermediary in this case (*Indian Ocean Newsletter,* 1985).

The overall pattern is unmistakable: the more conservative regimes have always maintained contacts with Israel. This pattern has not changed in the 1980s. What is clear today is that conservative regimes, while ready to have hidden alliances with Israel, are nonetheless reluctant to have official relations. Israel is making every effort to regain diplomatic assets in Africa—but from a position of pronounced weakness and isolation, nothing like the good old days of the early 1960s. By contrast, there are now PLO representatives in twenty African countries.

Several of the regimes supported by Israel face serious internal problems, display blatant corruption and repression, and are not likely to last much longer. The Israeli diplomatic offensive in search of open and formal ties has been coordinated with the United States and South Africa. The end of the apartheid regime in South Africa will send a shock wave over the whole continent. Such regimes as those in Kenya, Zaire, and the Ivory Coast—the very ones Israel has ties with—are not likely to survive it.

4

The Friendly Hemisphere

hile Israel seems quite isolated in the Eastern Hemisphere, it is in much better shape in the Western Hemisphere, where it has diplomatic relations with almost all nations. Israel has gained not only friends but real admirers in Latin America. General Augusto Pinochet Ugarte of Chile, General Romeo Lucas García of Guatemala, Roberto D'Aubuisson of El Salvador, and General Alfredo Stroessner of Paraguay are all admirers. So was the late Anastasio Somoza Debayle of Nicaragua. The Latin American military admires Israel for its machismo, for its toughness, ruthlessness, and efficiency. Israel does have its civilian friends here, of course, but the military class of Latin America is where most of its friends and admirers are.

CENTRAL AMERICA: ISRAEL'S DISTANT SHADOW

Over the past decades Central America has been in the throes of war, and Israel has become a party to it. Central America became a top-priority region for Israel in the late 1970s. The Mossad station in

Central America, based in Tegucigalpa, was headed by a deputy chief of the Mossad—an indication of the importance of the region in the eyes of the Israeli leaders. The Mossad was in charge of all the delicate Israeli operations in the region, such as the training of the contras. Israel has become part of the history of Central America, and history books will have to refer to it in analyzing the stormy events of revolutions and struggles in the last quarter of the twentieth century (Dunkerley, 1982). What is Israel up to in Central America? Why has it become involved in such a distant war?

By 1975, Israel had entered the region as a major arms supplier. Since then, Israeli weapons have become commonplace in Central America. *Time* magazine appraises Israeli arms sales in the region in 1984 alone at $22 million (1984a). This figure may not seem huge, as arms budgets go, but in impoverished Central America the numbers and the technology we are used to when we discuss modern arms are almost irrelevant. We are dealing here with a region that is underdeveloped and poor not only in terms of the basic standards of living for its people, but in military technology as well. If we compare Central America to the Middle East, this is immediately evident. In the whole of Central America, there are less than two hundred tanks, compared to about ten thousand in the Middle East. The region is so "underdeveloped" when it comes to military technology that five hundred rifles, one transport airplane, and several jets, make a huge difference in the technology of death and oppression. Thus, anybody wanting to interfere in the violent struggles in this region can do so without substantial investments. A few million dollars may mean the arming of thousands of fighters, as in the case of the CIA contras.

Actually, some of the military hardware sold by Israel in Central America was not made in Israel. French-built jets—the Marcel Dassault Ouragan and the Super-Mystère B2—were sold to El Salvador and Honduras when they became too old-fashioned for the Israeli air force. Mauser-98 rifles, made in Germany, were sold to Guatemala after they became obsolete. Arms captured during the Israeli invasion of Lebanon in 1982 were sold in Central America. Israel had no use for them, and besides, they had the advantage of being Soviet-made, so Israel and the United States could claim they had been captured right there in Central America, from Nicaragua.

Central American generals often say they admire Israel because they view the Israelis they know as practical, efficient, and tough, and because they see Israel as "unencumbered by issues of human rights." They find them much easier to deal with than North Americans, who are too concerned with public opinion. "The Israelis do not let this human rights thing stand in the way of business," a prominent right-wing Guatemalan politician said in a recent interview. "You pay, they deliver. No questions asked, unlike the gringos" (Debusmann, 1984, p. 5).

"Personal connections between retired high-ranking Israeli officers and the generals of the region" grow out of a close working relationship before retirement; "Many former officers have been traveling through Central America offering their personal services as anti-terrorist consultants, permanent advisers, trainers, and even as simple bodyguards" (Kaufman, 1984, pp. 46–47). Israeli mercenaries arrive in the area as the result of official contacts. Talking about defenses against kidnapping in Guatemala in November 1981, one informant says: "If money is no object, I recommend Israelis, former paratroopers, or commandos for choice. The trouble with the local chaps is that you never know whose side they are on" (Buckley, 1984, p. 241). The Israeli mercenaries in Central America have become known for their reliability. You always know whose side they are on.

Another reason for contacts with Israel is the strong pro-Israel lobby in the United States, which is believed able to do wonders for a reactionary regime in the dangerous waters of U.S. public opinion. For example, in 1983 there were "hopes in the Salvadoran government that the influential pro-Israel lobby in the United States [would] lend a discreet hand in congressional debates over the wisdom of administration policy on Central America" (Cody, 1983, p. 7). Israel's actions obviously are not the decisive factor in any of the struggles going on in Central America, but at the same time, its intervention tells us something quite significant about the Israeli view of the world today.

"In Central America Israel is the 'dirty work' contractor for the U.S. administration," wrote Knesset member Matityahu Peled (1985a, p. 9); "Israel is acting as an accomplice and arm of the United States" (Toriello, 1984, p. 28). By supporting the military regime in Guatemala, for example, Israel was performing a crucial service for the United States, which could not offer direct and open support to this regime. But Israel could, as it did in similar cases where the United States could not operate directly (Rhodesia, South Africa, Iran). Only once have U.S. sources admitted to making a direct and explicit request to Israel (by Secretary of State Alexander Haig in 1981) to help a regime in Central America (Guatemala). Otherwise, U.S. officials admit only a "convergence of interest" (Greve, 1984). When asked about Israeli involvement in Central America, an unnamed high State Department official said, "We've indicated we're not unhappy they are helping out" (Gelb, 1982). Clearly the United States regards whatever Israel does in the region as "help" in terms of its foreign-policy goals. The Israeli ambassador in Washington, Meir Rosenne, reportedly met early in 1984 with General Vernon Walters of the CIA who asked for a greater Israeli involvement in "defending the Free World" in Central America; Rosenne agreed with his ideas and spirit (*Smol,* 1984).

But more recently, the level of Israeli involvement in Central America has been decreasing as the United States has increased its direct involvement in Honduras, El Salvador, and Costa Rica. As of 1987, it seems that Israel's heyday in Central America is over. Israel is no longer needed as a U.S. proxy.

Guatemala

Even in the midst of the endless misery and cruelty of Central America, Guatemala stands out as a country where those in power have been fighting the powerless with an unusual degree of ruthlessness and bloodiness. Over the years, reports of the horrible realities of Guatemala have been numerous and the judgments harsh. What is unique is the extent to which those who carried out the deliberate policies of endless killings have proclaimed their indebtedness to Israel, as the source not only of their hardware, but of their inspiration. Israel became the main support of the Guatemalan military regimes, as attested to by both General Romeo Lucas García and General Efraín Ríos Montt in no uncertain terms. It was Ríos Montt, born-again Christian and dictator of Guatemala in 1982–1983, who explained the ease with which he took over in March 1982 simply: "Many of our soldiers were trained by Israelis" (Greve, 1984). The chief-of-staff of the Guatemalan army praised Israel for its support to the regime, and declared that "the Israeli soldier is the model for our soldiers" (Karny, 1981b).

Israel became Guatemala's largest arms supplier in the mid-1970s, and earned a near-monopoly position after 1977 (LaFeber, 1983; Perera, 1985a). Over the years, representatives of Israeli government corporations and private firms involved in arms sales have achieved positions of power and influence in Guatemala (Kessary, 1985).

Israel carried out its first major arms deal with Guatemala in 1975, delivering eleven Arava planes, artillery pieces, and light weapons (Lemieux, 1984). In November 1977, the Guatemalan army replaced its old Garand M-1 rifles, made in the United States, with Galil rifles from Israel—part of a program to refit the army completely with Israeli equipment. Between 1977 and 1981 Israel sent fifty thousand Galil rifles, a thousand machine guns, and five large helicopters. According to SIPRI (1981), Israel also delivered large quantities of Uzi submachine guns, grenade launchers, ten Reem RBY-MK1 armored cars, and three Dabur patrol boats. Several reports say an industrial plant, built with Israeli help in the city of Cobán, has been producing ammunition for the Galils and Uzis.

One shipment of Israeli arms to Guatemala received much unwanted publicity on December 22, 1983, when U.S. customs officers in Fort Lauderdale, Florida, discovered that four containers on the Israeli Zim freighter *New Orleans* were not in fact carrying "general freight," as listed, but twelve thousand rifles (Barak, 1983b). The containers, sent by Eagle Exports of Ashdod, Israel, were en route to Guatemala. The rifles were a story in themselves. These were Mauser 7.62mm rifles, of a model that dates back to 1898. These rifles—first made in Germany—were so successful that they were manufactured in several other countries. The Mauser 98 was used by the German army in the two world wars. In 1948, a shipment of them was sent from Czechoslovakia to Israel, where they became the standard army infantry weapon during the 1948 war and for years afterwards. In the 1960s and 1970s, its place was taken by several other guns—the Israeli Uzi, the Belgian F.N. automatic rifle, the American M-16, the Soviet AK-47, and the Israeli Galil—except in basic training. Finally the old

Mauser rifle was declared too obsolete even for that and was put in storage.

Then, in 1983, the Israeli Defense Ministry decided to sell these obsolete weapons to Guatemala. The flap in Florida was brief. The president (1983–1986) of Guatemala, Oscar Humberto Mejía Victores, announced that the weapons were indeed on their way to Guatemala, where they would be used in basic training for the army. The U.S. government did not stand in the way of a little arms deal between two trusted allies, and the story was soon forgotten. Some of the ancient Mausers were used to arm members of the civil patrol system (PAC), which involved the rural populace in coerced paramilitary service (Simon, 1986). Others found their way to Honduras, to be used in basic training by the CIA's contra forces.

In Guatemala, Israeli advisers are not just instructors: "Israeli advisers—some official, others private—helped Guatemalan internal security agents hunt underground rebel groups" (Cody, 1983, p. 7). They have been directly engaged in counterinsurgency campaigns against the Indian communities. General Rodolfo Lobos Zamora, army chief-of-staff, traveled to Israel in February 1985. According to Mexican sources, a new agreement was reached during this visit to arrange for Israeli military advisers to train the special Kaibil troops for counterinsurgency against the Indians.

Israeli advisers have also been working with the notorious Guatemalan secret police, setting up the internal intelligence network (Simon, 1983). Another important Israeli contribution to streamlining the Guatemalan counterinsurgency offensive was the development, maintenance, and operation of a computerized data processing system for the police. Reportedly, 80 percent of the Guatemalan population are covered, with their names and other details stored in the computer's memory. Guerrilla sources claim that the computerized system has been used to provide lists of names for the right-wing death squads. Some sources have claimed that there was another Israeli-installed computer system, capable of tracking "suspicious activities" by noting excessive electricity consumption in a particular building overnight. All this draws upon the Israeli experience in using the same technology to control the occupied territories. Israeli involvement in the creation of computerized intelligence systems in Guatemala was confirmed by Matityahu Peled, member of the Knesset, on December 10, 1985, in a letter to Abba Eban, chairman of the Knesset Defense and Foreign Affairs Committee. According to Debusmann (1984) twenty-five to forty Israelis worked in the Guatemalan intelligence services. Benedicto Lucas García, Guatemalan chief-of-staff (1978–1982), confirmed in a 1985 interview the deep involvement, including the presence of Israeli military advisers and the creation of computerized control systems (Karny, 1986).

In the early 1980s, a whole worldwide right-wing network could be seen in action in Guatemala, offering aid in whatever form was needed. Taiwan and South Korea were heavily involved (Perera, 1985b). General Rodolfo Lobos Zamora mentioned the United States, Israel, and Argentina as countries that offered Guatemala military aid "spontaneously" (*Enfoprensa,* 1984). Since 1975, Guatemala has received arms from the United States, Israel, France, Switzerland, Taiwan, Italy, Belgium, and Yugoslavia. Israel and Taiwan have been the most active in training Guatemalan officers, who often travel to both countries (Fried et al., 1983). A newscast on Israeli state television of March 7, 1982, said both Israel and South Africa were supplying arms to Guatemala. A South African military delegation, headed by J. B. Erasmus and Alexander Potgeiter, two of that country's most influential generals, visited Guatemala in November 1984, indicating South Africa's continuing support. Furthermore, "there are close ties with Argentina and Chile. Israel has traditionally supplied arms, and now South Africa is helping build a weapons factory. Taiwan has the second-largest diplomatic mission and provides technical aid" (Lewis, 1981, p. 29).

Israel is not the only adviser on counterinsurgency; "according to Guatemalan opposition sources, the government is being helped in sophisticated counterinsurgency techniques by advisers and experts from Argentina, Chile, Israel and the United States as well as by former agents of the late Nicaraguan dictator, Anastasio Somoza" (Rettie, 1981, p. 6; Toriello, 1984; Molina, 1984). The secret police were also being trained in interrogation techniques by advisers from Chile and Argentina (Lemieux, 1984). Argentine-Israeli cooperation created the Intelligence Center—notorious for its brutal methods of interrogation—in Guatemala City (Dabat and Lorenzano, 1984), though after the Falklands war of 1982, Argentina ended its involvement.

Israel has also offered Guatemala a variety of civilian training programs, run by the Foreign Ministry's International Cooperation Division, focusing mainly on agriculture (Black, 1983). It was involved in the large-scale government pacification program—similar to the well-known U.S. program in Vietnam—intended to control the Indians of the highlands. *Latin American Regional Reports* quotes one of the leaders of the program, Colonel Eduardo Wohlers: "The model of the kibbutz is planted firmly in the minds of my officials. I think it would be fascinating to turn our highlands into that kind of system" (1983, p. 8). There is, however, little similarity between the kibbutzim and the army's "strategic hamlets."

But Colonel Wohlers, like many of his colleagues in the Guatemalan army, does have an abiding admiration for things Israeli, and Guatemalan leaders have indeed been inspired by the Israeli kibbutz (Peckenham, 1984). These planned communities are based on communal agriculture, which clearly should be more efficient than traditional farming. They also have a communal household: "Women cook for the entire community in a newly built communal kitchen and leave their children in a daycare center so that, according to military planners, they can become 'productive' members of society. A communal hall for organized adult and youth educational civic activities has been built" (p. 17). This is indeed a remarkable restructuring of communal life for the Indians—but it is not a kibbutz, which is a socialist commune, a voluntary organization, led by its own members. What is happening in Guatemala is clearly directed from above. The founders and members of the kibbutzim in Israel are light-years removed in their cultural traditions from the Indians of Guatemala.

The close contacts between Israel and the military juntas of Guatemala have been discussed widely in the Israeli media. One of the most interesting manifestations is a short story, written as the first-person account of an Israeli operative in an unnamed Central American country. The narrator, stationed at the Israeli embassy and working with a colonel named García who is involved in fighting

"Indian terrorists," expresses his guilt and rebels against his superiors. To everybody's surprise, he finds himself identifying with the terrorists, which means the end of his career in the Israeli foreign service. The story refers to the computerized intelligence systems and alludes to the similar actions against the Palestinians and against the "terrorists" in Central America. Since it was presented as a work of fiction, the story was not censored (Dankner, 1982).

On January 25, 1982, Israeli state television carried a British report on conditions in Guatemala. The announcer in Jerusalem referred to the regime in Guatemala as a "right-wing dictatorship," guilty of atrocities. The announcer also added that both Israel and Argentina were arming this regime.

An Open Letter to the People and Government of Israel, asking them to stop their support for the regime in Guatemala was sent on February 16, 1983, by the International Fellowship of Reconciliation and by Servicio Paz y Justicia en América Latina (signed by Adolfo Pérez Esquivel, Nobel Peace Laureate) to the Israeli government. The letter was ignored by both the government and the Israeli media.

The election of Marco Vinicio Cerezo Arévalo on January 14, 1986, as the first civilian president of Guatemala after thirty years of military rule seemed to end an era for Israel in Central America (Perera, 1985b; Kessary, 1985). In an interview with an Israeli journalist a month earlier, Cerezo announced that he would investigate Israel's military role in Guatemala, and would not allow foreign domination of Guatemala's security (Karny, 1985b). Even under the regime of Cerezo, many Guatemalans still live in fear. People still are assassinated or disappear. The military has not lost its power. While the victory of Cerezo has created much hope in Guatemala for a new era in national life, for Israel the decline of the army means the end of an era of extensive involvement.

El Salvador

Most of the people of El Salvador "remain lost in the dust of poverty and war" (Rivard, 1985). The oligarchy, with the help of the United States, is very much in control. The struggle inside El Salvador has become an international one, "a crisis involving everyone from Sandinistas to the Pentagon, from Israel to Venezuela" (Schmidt, 1983,

p. 29). "Today, one would be hard pressed to find five countries in the world which support the Salvadoran regime. The United States under Ronald Reagan is at the head of the list of supporters. . . . In this honorable company, one can find Guatemala, a huge concentration camp masquerading as a state; one can also find the State of Israel" (Karny, 1984b, p. 6).

Israel's support for Salvadoran regimes has been expressed in several forms, mainly military and economic. The first major military agreement with El Salvador was signed in 1973, when Israel under-took to make the Salvadoran air force the best in Central America (Karliner, 1983). Israel agreed to sell to El Salvador forty-nine planes —eighteen 1950s French Ouragan jet fighters, six French Fouga Ma-gister jet trainers, and twenty-five Israeli Arava transports, usable for both military and civilian purposes—a major deal by Central American standards. The planes were all delivered by 1975; the Ouragans were the first fighter jets in Central America.

Israel may already have been El Salvador's main arms supplier before 1977 when it also sent counterinsurgency experts (Russell, 1984). It became more prominent between June 1977 and November 1979, when U.S. aid was cut off, after "U.S. authorities caught Sal-vadoran officers selling surplus weapons to North American gang-sters" (LaFeber, 1983, p. 246). When the Carter administration called El Salvador a human-rights violator, Israel became unquestionably its main source of military aid. Israeli-made napalm bombs were used by El Salvador, according to air force colonel Rafael Bustillo, who re-ported that the bombs were purchased in the late 1970s (Biddle, 1985b).

During the 1970s, 80 percent of arms imports to El Salvador came from Israel (SIPRI, 1981), but after the United States resumed sales in 1980, Israel became only its second largest supplier. Later, Israel played an official role in the channeling of United States aid to El Salvador, when it agreed in 1981 to give El Salvador $21 million, to be refunded by the United States (Lusane, 1984).

With so much hardware floating around, though, some of it is bound to get lost. The *Newsweek* cover of March 18, 1981, headlined "Storm over El Salvador," showed a picture of a guerrilla holding an Israeli Uzi submachine gun. On February 8, 1982, the *Jerusalem Post* carried a picture of Juan Ramone Medrano, a guerrilla leader in El

Salvador, speaking to his troops while armed with an Israeli Galil rifle. Israeli weapons do change hands in El Salvador, as in other places; they may become the weapons of the oppressed, used against the oppressors, to the chagrin of both seller and buyer.

Allegations about Salvadoran military being trained in Israel, and Israeli military advisers in El Salvador, were first made as early as 1979 by Shafik Handal, secretary-general of the Salvadoran Communist Party (*New York Times,* 1979). But in the early 1980s, it became widely known that El Salvador had secret agreements with Israel for "anti-guerrilla security assistance" (Woodward, 1985, p. 254). Arnoldo Ramos, the representative of the Salvadoran Democratic Revolutionary Front, claimed that Israel had fifty military advisers in El Salvador (Faro, 1983); other reports put the number at a hundred (Karliner, 1983). Israeli instructors were partly responsible for the changing tactics of the Salvadoran army in its war against guerrillas (Dickey, 1982). Inspired by his Israeli mentors, Colonel Sigifredo Ochoa earned a reputation as an aggressive tactician, the kind of officer the United States would like to see more of in Central America. During 1977–1979, when Israel was most active, it was also training counterinsurgency teams—less elegantly known as death squads. Francisco Guerra y Guerra, an undersecretary of the interior in the Salvadoran government in 1979, reported in an interview that Israeli intelligence advisers, stationed in El Salvador permanently, were working with the notorious ANSESAL death squads (Hunter, 1985). A computerized intelligence system, similar to the one in Guatemala, was reported in El Salvador (Lemieux, 1984).

There were reprisals. In 1979, Ernesto Liebes, Israel's honorary consul in San Salvador, was kidnapped and killed by guerrillas. Rebel leader Germán Cienfuegos declared that the consul was treated as a "war criminal" because of his involvement in the sale of Israeli planes to El Salvador. In November 1979, when guerrillas kidnapped South Africa's ambassador, they demanded that the government sever all links with Jerusalem and Pretoria, and recognize the PLO; a month later the Israeli embassy was bombed (Klich, 1982b).

In May 1982, a representative of the Democratic Revolutionary

Front of El Salvador, Joaquín Antonio Aguilar, visited Israel and asked the individuals and groups he met to influence their government to stop its support for the regime. Naturally, since most of the people he met with belonged to opposition groups—no more popular with the government of Israel than the Democratic Revolutionary Front is with the government of El Salvador—the meetings did not change Israeli policies (Klich, 1982b). On August 2, 1982, a high-level delegation from El Salvador arrived in Israel, headed by Ernesto Magaña, the son of El Salvador's provisional president, and including two government ministers. The delegation met with Prime Minister Begin, and reportedly discussed economic aid. The delegation announced El Salvador's decision to move its embassy to Jerusalem—becoming one of the few nations to recognize Israel's claims there. Mr. Begin, upon hearing the good news, reportedly embraced Ernesto Magaña (Strauch, 1983). President Álvaro Magaña was said to expect increased Israeli aid to El Salvador after its embassy was moved from Tel-Aviv in April 1984 (Benziman, 1984a).

Opposition members of the Knesset acted on events in El Salvador twice in 1984: in March, Shulamit Aloni and Amnon Rubinstein declined an invitation to visit El Salvador as observers for the general elections; and in October, two well-known members of the Zionist left opposition, Victor Shemtov and Yossi Sarid, sent a telegram to President José Napoleón Duarte. The telegram congratulated him "on your historical initiative for reconciliation with the labor unions [sic] in your country, after five years of civil war." It continued, "We want you to know that in Israel many are looking up to your brave and responsible leadership, which shows itself capable of rising above the sediments of the past and to devote itself to dialogue and understanding. Would it be that your initiative will inspire leaders in our region, of all countries, who are able, if they want and dare, to end bloodshed and start a new age of prosperity and peace" (*Al Hamishmar,* 1984, p. 8). This anecdote shows again how different Israeli left-wingers and liberals are from all those who are known by these labels in other parts of the world, and whose side they are on in Central America.

The Tel-Aviv paper *Davar* carried a letter to the editor on December 22, 1981, signed by 144 students in a nearby agricultural high school, protesting Israeli arms sales to El Salvador. Such a letter is a very unusual occurrence in Israel, but it indicates, nevertheless, that the facts of Israel's military contacts in Central America can easily be known, even by high-school students.

Salvadoran army officers have often expressed their admiration for Israel. For example, Sigifredo Ochoa "credits his training in Israel and by Israeli advisers in El Salvador in the mid-1970s for his military development. His personal rifle is an Israeli Galil" (*Israeli Foreign Affairs,* 1985a). Right-wingers in El Salvador, such as Ochoa and D'Aubuisson, often mentioned Israel and, to a lesser extent, Chile, Taiwan, and South Africa as their models. The Salvadoran military has taken Israel as its model ever since the 1969 "Soccer War": "the Salvadorans had what was for them a reliable model—the intense ferocity of the Israeli military in the June 1967 Six-Day War. . . . In their posture toward their neighbors the Israeli analogue is a convenient one" (Langley, 1985, p. 184).

Relations between Israel and El Salvador were closest from 1977 to 1979, under the regime of General Carlos Humberto Romero. Since 1981, the Reagan administration has given to El Salvador more than $500 million in military aid, thus making a serious Israeli involvement unnecessary.

Honduras

Honduras has the distinction of being the poorest country in one of the poorest regions of the world. This lack of resources does have its positive aspects, though; for instance, it has sometimes prevented Honduran generals and their Israeli friends from carrying out grand designs for spending on new and sophisticated weapons.

Honduran ground forces have been equipped with Israeli Galil rifles and Uzi submachine guns, and both the air force and ground forces have had Israeli advisers (Cody, 1982). Israel has played a crucial role in making the Honduran air force the strongest in Central America, by sending Israelis to train Honduran pilots, and by selling rebuilt French Dassault Super-Mystère B2 jets equipped with American engines. These jets, originally built in the 1950s and considered obsolete anywhere else today, are considered sophisticated in Central America—they were the first supersonic jet fighters in the region. Since 1977, Israel has sold twelve Super-Mystères, three Arava trans-

ports, and a Westwind jet transport to Honduras, making it the leading air power in the region. (Israel wanted to sell its Kfir jet fighters
to Honduras, but since their engines are made by General Electric, the
United States used its authority to block the sale.)

The December 1982 visit to Honduras by Defense Minister Ariel
Sharon received much attention. "During my brief stay, I could take
advantage of the opportunity to sign agreements of a military nature
with Honduras, as well as some agreements on agriculture, health, and
cultural assistance," he said at a news conference in Tegucigalpa
(Cuevas, 1982). Sharon came only two days after President Ronald
Reagan left—and according to a Honduran functionary, "Sharon's
trip was more positive. He sold us arms. Reagan only uttered plati-
tudes, explaining that Congress was preventing him from doing more"
(Morgan, 1982, p. 12). The Sharon entourage included General David
Ivri, commander of the air force, and General Aharon Beit-Hallahmi,
then director-general of the Defense Ministry. Besides signing a military accord, including weapons deliveries and training by Israeli advisers, Sharon visited military bases—and contra units based in
Honduras.

Interestingly, Sharon was invited not by the Honduran government, but by the commander-in-chief of the armed forces and strong-
man General Gustavo Alvarez Martínez, who had told the world
about his admiration for two great modern generals: Irwin Rommel
and Ariel Sharon (Karny, 1984a). The Sharon visit reciprocated Alvarez Martínez's secret visit to Israel in July (Goldfield et al., 1983).
The major arms deal envisioned by Sharon did not materialize, apparently because of the Hondurans' lack of hard currency. Sharon's aides
had proposed a rearmament program worth $200 million, while im-
poverished Honduras could offer only $1 million (Schiff, 1983b).

Three years later, in August 1985, Honduran foreign minister
Edgardo Paz Bárnica visited Israel and announced that his country
was interested in Israeli civilian aid, but not in arms or military
advisers. He acknowledged that Israel had sent military aid and advisers in the past.

Nicaragua

Nicaragua was under partial or complete American control between 1856 and 1979. It was occupied by U.S. forces between 1912 and 1933. To replace the U.S. marines, a national guard was created, and after 1936 members of the Somoza family headed the national guard and owned much of the country. The form of government there was heriditary dictatorship. Shirley Christian, no friend of the later revolution, describes the rule this way: "From the overthrow of Sacasa in 1936 until July 17, 1979, Nicaragua belonged to Anastasio Somoza García and his sons and a circle of relatives and collaborators" (1985, p. 23). One son, Anastasio Somoza Debayle, the last private owner of Nicaragua, was a typical Latin American dictator—except that most of them are military men who replace each other in rapid succession, while the Somoza family ruled Nicaragua for forty-three years. Somoza's Nicaragua was fervently anticommunist and pro-American, maintaining ties with South Africa and Taiwan (Somoza, 1980). Somoza's regime came under more and more resistance from the Nicaraguan people in the late 1970s, and by 1977 the country was in the throes of a full-scale civil war.

Israeli military aid to Somoza was offered as early as the 1950s. Shimon Peres, then director-general of the Defense Ministry, wrote to Anastasio Somoza Debayle in 1957, promising him any help that might be needed (Golan, 1982)—even though the Israeli Foreign Ministry expressed reservations about being tied to a notorious tyrant. As of 1961, the Somoza National Guard had three Sherman tanks and forty World War II amored cars purchased from Israel (Diederich, 1981). An exhibition of Israeli arms was organized in Managua in early 1974 for the benefit of Ansatasio Somoza (Kaufman et al., 1979). The contacts after 1975 were intimate and leisurely enough for Israel Galili, the inventor of the Galil rifle, to visit Nicaragua with Somoza (Walter, 1984). General Yigal Allon—Labor Party leader, deputy prime minister, and foreign minister—reportedly joined other Israeli guests for breakfast with Somoza in his Managua bunker (Lichtman, 1983).

There were "sketchy reports" of an arms deal between Israel and Nicaragua in the early 1970s (Hoffman, 1975). But Israel did not become a major supplier until 1978, when all military and civilian aid from the United States was cut off. Israel and Argentina filled the gap until Somoza's last day (Buckley, 1984; Diederich, 1981; LaFeber, 1983). In September 1978, Somoza was expecting a shipment of ten thousand Galil rifles (Diederich, 1981); the delivery included only five thousand Galil rifles, plus five hundred Uzi submachine guns, ammunition, flak jackets, trucks, mortars, and four patrol boats.

"During the early months of 1979, Somoza's own arms situation suffered surprisingly little damage from the cutoff of U.S. military assistance. . . . Somoza had turned to Israel, which was filling the gap. . . . Diplomats who were involved in the mediation believed that one reason Somoza was so cocky in resisting pressure to resign was the knowledge that Israel . . . could and would supply whatever the national guard needed" (Christian, 1985, pp. 91–92). In Somoza's last six months, Israel kept supplying new equipment, ammunition, and arms. The Somoza national guard used the Arava transport planes as bombers—possible only because the Sandinistas had no planes. The Israeli press reported, on June 26, 1979, that Israeli-made Arava planes were being used to bomb the poor neighborhoods of Managua (Cohen, 1979). Following many press reports on the use of Israeli arms by Somoza's National Guard, and television films that showed them clearly, the matter was raised in the Knesset by Amnon Rubinstein, a member of the Defense and Foreign Affairs Committee for the Shinui Party (a small, "liberal" centrist group). On June 28, Rubinstein announced that Israeli arms were no longer being supplied, but other sources indicate that the supply lines were open right up to the last minutes of the Somoza regime in July.

As the Sandinista forces were making their way toward Managua that summer, they captured large quantities of brand-new Israeli arms and equipment. On their last days "the *guardias* on the barges looked like nothing so much as Israeli soldiers, with their Israeli Galil rifles and, for those who had not thrown them away, their Israeli paratroopers helmets" (Dickey, 1985, p. 41). When the Sandinistas finally took over, they found additional large quentities of Galil rifles, sent during the summer (Hoge, 1979); they gave some as souvenirs to friends such as General Omar Torrijos of Panama. A famous picture showed the first delegation of Sandinistas to visit Cuba presenting Fidel Castro with his own Galil rifle. When the Sandinistas took over, they announced that as the legitimate government of Nicaragua, they would honor all of the nation's debts. There was only one exception: the $5.1 million owed to Israel and Argentina for arms delivered to Somoza in his hour of need.

Many stories have appeared in the media about the debt owed by Israel to the Somoza family for its help during the 1948 war. Any sentimentality related to the real help offered by Anastasio Somoza, Sr., to Israeli agents in 1948 is laid to rest by Slater (1970). The help, in the form of Nicaraguan diplomatic passports and fake Nicaraguan receipts for arms shipped to Palestine, was offered on a business basis; $200,000 was paid into Somoza's private account in the Bank of London and South America in New York City (Heckleman, 1974).

"Until the United States came along," a sympathetic American wrote in 1982, "the *Contras* could hardly be considered a threat to Managua. In the years following Somoza's downfall, small bands of former national guardsmen operated along the Honduran border, making hit-and-run attacks inside Nicaragua. The Somocistas, as they were known, were demoralized and poorly organized. The United States set about forcing the various factions to unite under a central command, while the CIA began recruiting students, farmers and other civilians to beef up the force. Then, early this year, the FDN [Nicaragua Democratic Force] was established to serve as a respectable political front group for the *Contras*" (Kelly, 1982, p. 32). There are several contra organizations, alternately cooperating and competing, all supported by the United States and other countries with money, arms, and military training.

Given Israel's earlier support to the Somoza regime, it is not surprising that it has been active in backing the contras. When the CIA was setting up the contra organization in 1981, the Mossad was there with members of one of Israel's leading commando outfits, training the first units. Comandante Edén Pastora, based in Costa Rica, then one of the contra leaders, refused to accept direct CIA aid, but accepted Israeli aid, though the connections were obvious.

Evidence of Israeli support for the contras has come from four sources: Nicaragua, the United States, the contras themselves, and Israel. Nicaragua first stated its concern about Israeli involvement during the visit in December of 1982 by Ariel Sharon, then Israel's defense minister, to Honduras during the first stage of the American buildup there (Cuevas, 1982). According to *Israeli Foreign Affairs* (1985c), Sharon met the directorate of the contra FDN. Since then, Nicaragua has consistently pointed out Israeli support for the contras. Nicaraguan president Daniel Ortega has claimed many times, publicly and privately, that Israeli advisers have been aiding the contras (Karny, 1985a). An information service based in Managua has reported that Guatemalan right-wing organizations, together with the embassies of Israel and Taiwan, have been involved in money transfers to the contras (SIAG, 1984).

Official United States sources first reported Israeli support in 1983. "Senior Reagan administration officials" told the *New York Times* in July 1983 that "Israel, at the request of the United States, has agreed to send weapons captured from the Palestine Liberation Organization to Honduras for eventual use by Nicaraguan rebels. . . . The arms shipments, which began recently, include artillery pieces, mortar rounds, mines, hand grenades and ammunition" (Taubman, 1983). According to CIA sources, the Israeli effort to help the contras was based mainly in Honduras, and financed by the CIA (Lathem, 1983). The *Washington Post* reported that the CIA asked both Israel and Saudi Arabia to aid the contras; Saudi Arabia refused, but Israel "provided some type of well-concealed financial assistance to U.S.-backed guerrillas. . . . According to U.S. sources, the Israeli assistance reportedly totals several million dollars and appears to be reaching the Contras through a South American intermediary" (Woodward, 1984, p. A8).

Israel first supplied arms to the contras in July 1983 (Anderson, 1984). "Knowledgeable sources both inside and outside the U.S. government" were quoted as saying that "Israel would help U.S. allies in Central America if Congress cuts military assistance" (Greve, 1984). "Several major U.S. allies—including Israel, Taiwan, South Korea and possibly Saudi Arabia—are secretly helping to support the *contras,* . . . a source with direct access to U.S. intelligence information said"; Israeli aid consisted of military hardware and training (McCartney, 1984). All these reports include the obvious observation that by persuading Israel (or any other party) to aid the contras, the administration could circumvent the congressional ban on direct U.S. aid—which explained how the contras managed to continue functioning even when U.S. aid was stopped for a time.

Reagan administration officials have mentioned Israel, along with Argentina, Venezuela, Guatemala, and Taiwan, as contributing money to the contras (Taubman, 1985a, 1985b). A March 1985 report said that Israel had increased its aid to the contras "within recent months" (Weinraub, 1985). But there was a price: Israel charged the contras $230 for every captured Soviet AK-47 rifle it delivered; its price for the Soviet RPG-7 grenade launcher was unknown (Biddle, 1985a). Contra leaders in Honduras have asked Taiwan, Israel, and Japan for financial aid and training (Dillon and Anderson, 1984); the U.S. government expected Israel, South Korea, and Taiwan to chip in (Parry, 1985); Israel, Honduras, and El Salvador are in fact reported as supplying direct military assistance to the contras (Parry, 1985). Somehow, Israel is on everyone's list.

Contra leaders themselves have been the best source of information on Israeli support; they seem eager to publicize it. In any attempt to win over public opinion in the United States, they judge an association with Israel to be a definite asset. In this respect the contra leaders are just like any other Third World regime worried about their public image.

Reports from Costa Rica say that Edén Pastora and his group had Israeli weapons and advisers (Honey, 1983). The contra group FDN is based in Honduras and led by Adolfo Calero, former president of Coca-Cola in Nicaragua. An unnamed leader of the group said that they planned "to ask Israel for aid because Congress has failed to authorize any further CIA expenditures." Private aid would not be enough: "We need a government. We think the Israelis would be the best, because they have the technical experience" (McManus, 1984).

Enrique Bermúdez, another contra leader in Honduras, told NBC-TV on April 23, 1984, that his group was receiving weapons from the Israeli government. Another FDN leader, Edgar Chamorro, said the same to *Time,* which continued, "Israeli intelligence experts helped the CIA train the *contras* and retired or reserve Israeli army commandos have been hired by shadowy private firms to assist the rebels. 'The Israelis,' says a U.S. intelligence expert, 'know how to run a secret operation' " (1984a, p. 20).

Officially, Israel has always denied any contacts with the contras and declined to comment when more specific questions were raised— with one notable exception: in May 1984, Victor Harel, a spokesman for the Israeli embassy in Washington, would not rule out the possibility that Israeli arms might have reached the contras, and that "retired Israeli military personnel might be working in the region" (McCartney, 1984).

Numerous reports from Israeli sources mention either joint planning by the United States and Israel, or American pressure on Israel to support the contras.

One said the United States demanded that Israel support its anti-Sandinista activities both overtly and covertly; in return, the United States would bankroll Israeli activities in other parts of the Third World (Barak, 1984). The issue of Israeli support for the contras was raised in the Knesset by Muhamad Miari on November 14, 1984. He proposed putting this topic on the agenda for urgent discussion; the request was turned down by the Speaker. On August 8, 1985, the foreign minister denied that Israel sells directly to the contras, according to Israeli state radio.

Israeli aid to the contras was reported to have grown tenfold after Peres became the prime minister in late 1984 (Fishman, 1985a). The increasing role has been acknowledged by a senior adviser to Peres, Amnon Neubach (Martin, 1985).

In December 1985, the United States government hailed an important victory for the contras, the shooting down of a Nicaraguan helicopter. The missile used was a Soviet SA-7 Strela missile, a light, shoulder-held, heat-seeking weapon. Such weapons have been captured by Israel on various occasions since 1973, and indeed Israel supplied the contras' missiles, as it has supplied all the contras' Soviet-made weapons.

And in 1986, a roving photographer in remote Honduras took pictures of contra recruits in basic training, proudly carrying the ancient Mausers that had been shipped from Israel to Guatemala in 1983. They have been used in World War I, World War II, and in the Middle East wars of 1948, 1956, 1967, and 1973. In Israel, old weapons never die. They don't even fade away; they just get recycled to some remote corner of the Third World.

Revelations since November 1986 in the Iran-contra affair have not told us much of substance that was not known before. What they have underscored again is the major role played by Israel in the survival of the contra forces. Israel was always ready to help—with money matters, arms, or training. Israel was fully committed to this ill-fated American scheme to stop another revolution in the Third World. And as it was becoming clearer that the whole contra effort was the Bay of Pigs of the 1980s, Israel was becoming tied to another American failure, and another of its own misreadings of world developments.

CARIBBEAN PARADISE: HAITI UNDER THE DUVALIERS

The poorest country in the Western Hemisphere holds many distinctions in the annals of misery and inhumanity. For the past century, Haiti has been a miserable, hellish U.S. colony. Between 1915 and 1934 it was occupied by U.S. forces. Franklin Delano Roosevelt, as assistant secretary of the navy, drafted its constitution. Later on, as president, he ordered the marines removed, but everything left behind was set up to ensure continuing American control. Haiti's government between 1957 and 1986 was a hereditary dictatorship: Jean-Claude Duvalier, known as Baby Doc, inherited from his father, Papa Doc, the title of President-for-Life, with the right to designate his successor —though he was confirmed in what locally passes for an election.

Recent diplomatic contacts between Israel and Haiti included a visit by the Haitian foreign minister, Jean Robert Estimé, in November of 1983, and a cultural-cooperation-and-exchange treaty, signed by the two countries on March 8, 1982. Not too many nations in the world had treaties with Haiti, and no other nation except Israel has a treaty in the area of culture. One might wonder what this treaty means, but its details are kept secret. While the signing of a treaty for cultural exchange and cooperation with Haiti would have aroused at least derisory interest in the United States, France, or West Germany, no interest was displayed by either the public or politicians in Israel. The last foreign dignitary to visit Haiti under the Duvalier rule, in January 1986, was David Levy, deputy prime minister of Israel. By that time it was clear to most observers that the regime would topple in a matter of a few more weeks.

Haiti's military needs were quite limited, and Israel could supply them all. There were Israeli military advisers in Port-au-Prince, and the guards watching over the security of President-for-Life Jean-Claude Duvalier carried the ubiquitous Uzi. When Duvalier became more concerned about attacks by rebels, he bought antiaircraft guns from Israel (Egozi, 1984). Israeli advisers were reportedly helping the Haitian government in maintaining "internal security" (Bahbah, 1983). Officers of the Haitian military have visited Israel for training. The elite Leopard counterinsurgency unit, created by Baby Doc, was trained by Israel.

Israeli entrepreneurs have become active in Haiti; the Israeli foreign office has been giving "high priority" to these contacts (Levin, 1983). These entrepreneurs were all doing business with the Duvalier family and its friends—as did all foreign investors in Haiti, since no one else owned anything worth owning in the country. Israelis have launched profitable agricultural ventures in Haiti and other Caribbean islands (see Peri, 1985).

Among Israelis active in Haiti were two former government officials. One is General Efraim Poran, formerly military liaison officer to Prime Minister Menahem Begin (1977–1980); the other is Eli Mizrahi, former chief-of-staff to Begin and to Prime Minister Yitzhak Rabin (1974–1977). There can be little doubt that the ability of these two gentlemen to procure business in Haiti and elsewhere (they are also active as entrepreneurs in South Africa) has something to do with connections established during their years of government service. A former ambassador to Haiti, Rafael Bashan, had become honorary consul-general of Haiti in Israel, where he represented Jean-Claude Duvalier and his business interests (Perera, 1985a).

The Duvalier regime was replaced in January 1986 by a new government, in a transfer of power successfully engineered and carried out by the CIA. The actual transfer of power was supposed to take place on the morning of January 31. Jean-Claude Duvalier was to leave Haiti on a U.S. air force plane, and the new government was supposed to be introduced.

Something went wrong; as a result the White House announced that Duvalier was gone, while he was still in Port-au-Prince. What went wrong? The U.S. media blamed poor coordination between the State Department and the White House. But CIA sources say the reason for the delay was Israeli intervention. According to this un-confirmed story, the Mossad station in Haiti was concerned about the harm to Israeli interests in the region, and managed to convince Duvalier to stay. American pressure prevailed, of course, and Baby Doc left a few days later. What this story reflects, even if untrue, is the reality of Israeli involvement in Haiti, to the extent that it can be construed as influential in such situations.

In any case, the new government did not seem to change the nature of politics in Haiti in any significant way, or the life of the Haitian people.

SOUTH AMERICA: ADORING GENERALS

South American generals, Israel's admirers in that part of the world, come from military establishments that are significantly different from those of Central America. Most South American armed forces are bigger and have more sophisticated equipment. In the past, Israel has offered civilian-aid programs to almost all South American nations (Laufer, 1967). As in other parts of the world, however, Israeli civil-ian-aid programs have lost their importance; military aid is the order of the day. Since 1973, Israel has had close relations with those coun-tries in South America that adopted "the South American mix" of conservative, supply-side economic programs set up by military regimes (Jameson, 1984). These socioeconomic experiments, favored by the Reagan administration, were carried out in Chile, Uruguay, Brazil, and Argentina, and placed those countries squarely in the worldwide right-wing camp.

Chile

The military regime of Augusto Pinochet Ugarte, in power since September 11, 1973, now represents almost an anomaly in Latin America, where several juntas have been replaced by civilian govern-ments since 1980. Augusto Pinochet himself is second in tenure only to Alfredo Stroessner of Paraguay. A former military attaché in Washington and a devout Catholic, he models himself after Francisco Franco of Spain. Salvador Allende appointed Pinochet chief-of-staff two weeks before the military coup of September 1973. Like Franco, who was considered a loyal officer by the leaders of the Spanish Republic, Pinochet turned out to be not only eminently disloyal but a tough and tenacious ruler.

Israel became a major arms supplier to Chile after the Carter administration suspended all U.S. military aid to the Pinochet regime in 1977. (This was partly reversed by President Reagan in July 1981.) Later on, Chile suffered a British arms embargo (imposed in response to the torture of Sheila Cassidy, a British citizen). After the Carter administration refused to deliver promised Sidewinder missiles, Israel sent 150 Shafrir air-to-air missiles in 1977 (Klich, 1982a).

Friendship has blossomed between General Pinochet and his colleagues, and the Israeli leaders and generals. In January 1979, the deputy defense minister of Israel, Mordecai Zippori, visited Chile. He concluded an arms deal, which included six Reshef patrol boats, now the mainstay of the Chilean navy. Over the years, Israel has sold Chile an electronic radar system and a thousand Shafrir air-to-air missiles, and large quantities of spare parts, light arms, ammunition, uniforms, and helmets. Another agreement was reached to service U.S.-made C-130 transport aircraft. Israel is reported to have supplied the Chilean army with antitank weapons and related training (Sharif, 1977). In one $170,000 deal for nonlethal military equipment, Kibbutz Beit-Alpha, of the left-Zionist Hashomer Hatzair kibbutz federation, sold firefighting equipment to Pinochet's army (Handwerker, 1983). An Israeli corporation has developed a special crowd-control vehicle for the Pinochet government, carrying four water cannons. These vehicles can be observed quite often on the streets of Santiago.

Especially close contacts seem to exist between the two countries' air forces. Israeli air force commander General David Ivri visited Chile in October 1982. There are regular visits by delegations, such as the visit in January 1985 by the Chilean Air Force Academy group. We can be sure that there are many friendly secret visits. The Chilean newspaper *El Mercurio* reported that Israeli experts have helped Chile in developing its own aircraft industry, which started producing a light jet fighter-trainer (Tzur, 1984). In addition, Israel sold Chile the technology needed to produce cluster bombs. *Time* magazine says that some of them ended up being sold to Iraq, to be used against Iran (1984b). One can imagine no Israeli objections to the agreement, since

Israel is interested in keeping the Iran-Iraq war going. Israel has been especially active in helping the Pinochet regime with intelligence, counterintelligence, and secret police (Weir and Bloch, 1981; Ghilan, 1984).

Chilean leaders have expressed positive feelings toward Israel and Israeli-Chilean relations. Jaime del Valle, a professor at Chile's national university who became foreign minister in 1983, spoke of the similarities during a visit to Israel in 1974: "You are attacked systematically by Arab countries and the Soviet bloc, and Chile is subject to worldwide Communist defamation. The enemy is the same enemy" (Kaufman et al., 1979, p. 50). The director-general of Chilean state television visited Israel in May 1980 at the invitation of the Foreign Ministry; the visit attracted some attention because the director's wife, Inez Pinochet García, is the daughter of Augusto Pinochet. Chilean foreign minister Miguel Schweitzer, in Israel for an official visit in November 1983, enjoyed the attention of the mass media; on state television, he praised the close relations between the two countries.

Israeli leaders have returned the visits—and the compliments. General Mordecai Gur's visit to Chile in July 1978 received much publicity, especially because he lavishly praised the local army, which he described as "accustomed to victories." There was a meeting between Likud deputy prime minister David Levy and General Pinochet in 1982 (Baram, 1982). Mordecai Zippori, who had visited Chile as deputy prime minister in 1978, visited again as minister of communications in 1984. During the second visit, Zippori commented in a radio interview on what he saw as a problem common to Israel and Chile —the way they are misrepresented in the international media: "If I were to base my judgment of the Chilean situation on images shown on television or information aired on radio, I would not come to Chile, because I would only think that there are shootouts in the street all the time. The same thing happens with the state of Israel because, seen through the communications media, the Palestinian terrorists are serving a just cause and are therefore persecuted by Israel. But neither Chile's nor Israel's image is correct."

The friendship between Chile and Israel is expressed in cultural contacts and cooperation. One example: the city of Bat-Yam, south of Tel-Aviv, has a twin-city treaty with Valparaíso in Chile, and the twinship leads to mutual visits and exchanges of art exhibits (Blumenkrantz, 1985c). A commercial-aviation treaty was signed in 1981. Cooperation in the purely civilian field of tourism was reported in 1985, following a visit to Israel by Chilean tourism officials (Blumenkrantz, 1985b).

During the Statue of Liberty Weekend celebration in New York in July 1986, a tall ship from Chile achieved a measure of notoriety: the *Esmeralda,* which took part in the naval parade, had a past. It had served as a prison following the Pinochet coup of September 1973— a prison and a center for brutal torture and killings. When its history became known to American journalists and leaders, plenty of voices were raised in protest. Senator Edward Kennedy and Mayor Edward Koch of New York City joined the opposition to the visit. Mayor Koch canceled his personal invitation to the ship, and the matter was debated in the U.S. House of Representatives, where a motion to stop the visit was defeated 223 to 194. The visit of the *Esmeralda* brought a sound denunciation of the United States and its ideas of democracy and liberty from the daily newspaper of the Mapam party, the last bastion of socialist Zionism in Israel (Slucki, 1986). What the newspaper forgot to tell its readers was the story of the *Esmeralda'*s visit to Israel in 1976. At that time, Mapam was part of the Israeli government, and it voiced no protest. When the *Esmeralda* visited the port of Haifa, the only opposition—from small, left-wing groups—was almost unnoticed.

Argentina

President Isabel Perón was overthrown by the Argentine military in March 1976. Thus began eight years of military rule, during which the relations between Israel and Argentina were cordial and intimate. The first junta, in control to 1981, was headed by General Jorge Rafael Videla, and included also Admiral Emilio Massera and Brigadier General Orlando Agosti. Lieutenant General Roberto Eduardo Viola succeeded Videla in April 1981 as Argentina's president, and ruled with the help of Admiral Armando Lambruschini and General Omar Graffigna. The third and last junta was made up of General Leopoldo Fortunato Galtieri, Admiral Jorge Isaac Anaya, and Brigadier General Basilio Lami Dozo. The last junta had to relinquish power after a long series of economic and military fiascos, and Argentina was returned to civilian rule.

Generals Viola, Videla, Valín, and Galtieri became gracious hosts to Israeli military and civilian leaders, and their names grew familiar to their Israeli counterparts during the years of military rule. Israeli generals Peled and Lahav and Reshef and Rahav, names as interchangeable and forgettable as their Latin American colleagues', had many good meetings with the Argentines. They were liked and admired; they enjoyed the friendly times. There were "three countries that enjoyed a special sympathy in Argentine military circles: the United States, South Africa, and Israel" (*Yediot Aharonot,* 1983a, p. 7).

Argentina has been one of Israel's major arms customers, especially since President Carter suspended U.S. military aid in 1977 (a move partly reversed by President Reagan in July 1981). The script is familiar to us from Nicaragua, Guatemala, and other places: Israel filled the demand. It sold Argentina nearly a hundred jet fighters— mostly improved versions of the French Mirage, plus twenty-four U.S. A-4 Skyhawks—and Shafrir missiles to arm them. The navy received four Dabur-class patrol boats and fifty Gabriel missiles. Spare parts, ammunition, and small arms were also sold in large quantities.

Israel's supplying arms to Argentina during the Falklands-Malvinas war of 1982 brought much comment and understandable British concern, but it merely reflected a long-standing relationship (Taubman, 1982). Judging by reports of arms delivered, Israel played a major role in helping the Argentine armed forces to replace armaments and aircraft lost during the war, with Nesher planes, Mirage planes, Gabriel missiles, spare parts, and ammunition (Schumacher, 1982). Supplies also came from South Africa (Dabat and Lorenzano, 1984) and numerous other countries, including Libya.

Although many Israeli leaders visited Argentina during the years of the generals, former military leaders drew the most attention. General Mordecai Gur followed up his visit to Chile in 1978 with one to Argentina, and was warmly received by General Alfredo Ciola, Argentine chief-of-staff, and other generals. The former chief-of-staff (1964–1968) and prime minister (1974–1977) Yitzhak Rabin visited Argentina in August 1980, and lectured at the Argentine Armed

Forces National College. Lately it has come out that after the Malvinas War of 1982, when the military regime was on its last legs, its Israeli friends came up with a grand rescue plan, designed to make Argentina into a "South Atlantic power," and to save the generals' future (Shipler, 1986).

Of course, with the return to civilian government under President Raúl Alfonsín, Argentina began moving out of the Pariah Club, and away from a close association with Israel, South Africa, and the United States. President Alfonsín refused to continue military support for the contras and for military regimes in Central America. Contacts between Israel and Argentina have continued under the Alfonsín administration, though at a much reduced level—mainly sales of arms and agreements licensing the production of Israeli military equipment in Argentina.

But even though Israel has continued to supply Argentina with military equipment, relations are much cooler now. Most of Israel's friends among the Argentine military leadership were sentenced to prison terms in December 1985: Videla and Massera were sentenced to life imprisonment, Viola was sentenced to seventeen years, Lambruschini to eight, and Agosti to four. As far as Israel is concerned, Argentina was a much better place between 1976 and 1983, the good old days of the Israeli-Argentine honeymoon.

Paraguay

Paraguay boasts Latin America's oldest dictatorship. It has been ruled since August 15, 1954, by El Excelentisimo, General of the Army Don Alfredo Stroessner, and his regime remains largely unchallenged. President Stroessner claims to offer his people "democracy without Communism." While there is no doubt about the absence of the latter, there is no sign of the former, under one of the most brutal regimes in the world. It is estimated that 10 percent of Paraguayan citizens have passed through the country's prisons (Americas Watch Committee, 1985). South Africa is a close ally of Paraguay (see chapter 5). The new Supreme Court building in Asunción was funded by the Republic of South Africa as a token of friendship (Vinocur, 1984). Another close ally is General Augusto Pinochet of Chile. Storessner is known for his hospitality to other Latin American dictators in retirement.

Anastasio Somoza of Nicaragua was assassinated in Asunción in September 1980, after finding a comfortable exile there. Some dictators buy homes in Asunción for possible future use.

Israel's relations with Stroessner have been described in the Israeli press as "excellent." El Excelentisimo uses only Israeli weapons to equip his bodyguards, and is a good customer of the Israeli arms industry. The Paraguayan voting record at the United Nations is the most consistently pro-Israeli of any nation in the world (Shohat, 1985). Paraguay is another country whose officers warmly receive their Israeli counterparts and admire them for their toughness and efficiency (Rosen, 1982). In a CBS interview with Mike Wallace, President Stroessner, in response to criticism of his regime, mentioned his good relations with Israel (*60 Minutes,* January 5, 1986). In this case, as in many others, El Excelentisimo showed his shrewdness: his friendship with Israel will always serve as a saving grace with an American audience.

Bolivia

Beginning in the early 1970s, Israel developed close relations with the successive military regimes in Bolivia, but the relationship reached its height under the regime of Luis García Meza. The coup of July 18, 1980, following the elections which gave Hernán Siles Zuazo a plurality, was a shock. "Neighboring Peru and Ecuador had already chosen civilian leaders, and Bolivia was to have been next. Once Bolivia inaugurated its civilian leader, the loose and unofficial scenario called for a movement toward greater civilian influence in both Argentina and Uruguay—and perhaps Chile, as well. But by grabbing power, Bolivia's military has shattered the scenario" (Goodsell, 1980, p. 4). The leader of the junta, García Meza, declared Augusto Pinochet to be his model in government; as ruler of Bolivia, García Meza really represented the cocaine dealers of his country. It was not just another South American putsch. It "was supposed to complete a 'stable axis' in South America—from Chile, through Argentina, Uruguay, and Paraguay, to Bolivia. The coups in Chile in 1973 and in Argentina in 1976 were examples" (Hermann, 1986, p. 16). The United States, still under President Carter and Secretary of State Edmund Muskie, recalled its ambassador and most embassy staff and started an economic and diplomatic boycott. Most European and Latin American countries followed suit. The Organization of American States condemned the coup, with Chile and Paraguay dissenting and Argentina and Brazil abstaining. "For the next year . . . Bolivia was a pariah state" (Levine, 1984, p. 16). Even the incoming Reagan administration maintained the boycott as long as García Meza was in power.

At the same time, Israel was one of only nine states that extended recognition to the military regime. The others were Argentina, Paraguay, Uruguay, Brazil, Taiwan, South Africa, the USSR, and Egypt. The list speaks for itself, being made up mostly of pariah states. Uruguay, Argentina, and Brazil were then under military regimes. According to Israeli sources, the García Meza group asked for Israeli support and got it immediately (Samet, 1981). While the Carter administration was applying economic sanctions against the regime, Israel offered not only diplomatic and moral support, but also economic and military aid, sometimes in partnership with South Africa (*Maariv,* 1980). The two offered aid as soon as the García Meza regime took over (Hoge, 1980). The Argentine junta of Jorge Videla also offered its help. An educational-cooperation agreement between Israel and Bolivia was signed in July 1981. According to some sources, Israel was involved in training a short-lived anticommunist "people's army" (Hermann, 1986).

CONCLUSION

Israel has staked its future relations with Latin America on an alliance with the military, the traditional locus of power in the region. In return, the Latin American military class has a positive attitude toward Israel, and especially toward the Israeli military. From the "professional" point of view, "there is little doubt that Latin American military [leaders] have been profoundly impressed by Israel's military capacity" (Kaufman et al., 1979, p. 48). Moreover, Latin American military men see Israel "as a Western outpost standing in the way of the Soviet Union and revolutionary left governments. . . . Israel's triumph in the Six-Day War was seen by the more conservative and pro-Western establishments as a victory over a common enemy" (p. 50).

An Israeli journalist unequivocally states that his country "is identified with the most reactionary elements in [Latin America]. And at the same time it is doing nothing to lay even the most modest foundations for an understanding with the formidable forces which will form the destinies of more and more countries in the area within the next few decades, in an area undergoing a tremendous shock. In the margins of writings on the Latin wall, Israel scribbles: 'Business as usual' " (Samet, 1981, p. 7). This Israeli position, he says, is based on the hope that business will continue as usual. Israeli diplomats in Central America clearly did not share his concerns. He describes them as praising the military regimes in Chile and Uruguay for bringing back "law and order."

Despite close ties with many Latin American countries, Israel enjoys less diplomatic support from that region than it did twenty years ago. Even some of the right-wing regimes in the region do not stray from the Third World consensus on the Palestinians, as can be easily observed at the United Nations.

Israeli activities in Latin America, like Israeli activities everywhere, should be seen in the context of U.S.-Israeli relations, and especially so in a part of the world so obviously living under the U.S. shadow. More than a century and a half ago, Simón Bolívar said, "The United States seems destined by providence to plague [Latin] America with miseries in the name of freedom." Total North American domination of the hemisphere was described by Secretary of State Richard Olney in 1895: "Today the United States is practically sovereign on this continent, and its fiat is law upon the subjects to which it confines its interposition" (Smith, 1984, p. 46). U.S. leaders' attitudes were clearly expressed by President Franklin Delano Roosevelt, when he said, "We could stage a revolution in any Central American government for between a million and four million dollars. In other words, it is a matter or price" (LaFeber, 1984, p. 29). The U.S. marines have been used to assert U.S. domination here more often than anywhere else in the world. Even before 1900, marines had landed in Haiti, Panama, Uruguay, Paraguay, Argentina, Chile, Nicaragua, Mexico, and Cuba. They always came to support law and order.

Israel's deepening entanglements in Latin America since the 1960s can be understood only as related to North American domination—and its relative decline in the hemisphere since 1960. Among the factors that created an increased Israeli attention to Latin America

are "the Cuban Revolution under Fidel Castro in 1959 which sig-
nalled that in the future Latin American countries might not automat-
ically follow U.S. instructions" (Kaufman, 1976, p. 122). Three
commentators who cannot be suspected of anti-Israeli sympathies
state, "On the whole, it is noteworthy that Israel's assistance activism
in Latin America followed the launching of the Alliance for Progress
—President Kennedy's new policy for Latin America" (Kaufman et
al., 1979, p. 7). Israel's activities in Latin America—even at an early
stage, and even when these activities were mostly civilian—were part
of an American strategy to counter radicalism in the area.

*CIA contra recruits in basic training with Mauser 98 rifles, photographed near
the Nicaragua-Honduras border in the summer of 1986. (Photo © 1986 by
Paul Larkin, Gamma/Liaison.)*

5

South Africa and Israel: An Alliance of Desperation

The common journey of South Africa and Israel is the most important history told in this book. We have here a unique alliance. Here we can observe the most comprehensive and the most serious Israeli involvement anywhere in the world, and see Israel playing a crucial role in the survival of the apartheid regime, a role that is becoming more crucial every day.

The alliance between South Africa and Israel has been one of the most underreported news stories of the past four decades, though many of its significant details have been covered by the world media and are a matter of public record. What has not been done is to assess the true extent and meaning of the relationship. Any portrayal of the

Israel–South Africa alliance is bound to be partial and limited, because the scope of this alliance is so broad, and the relationship so multifaceted.

There has been nothing like it in Israel's history; an intimate, close, long-term match. The alliance with France in the 1950s and 1960s pales in comparison to the "Jerusalem-Pretoria Axis" (Karny, 1981a). The leading political commentator of *Haaretz* called South Africa "Israel's second most important ally, after the U.S." (Marcus, 1982, p. 5). Even as a prisoner in his native land, South African anti-apartheid writer Breyten Breytenbach discovered the magnitude of the alliance: "Americans and Israelis never stayed very long [in prison]—theirs were the only two governments with the prerequisite influence to have their nationals repatriated rapidly" (1984, p. 285).

The South African government itself, in characterizing the relations between the two countries, chooses the phrase "continuing high-level contact between South Africa and Israel" (South Africa, 1984). Israel is mentioned, together with the United States, Taiwan, Paraguay, and Argentina (under the military regime) as countries with which South Africa has close relations.

The "special relationship" between Israel and South Africa has now existed for more than thirty years, and the contacts are so numerous and intricate that only a sampling of significant events is needed to suggest the nature of this partnership. On November 5, 1984, reporting on the visit of P. W. Botha to Israel, Israeli state television reporter Victor Nahmias said, "In South African–Israeli relations, what is hidden is much more than what is known"—an expression often used in Israel. Some of the many aspects of the alliance have so far received only limited coverage.

FORMAL CONTACTS

The history of South African support for the Zionist movement in Palestine before 1948 is well known; streets—and even a kibbutz—in Israel are named for General Jan C. Smuts. But after 1948, relations became formal and tangible. The highlights of diplomatic contacts between the two countries are covered in table 2. The first formal contacts were not particularly warm; in those bygone days, the Union of South Africa expressed reservations about Israel's borders. On May

24, 1948, the formal note according *de facto* recognition included this sentence: "In view of the resolution of the United Nations General Assembly of 29 November 1947, which is based on partition, this recognition is not in respect of any particular boundaries, and the Union government will be prepared to accord similar recognition to an Arab area in Palestine either as a separate state or as incorporated into neighbouring Arab states" (Eytan, 1958, p. 13). *De jure* recognition was accorded only a year later, after Israel had been admitted to the United Nations.

An official South African source is not alone in claiming that Daniel F. Malan visited Israel in May of 1948, but there seems to be no evidence for that claim (South Africa, 1984; Hoagland, 1972b). Malan actually visited Israel in September of 1953; he was the first foreign prime minister ever to do so. (South African sources consider the visit official [Geldenhuys, 1984]). Just like John Vorster twenty-three years later, Malan was described as a devout pilgrim to the Christian holy places, but his admiration for Israel and his apartheid philosophy were noted in the Israeli press at the time. The first publicly recorded visit by an Israeli leader to South Africa was that of Foreign Minister Moshe Sharett in 1950.

Israel established a consulate-general in Pretoria in 1949, which became a legation in 1950 (Geldenhuys, 1984). But a South African consulate was established in Tel-Aviv only in 1961, after South Africa left the British Commonwealth—until then, consular matters were handled in Tel-Aviv by British representatives. Lines of communication between the two governments were open, through the Israeli consul-general in Pretoria, who in the 1960s held the personal rank of ambassador.

At the same time, in line with its diplomatic campaign in black Africa in the 1960s, there were public Israeli actions against South Africa. On November 6, 1962, Israel voted at the United Nations for a resolution supporting sanctions against South Africa. In September 1963, the head of the Israeli mission in Pretoria, Simha Pratt, was recalled, and the rank of his successor was downgraded to *chargé d'affaires* (Metrowich, 1977).

The South African reaction to Israel's ties in black Africa during the 1960s, however, was one of benevolent forgivingness. On numerous occasions Israeli representatives were told that black Africans

TABLE 2
MAJOR EVENTS IN THE
ISRAEL–SOUTH AFRICA ALLIANCE

1948	*De facto* recognition, May 24, 1948
1949	*De jure* recognition, May 14, 1949
1950	Visit by Israeli Foreign Minister Moshe Sharett to South Africa
1953	"Private" visit by Daniel F. Malan to Israel
1955	First nuclear collaboration? Uzi submachine gun in use in South Africa
1957	First uranium shipment?
1962	Shipment of ten tons of uranium to Israel
1967	South African military delegation in Israel (public)
1972	Secret agreements on nuclear and conventional collaboration Opening of a South African Counsulate-General in Tel-Aviv Decision to upgrade diplomatic representation to embassies
1974	South Africa cancels the Merkava agreement for the development of main battle tank
1975	Diplomatic representation raised to embassy level by two countries
1976	Public visit by John Vorster Secret agreements signed Joint Ministerial Committee announced Israeli involvement in South African "Public Relations" campaign ("Muldergate")
1977	Visit to Israel by R. F. Botha, foreign minister
1979	Secret nuclear test by the two countries
1984	Public visit by R. F. Botha to Israel
1985–1987	Secret visits to South Africa by Israeli Ministers Rabin, Arens, and Sharon

were not to be trusted. "You will see in time who your real friends are," the South Africans said. In the 1960s, not much happened in terms of formal relations. As an American observer noted, it was a "strange nonalliance," less of formalities than of serious substance.

"There is a remarkably close if little known partnership between Israel and South Africa. This relationship between the nation controlling Africa's southern tip and the nation still holding gate to its northern tip affects political, economic and military matters. . . . Prime Minister Vorster even goes so far as to say Israel is now faced with an apartheid problem—how to handle its Arab inhabitants. Neither nation wants to place its future entirely in the hands of a surrounding majority and would prefer to fight" (Sulzberger, 1971, p. 39).

In a speech given (in Afrikaans) in May 1971, Yitzhak Unna, then Israel's consul-general in Johannesburg, reported that relations between the two countries had grown deeper and stronger over the previous year (*Jewish Chronicle,* 1971). A South African consulate-general was opened in Tel-Aviv in March 1972. According to Tamarkin (1980), the decision to upgrade diplomatic representation to ambassadorial level was made as early as 1972, and that fits with other reports of the alliance being further cemented through several treaties for military and nuclear collaboration. In the summer of 1973 there was a publicized visit to Israel (there were probably secret ones as well) by General Hendrik J. van den Bergh, the director of the Bureau for State Security (BOSS)—"probably Vorster's closest confidant and key adviser . . . in both domestic and foreign affairs" (Geldenhuys, 1984, p. 87). Diplomatic missions were officially elevated to ambassadorial level in June 1974, when Israel opened an embassy in Pretoria. South Africa opened an embassy in Tel-Aviv in November 1975.

Formal secret agreements specifying procedures for cooperation have been signed on several occasions. Cornelius P. Mulder, one of South Africa's rising young stars of the 1970s, frequently visited Israel on secret missions, and signed several of them. As South Africa's interior minister, he visited Israel in September 1973, reportedly to study Israeli counterinsurgency tactics (Gitelson, 1976). In June 1975, he was in Israel to prepare the public Vorster visit of 1976, which came about as the result of Israeli initiatives (de Villiers, 1980). Reportedly Shimon Peres invited Vorster during a secret visit to South Africa in March 1976 (Alfon, 1986). (Defense Minister Peres had written to Eschel Rhoodie of the South African Department of Information on November 22, 1974, thanking him for helping in "a vitally important co-operation between our two countries" [Geldenhuys, 1984, p. 268].)

South Africa's foreign minister at the time, Hilgard Muller, had reservations, and so did Vorster, but pressure from Mulder and van den Bergh carried the day. The visit turned out to be a triumph for South African diplomacy (Joseph, 1987). The establishment of a joint ministerial committee charged with overseeing the affairs of the alliance was made public during the visit (Landau, 1976). Vorster described the topics of his official discussions in Jerusalem as "ways to expand trade, encourage investments, the setting up of joint scientific and cultural ventures, and loans for the joint utilization of South African raw materials" (Farrell, 1976).

In June 1976, U.S. secretary of state Henry Kissinger, South African prime minister John Vorster, and Israeli foreign minister Yigal Allon met in Germany to discuss the situation in southern Africa, following the South African debacle in Angola. In September 1977, Roelof F. Botha, the foreign minister, paid a weekend visit, shrouded by official secrecy, but covered by the media in Israel and abroad (Morris, 1977). Botha met with his Israeli counterpart Moshe Dayan, and with Prime Minister Menahem Begin.

The leaders of South Africa are hungry for public acceptance and recognition. They are not satisfied with secret contacts, as warm and frequent as they may be. Secret visits by Israeli leaders to South Africa are frequent. Likewise, visits by South African leaders to Israel. But from time to time the South African side demands, and gets, a public visit. The 1984 visit by Foreign Minister R. F. Botha is a case in point. The visit was first described as private, but the visitor was met at the airport by his Israeli counterpart, Shamir, and a red carpet was rolled out for him. The visitor had several working sessions with Shamir, a festive luncheon with Abba Eban at the King David Hotel in Jerusalem, and a meeting with the defense minister, Yitzhak Rabin.

When Denis Goldberg, a Jewish leader of the outlawed African National Congress, was released from prison after twenty-two years through the intervention of Israeli officials and private citizens, it was another indication of the intimacy of the relations between the two countries. Israel's president Haim Herzog and a senior minister in the Shamir government "sounded out their contacts in the South African government and its ruling National Party" (Isacowitz, 1985a, p. 2). Not many foreign leaders have such connections in South Africa.

Israel's alliance with South Africa has been mentioned and condemned by various international organizations. The U.N. General Assembly has passed resolutions condemning the Israeli–South African alliance every year since 1974. The topic has come up in meetings of the Organization of African Unity, but Israel has not (between 1963 and 1979) been condemned more often than the United States, Britain, France, West Germany, Japan, or Italy (Nzuwah, 1981). At the OAU, Israel was singled out for condemnation for its nuclear cooperation with South Africa in 1977, but the United States, West Germany, France, and Japan have had the same treatment.

The South Africa–Israel alliance was the subject of a motion for debate by Yair Tzaban in the Knesset in July 1983. Tzaban, a member of Mapam, the left-Zionist party, specifically mentioned nuclear cooperation between the two countries and Israel's refusal to sign the nuclear nonproliferation treaty. This motion failed to receive the necessary support.

On June 19, 1986, the Knesset discussed the situation in South Africa, in response to the State of Emergency declared on June 12. Participants in the debate—which did not lead to any resolutions—were unanimous in condemning apartheid, but the Israel–South Africa alliance was never mentioned. While all parliaments in the West, including the U.S. Congress, have expressed their strong condemnations of apartheid in special, often unanimous resolutions, the Israeli Knesset has remained officially silent.

IDENTIFICATION AND SUPPORT

While no leader in Israel will come out and openly admit a commitment to the survival of apartheid, the style used in Israel when discussing South African realities is unique. In a 1960 interview, Yaakov Meridor, leader of the Herut Party, claimed that Herut openly supported the apartheid policy (Brecher, 1972). In 1981, as economic planning minister in the Begin government, Meridor had many opportunities to express his support for South Africa and to offer Israel's services, as U.S. proxy, in aiding apartheid (see chapter 6). Moshe Dayan visited South Africa in 1974 and expressed his admiration of the "great civilization" being created there (Joseph, 1987). Israel's prime minister in 1976, Yitzhak Rabin, said, "Our countries have in common the problem of initiating dialogue, coexistence and stability in our respective parts of the world, in the face of foreign-inspired instability and recklessness"—exactly the language of apartheid's leaders (*South Africa Digest,* 1976, p. 11). Yitzhak Unna, then Israel's ambassador, said in 1979: "We carefully refrain from joining in the sterile symphony of blanket condemnation of South Africa that emanates from the United Nations—that complete lack of recognition of positive symptoms of change in South Africa. . . . South Africa must be seen as having special values for the free world—which is already being blackmailed and held for ransom by the Arabs in terms of oil and energy. . . . It would be a disaster if South Africa were lost as a constructive and active member of the free community of nations" (United Nations Centre Against Apartheid, 1980).

The *Jerusalem Post* of February 10, 1968, carried a large advertisement by the newly founded Israel–South Africa Friendship League, asking the government to work toward closer relations between the two countries. Among the organizers of the league were Menahem Begin, later prime minister (1977–1983), Eliezer Shostak (minister of health in Begin's cabinet), and Shmuel Tamir (his minister of justice). Visiting South Africa in 1982, Israeli industry and commerce minister Gideon Patt complacently declared that "Israel and South Africa are two of the thirty democracies in the world" (Karny, 1983b, p. 6).

Israeli right-wing leaders describe South Africa as a model to follow—usually in private conversations. At a closed meeting of professionals hosted by a law professor at Tel-Aviv University, General Rafael Eitan, a popular right-wing speaker since his retirement as chief-of-staff of the Israeli Defense Force, presented the South African Bantustan policy as a possible solution to the Palestinian problem facing Israel (Nakdimon, 1983). General Eitan has visited South Africa many times.

Visits to South Africa by Israeli politicians of all stripes and levels have been too numerous and too commonplace to mention. Leaders of the Labor Party have been regular guests; in 1980, MK Haim Bar-Lev, then secretary-general of the opposition Labor Party, visited

Pretoria and met officially with leaders of the ruling National Party. In 1983, Yitzhak Rabin, another leader of the Labor Party (still in opposition) visited South Africa and met with R. F. Botha and P. W. Botha (South Africa, 1984). Name any Israeli leader of the first rank, and the record will show many public visits to South Africa—besides those kept secret (Joseph, 1987). Visiting South Africa has become so routine for Israeli politicians at all levels that the story is told of two members of the Tel-Aviv city council holding a caucus in Pretoria. The two—Dov Ben-Meir, of the Labor Party, and Nathan Wolloch of the Zionist-Socialist Mapam Party—found themselves there at the same time, so the business of the left-wing block in the Tel-Aviv city council could be conducted right there (*Maariv,* 1983).

A debate that erupted in the Knesset Foreign Affairs and Defense Committee during the 1980 visit of Owen Horwood, South Africa's finance minister, reveals something of the way "liberal" and "left-wing" Israelis view the alliance with apartheid. Yossi Sarid, Israel's best-known dove, and Amnon Rubinstein, one of Israel's leading liberals and a professor of constitutional law, criticized the government for its treatment of the visit. What Sarid and Rubinstein objected to was not the visit itself, or the alliance with South Africa. What upset them was the publicity given the visit, and the coverage on television, which might harm "Israel's image" abroad (Krivine and Maoz, 1980). This is the typical position of the Zionist doves—more concerned about "Israel's image" than about the reality of an Israeli commitment to the survival of apartheid.

THE MILITARY ALLIANCE

The alliance between South Africa and Israel is symbiotic in many areas of military endeavor, with Israel usually the more vital element. Israel is South Africa's closet military ally and its source of inspiration and technology. The Uzi and Galil weapons are as visible in South Africa today as they are in Haiti and Guatemala (Leonard, 1983).

Reports from a variety of foreign sources give indications of the level of military cooperation. In Israel, any reporting on military cooperation between Israel and South Africa is strictly forbidden by the military censors. However, Israeli journalists have an easy loophole—anything published abroad, beyond the reach of Israeli censorship, can then be quoted in Israel, since it has become public knowledge. Sometimes Israeli journalists will give information to their foreign colleagues, so that once it is published abroad, they can use it. When it comes to Israeli–South African cooperation, the Israeli media have been very active in quoting "foreign sources"—thus telling what, in most cases, they had first found out themselves. The South African press clearly knows that the alliance is military. Commenting on the Vorster visit to Israel, the Johannesburg *Star* wrote on April 17, 1976: "Clearly the pact goes well beyond the usual trade and co-operation agreements that normally round off a state visit between friendly countries. . . . At the root of the pact is a mutual exchange of materials and military know-how which both countries desperately need. For both, it is virtually a question of survival. Very likely that is the strongest imperative of all" (United Nations Centre Against Apartheid, 1977, p. 11).

And it is important to Israel: its military attaché in South Africa is a high-ranking officer, a general who is a member of the General Staff Forum, the highest decision-making body of the Israeli armed forces. (Only one other military attaché, the one assigned to Washington, is a member of the forum.) Various high officers have served in this position, including Admiral Benjamin Telem, former commander of the Israeli navy.

The history of the military alliance has been long and rich in joint projects and collaboration. Sulzberger reported on intimate military contacts between the two countries, which included manufacturing the Uzi submachine gun under license in South Africa (1971). The first Uzis were delivered as early as 1955. According to SIPRI, Israel sold South Africa thirty-two Centurion tanks as early as 1962 (1975). South Africa has proven itself a reliable friend in time of need: in 1967, when the French embargo stopped the supply of spare parts for French jets in Israel, South Africa supplied whatever Israel needed.

The first U.N. resolution on an arms embargo against South Africa was passed by the Security Council in August 1963. Resolution 181 called upon all states to stop all shipments of military equipment to South Africa. In November 1977, Resolution 418 repeated the call and made it mandatory. The 1977 embargo was observed by most nations—but not by Israel. Foreign Minister Moshe Dayan stated that

Israel would simply ignore the resolution. One Israeli journalist wrote, "According to various sources Israel will continue its current relations with South Africa, probably with some aspects of these relations under cover" (Golan, 1977, p. 9). Over the years, Israel stopped even pretending to pay attention to the embargo; a document prepared by Israeli Aircraft Industries in the early 1980s describes ambitious marketing plans for the Lavi jet-fighter in the 1990s, in Argentina, Chile, Taiwan—and South Africa (Babcock, 1986).

The political logic behind Israel's defiance is clear: "The Israelis, for their part, believe that should the United Nations Security Council impose a mandatory arms embargo against South Africa, Israel itself could be next in line; that if the West can be pushed into endorsing one against South Africa, it can equally be pushed into one against Israel. Israel, therefore, would not adhere to an arms embargo against South Africa" (*Economist,* 1977, p. 91).

A 1984 map indicates relative Israeli arms sales to fifty-three countries around the world with boxes of different sizes (Kartin, 1984b). The largest box (8.75 square inches) lists sales to South Africa; the next largest box, for Argentina, is only 3 square inches. Among military items listed as sold to South Africa were six missile boats, thirty-six Kfir jets, hundreds of Gabriel missiles, howitzers, communications equipment, radar systems and intelligence technology, airplane parts, and ammunition for tanks, jets, and artillery.

The International Defense and Aid Fund (1980) reported that four hundred M-113A1 armored personnel carriers, and 106mm recoilless rifles, both made in the United States, were delivered to South Africa via Israel. The Galil rifle is produced in South Africa as the R-4 under license, and became the standard weapon of South African ground forces in 1981 (Bunce, 1984). A reconnaissance drone was shot down over Mozambique in May 1983; it bore an Israeli Aircraft Industries identification number (IAI-P/N/ZVN 161003) and was being used by the South African Defense Force.

Sharon's visit to South Africa in December 1981 signaled Israel's commitment to helping South Africa even more: "The military relationship between South Africa and Israel, never fully acknowledged by either country, has assumed a new significance with the recent 10-day visit by Israel's Defense Minister, Ariel Sharon, to South African forces in Namibia along the border with Angola" (Middleton,

1981, p. 9). A secret visit to South Africa in October 1984 by Minister Without Portfolio Moshe Arens, former defense minister, was said to be related to military matters (Langellier, 1984). Undoubtedly, there have been scores of such high-level visits.

During R. F. Botha's November 1984 visit to Israel, Israeli journalists went out of their way (within the limits imposed by military censors) to indicate that the real substance of the visit was the discussion of military cooperation. One reported that the Israeli defense establishment was extremely interested in the Botha 1984 visit, but did not explain why (Eldar, 1984c); he also stated that the meeting between Botha and Rabin was the really substantive one of the whole trip, dealing with bilateral issues (1984b). *Haaretz* stated that in that particular meeting, scheduled long before the visit, the two ministers were to discuss "various topics related to the relations between the defense establishments of South Africa and Israel" (1984).

There is a basic difference in the military needs of Israel and South Africa. For both countries, the question is not just defense, but survival. But unlike Israel's neighbors, South Africa's outside enemies do not pose a threat in any conventional military sense. The Arab countries of the Middle East have modern, formidable military machines. In South Africa the real danger is one of internal insurrection. This causes a divergence in military planning. The South African Defense Force (SADF) does not need the same heavy weapons and sophisticated systems as the Israeli Defense Force (IDF). South Africa is developing its own military industry, to produce all light and heavy conventional weapons, including jets and armored vehicles (Shaw and Leppan, 1985). This industry was created with the help of Italy, France, West Germany, Britain, and Israel. The Armaments Corporation of South Africa (Armscor), which now provides most of South Africa's needs in military equipment, was created with Israeli inspiration and advice. Under Israeli licenses, South Africa produces missile boats and the naval missile Scorpion (a.k.a. Gabriel). South Africa and Israel have worked out a "division of labor" (Terrill, 1984). "What seems to work best is not the outright sale of large weapons systems, but rather: (a) provision of the building blocks of modern weaponry —components, unfinished assemblies and dual-use technologies; (b) licensing and co-production" (Klieman, 1985, p. 154).

Agreements on cooperation in the development of conventional weapons were signed in 1972. One of them covered the production of the Merkava (Chariot) main battle tank, designed by General Israel Tal of the Israeli General Staff. A year later, South Africa decided to cancel the agreement, and with good reason: it had no need for a main battle tank, given the kinds of enemy it would have to fight. But South Africa still played a major role in building the Merkava, because Iscor, the South African Iron and Steel Corporation, supplied the special armor plate for it, produced through the cooperation of South African and Israeli experts and steel industries. A special chemical mix imported from South Africa is used at the Urdan plant near Netanya in the production of reinforced steel (Allon, 1986).

All of South Africa's armored vehicles have been modernized by Israel, including the used British-made Centurion tanks Israel sold it in the 1960s. This modernization program included better engines and new Merkava armor plating for the Centurion tanks and Panhard armored cars.

As of the mid-1970s, Israel supplied equipment that reflected its greater experience and expertise: ground radar stations, antiguerrilla alarm systems, communication equipment, and night-vision equipment (*Economist,* 1977). An especially crucial area of military aid has been electronic equipment (Farrell, 1976). The Israeli electronics industry—mainly such corporations as Elbit and Tadiran—has been playing a major role in creating a military-electronics industry in South Africa. Furthermore, "Israeli military specialists have also seemed to play some role in more recent developments in the South African missile industry" (Frankel, 1984, p. 86).

The most significant part of the alliance involves training. Hundreds of South Africans have graduated from Israeli military schools. And Israeli military advisers serve in South Africa as instructors and models for the local ground forces. Knesset member Marcia Freedman, in a parliamentary question to Defense Minister Shimon Peres in 1976, charged that hundreds of Israeli military men were in South Africa in joint training with the South African army; the Ministry of Defense denied the claim. According to one report, there were two hundred Israeli military advisers in South Africa in 1981 (*Economist,* 1981).

The Israeli instructors have helped to create the elite South African Reconnaissance Commandos—the equivalent of their Israeli namesakes. In 1986, an Israeli journalist wrote in the Labor Party daily, "It is a clear and open secret, known to everybody, that in army camps one can find Israeli officers in not insignificant numbers who are busy teaching white soldiers to fight black terrorists, with methods imported from Israel" (Tavori, 1986, p. 5)—the very methods used against Palestinian guerrillas.

Military Strategy and Planning

What the South Africans get from Israel, as they wage their war for survival, is first and foremost inspiration. Second is practical guidance in every facet of their military endeavor.

Israeli military advisers were involved in planning the invasion of Angola, and have been stationed in Namibia since 1975. South Africa's current strategy—expressed in its invasion of Angola and its continued attempts to destabilize its African neighbor states—follows Israeli strategies against the PLO and neighboring Arab states. "Indeed, based on Israeli experience, the South Africans have not only undertaken 'hot pursuit' operations but also pre-emptive strikes against guerrilla concentrations in host states" (Beckett and Pimlott, 1985, p. 9). South African raids on Mozambique and Angola have been described in the Israeli media as "daring commando raids in the Israeli style" (Hamizrahi, 1981)—in other words, Israel is the source of both ideological inspiration and military tactics (Gann and Duignan, 1981).

The role of the IDF in inspiring the SADF is recognized by those who know the latter intimately: "The South African military also imbibed deeply, directly or indirectly, of the strategic experiences of both the Taiwanese and the Israelis. . . . Practical and intellectual ties exist between the South African and Israeli militaries. Independent of exchanges in matériel and military technology, many South African officers take their cues from the Israelis in the process of putting total strategy into operation. Many wax enthusiastic over the organizational ability of the Israeli Defense Force in actively combating 'terrorism,' and Israeli action against the PLO in her neighboring territories is an important source of inspiration for the SADF pre-emptive strikes against ANC bases in Lesotho, Angola, and Mozambique" (Frankel, 1984, pp. 65–66). According to some sources, Israeli officers have been observers during such raids (Bloch, 1985).

The raids against the capitals of Zimbabwe, Zambia, and Botswana on May 19, 1986, are a good example of Israeli inspiration and tactics. Helicopter-borne troops and bombers attacked targets said to be African National Congress bases—replicas of Israeli raids against targets described as Palestinian bases in Lebanon and Jordan since the 1960s. And the effect is the same, too: the raids forced the ANC to move its bases—but that has not reduced the African resistance, just as Palestinian resistance has not weakened because of PLO reversals.

Naval Warfare

The South African navy has acquired its strategy, its tactics, and its technology from Israel. A cooperation program in effect since the early 1970s has involved both surface craft and submarines. The South African navy enjoys the benefits of Israeli technology, from coastal radar stations (developed by ELTA, a subsidiary of Israeli Aircraft Industries) to patrol and missile boats. An Israeli flotilla visited South African navy bases in 1975. In 1976 South African navy personnel went to Israel for training on the Israeli missile boats, which were to become standard equipment in the South African navy. The French embargo has been a severe blow to the South African navy, which was expecting two new French submarines when the contract was cancelled in 1977 (Moorcraft, 1981). Israel came to the rescue. Israel developed light, swift, missile boats, which have now been produced in South Africa (SIPRI, 1978). According to SIPRI (1975), Gabriel sea-to-sea missiles were delivered to South Africa in December 1974; they are now produced there under license. By 1983 the South African navy had launched eight of its own Reshef-class boats, armed with six Gabriel missiles each; the first boat, SAS *Jim Fouche,* was commissioned on July 9, 1977. The two navies started cooperating in the development of the missile-boat strategy, and their boats and equipment are now almost indistinguishable. This makes joint training exercises not only practical, but extremely useful.

The intimacy in the military cooperation between the two countries was proven again in the Gerhardt affair. Dieter Gerhardt was a German who immigrated to South Africa in 1953 and joined the South

African navy. By 1976 he was the commander of the naval base at Simonstown. In 1983, he was put on trial as a Soviet spy. Reportedly it was Mossad agents, concerned about leaks of Israeli–South African secret initiatives, who exposed him (O'Toole, 1984). The Israeli press claimed that he passed Israeli military secrets on to the Soviet Union (Levite, 1984; Melman, 1983a, c).

The South African naval raid against the port of Namibe in southern Angola on June 5, 1986, was the outcome of Israeli inspiration and training. In the raid, South African boats hit oil tanks with their missiles, and Israeli-trained naval commandos sank one ship and damaged two.

The most ambitious joint naval project is the development of nuclear submarines. Designed by experts from both countries, the submarines are being built in South Africa, with the active involvement of Israeli navy officers and engineers. A smaller joint project is the Barak-1, a missile against naval missiles scheduled to become operational in 1988.

Air Forces

The air forces of South Africa and Israel have been working and training together for many years. This means mainly holding joint flying exercises, sending Israeli pilots as instructors in air combat, and providing Israeli advice on planning airbases and maintaining aircraft.

In the 1960s, South Africa, like Israel, based its air force on French technology and products. It bought its first supersonic jet fighters, Dassault Mirages, on Israel's advice. Since then the air force has operated with close Israeli support and guidance. Thus Israel and South Africa, using the same Mirage-3 jets, could share operational experience and spare parts; South Africa also acquired the license to manufacture them. Then, various new models of "Super-Mirage" were developed with the help of the original blueprints for the Mirage-5, obtained in Switzerland in 1969 in a highly successful Israeli intelligence operation. These blueprints facilitated a major production effort in Israel and South Africa (Steven, 1980; Sulzberger, 1971). In the 1970s, Israel produced two improved versions of the Mirage-3—first the Nesher (Eagle), then the Kfir. On July 16, 1986, in a festive ceremony near Johannesburg, President P. W. Botha unveiled the newest weapon in South Africa's arsenal, a modern jet fighter named the Cheetah—according to Botha, the product of South African ingenuity and hard work. But one look at the pictures shows that the Cheetah is simply the Israeli Kfir-2 jet—which in turn is based on the French Mirage. The unveiling of the Cheetah was in fact the culmination of a South African–Israeli joint project dating back to 1967, following the French arms embargo against Israel.

Since the late 1960s, Israel has been moving away from French equipment and concentrating on U.S.-made jets, but Israel can still help in providing maintenance and parts for the French-made Alouettes and Super-Frelon helicopters. And the Shafrir air-to-air missile, developed in Israel in the 1960s, has become standard equipment for South African jets (Bunce, 1984). By now, the South African air force is entirely an Israeli creation.

In 1986 Israel delivered two military refueling planes to the South African air force. These planes—originally commercial Boeing 707 jets, converted by the Israeli Aircraft Industries—will enable the South Africans to bomb at will all over subequatorial Africa. The strategy is clear, and adopted from Israel's actions against the PLO. If the ANC moves its bases out of the states bordering South Africa, the Israeli Kfir jets, refueled by these new planes, will be able to reach them even at a distance of two thousand miles.

Guarding the Borders

Since the late 1960s, Israelis have, by virtue of their campaign against Palestinian guerrillas, become the world's leading experts on electronic fencing and detection of ground movements. The development started after the 1967 war, and continued during the guerrilla war between 1967 and 1970 along the Jordan river.

Israel has been prominently involved in policing South Africa's border, to prevent guerrilla infiltration. "Israeli technicians are hard at work along South Africa's borders, erecting an electrified 'wall' and laying a carpet of electronic sensors" (Moss, 1977, p. 7). Work on the border project started around 1974, and a contingent of fifty Israelis is permanently stationed in South Africa to oversee it (Adams, 1984). The border defenses include electronic fences, microwave detection

The training version of South Africa's Cheetah (top) was unveiled with great fanfare in July 1986. Though—as many observers noted—it is not the same as the well-known Israeli Kfir C-2, it is virtually identical to the Kfir TC-2 trainer (bottom). The "real" Cheetah, the twin of the C-2, has not been publicized. (Photo top: AP/Wide World. Bottom: © 1981 Eshel Dramit Ltd., Israel.)

systems, radar systems, and minefields—"an exact copy of the Israeli system" (p. 93).

In May 1976, the SADF started sealing the border between Angola and Namibia. Two fences were erected along the thousand-mile border, then electronic warning devices were set up between them. This was done with Israeli assistance (Toase, 1985). In 1985, South Africa was also building an electronic wall on its border with Zimbabwe (UPI, 1985). By all indications, this wall, too, was produced and built by Israeli experts.

Intelligence and Counterinsurgency Collaboration

Intelligence operations for the government of South Africa are conducted by the National Intelligence Service (NIS, formerly known as Bureau for State Security, BOSS, and DONS—the equivalent of the Mossad and CIA), the Security Police, and the Department of Military Intelligence (DMI). All these organizations collaborate closely with their Israeli counterparts, with exchanges of information, transfer of technology from Israel to South Africa, and training of South Africans by Israelis. General Hendrik van den Bergh, former head of BOSS, and Dr. Lukas Daniel (Niel) Barnard, head of NIS, visited Israel many times, as guests of their colleagues and of such Israeli leaders as Shimon Peres (Ronel, 1985).

Cooperation between South Africa and Israel on intelligence operations dates back at least to 1964, when communication between the secret services of the two countries was routine, according to a former BOSS operative (Winter, 1981). As reported by Breytenbach, one field of joint operations for the Mossad and the South African DONS is the African continent itself: "Jiems Kont, alias Blue Eyes, proudly displayed a star of David on his finger, given to him—he insisted—by David Ben-Gurion himself, after a South African–Israeli 'dirty tricks' operation presumably somewhere in Africa" (1984, p. 47).

When a U.S. journalist visited the office of the commander-in-chief of the South African Police, General Johannes Coetzee, he noticed a plaque presented by the Dan Police District in Israel

(Lelyveld, 1985). Memories and souvenirs of pleasant visits with colleagues in Israel are common in the South African security forces. Hundreds of police officers have visited Israel for training. Brigadier "Rooi Rus" Swanepoel—the chief interrogator of the 1964 Rivonia trial (which put ANC head Nelson Mandela and others in prison for life), the founder of Koevoet (the notorious Namibian counterinsurgency unit), the man known as the Beast of Soweto for the way he crushed the 1976 riots there—was a welcome and honored visitor to Israel in the 1970s.

But General Coetzee and his comrades do not have to travel all the way to Israel to see their friends. SHABAK, the Israeli secret security police, has a permanent mission in South Africa. The Israelis are there to help their counterparts in the day-to-day operation of the apartheid system. SHABAK prides itself on its success in keeping the Palestinians under control, by using a network of informers, penetrating Palestinian organizations, and harrassing and arresting suspects. SHABAK operatives feel they can teach the South Africans (or anybody else) a thing or two about controlling the natives, and they have been doing that. Many of the recent actions of the security police under General Coetzee bear the unmistakable stamp of Israeli inspiration (Langellier, 1984). In the early 1980s, ANC leaders in exile began receiving parcel bombs and letter bombs in the mail; the terror campaign resulted from cooperation with the Mossad, which has used similar techniques against PLO leaders. The technology for the assassination campaign against the ANC leaders, according to Foy (1982), came from the United States by way of Israel.

There is a real camaraderie among Israeli and South African fighting men. Witness the testimony of Uri Dan, an Israeli journalist and an adviser to Ariel Sharon. Sharon and Dan joined a South African unit on a march into Angola, and they liked what they saw. "When I look at the South African officers, when they speak Afrikaans or English, and during operations, I imagine that soon they will give orders in Hebrew. Their physical appearance, their freshness and openness, their battlefield behavior, all remind me of IDF officers. And I never said that about the U.S. and South Vietnamese officers I met eleven years ago in Vietnam, during the war. 'Don't play down the effect of the IDF as an example to us as a fighting body,' said a high-ranking officer in Pretoria" (Dan, 1982, p. 88).

One anecdote can serve to illustrate the intimacy of relations. General Rehavam Zeevi was appointed commanding officer of the Central Command, which since the 1967 war has been in charge of the West Bank and the Gaza Strip. The headquarters of the Central Command was moved to the West Bank, where General Zeevi built it an imposing new structure that he named Fortress Lion Cub. In a final touch of grandiosity, two live lions were put in cages to guard over the entrance. Where did General Zeevi find his lions? In Pretoria, of course.

Terrorology

To judge by media reports over the past ten years, it would seem that a new academic discipline had been born: terrorology, the study of terrorism. Books have been written, scholarly conferences held, "models" and "typologies" presented, and a new discourse has bombarded us with warnings about the dangers of "international terrorism." But despite the fact that some of the proponents of the new terrorology are academics, the campaign has all the marks of what has become known as media hype, otherwise sometimes called propaganda or disinformation. The new discourse has not gained much respectability outside the narrow confines of places called "centers for strategic studies." The new terrorology represents only a handful of academics, a handful of journalists (for example, see Sterling, 1981), and a handful of governments, among them South Africa and Israel.

The only academic haven for terrorism research in Israel is the Jaffe Center for Strategic Studies at Tel-Aviv University. The center has a project on terrorism, headed by Dr. Ariel Merari, a psychologist. While Dr. Merari's early career was devoted to studying the sexual behavior of animals, he turned his attention to terrorism after 1973. His project is concerned with "international terrorism," which, he claims, flows from one fountainhead in the Middle East—the PLO (Merari, 1983). He lists the ANC and SWAPO (the South West Africa

People's Organization, the Namibian equivalent of the ANC) among "terrorist groups around the world" supported by the PLO.

There is, of course, cooperation between the terrorism project at the Jaffe Center and the Terrorism Research Centre in Cape Town. In an interview for South African state radio, Dr. Merari said, "The foundation of the struggle against terrorism has to be embodied in unity; the unity of the Western world against the phenomenon of terrorism itself —regardless of the motive or intention, declared or undeclared, of one terrorist group or another." (Raanan, 1984). While the statement does not show much originality, it does reflect an agreement with the South African view of "terrorism."

THE DOOMSDAY SECRET

Several times a year, the arrival in Israel of a relatively small shipment of expensive enriched uranium is a cause for high-level attention and celebration. "The package has been delivered" is the jubilant message to Israel's chief executive. The prime minister is the first to get the word, and sometimes he is at the scene himself. Part of the Israeli–South African nuclear program, these shipments keep Israeli nuclear-weapons production going.

It is the most guarded secret of the alliance, but there is little reason to doubt that nuclear development plays a major part in the joint survival strategy of both countries. Shlomo Avineri, a former director-general of the Israeli Foreign Ministry, referred to "commercial and technological dealing with South Africa" and stated that "they need us more than we need them" (1985, p. 8). One wonders what he is referring to here. What are the "technological dealings"? Why does South Africa need Israel?

The public record gives us some indications of large-scale activities in connection with nuclear energy. The Israeli nuclear effort started quite early, in 1949, and in the 1950s it was based on cooperation with France. A book written a generation ago provides the logic behind Israel's nuclear-survival strategy: "Nuclear weapons, as the most important form of power available to man, may thus appear as the greatest possible guarantee of existence of Israel" (Beaton and Maddox, 1962, pp. 168–69).

Israel's basic history of nuclear development started early: "Israel, like India, demonstrated an interest in nuclear research and development from the time it became a state in 1948. Almost immediately it initiated exploration for uranium within the country. Its Atomic Energy Commission was established in 1952 under the jurisdiction of the Defense Ministry. In 1966 it was reorganized and placed under the direct control of the prime minister, who became its chairman" (Lefever, 1979, p. 66).

The initial decision to develop nuclear weapons was made by David Ben-Gurion in 1956, when he realized that it was the only way for Israel to avoid the fate of the Crusaders (Perlmutter et al., 1982). In early October 1957, Shimon Peres, representing Israel, and the French government reached an agreement on nuclear cooperation after secret negotiations in Paris (Golan, 1982). Things quickly got rolling: "Under Shimon Peres, deputy defense minister from 1958 to 1965, the Ministry of Defense increased its efforts in the nuclear field. Its first success was the Dimona reactor and nuclear complex," built with French help between October 1957 and December 1960 (Perlmutter, 1978, p. 28). Another agreement came on Ben-Gurion's visit to Paris in June 1960 (Bar-Zohar, 1977).

The covert part of Israel's nuclear program has been active since the early 1960s at Dimona, in the Nuclear Research Center of the Negev (NRCN, also known by its Hebrew acronym KAMAG). NRCN was modeled after the Manhattan Project of World War II, which created the first atom bombs. Charles de Gaulle, in his memoirs, mentioned the center being built with French help as "a facility for transforming uranium into plutonium from which, one fine day, atomic bombs might emerge" (Golan, 1982, p. 94).

Israel was able to develop nuclear weapons first and foremost because of an outstanding group of scientists who provided the brainpower. Among them were Yuval Neeman, a world-class physicist, and Ernst David Bergmann. After Bergmann resigned, in May 1966, from three positions he had held since the early 1950s—chairman of the Atomic Energy Commission, director of the Research and Planning Division at the Defense Ministry, and scientific adviser to the Defense Minister—he won the State Defense Award in 1966 for "contributions to national defense," the exact nature of which was never disclosed (Feron, 1966). Bergmann was also a frequent visitor to South Africa, and a cheerleader for the Israel–South Africa alliance (Joseph, 1987). Apparently not wishing to divulge the secret of Israel's nuclear program, one writer refers to cabinet discussions about "the expansion of research projects aimed at qualitative changes in Israel's long-term military capability" (Brecher, 1972, p. 313).

The clearest indication of the Israeli leaders' decision to push ahead with the development of nuclear weapons was the formation of a group within the Israeli elite that opposed this policy. While Israeli censorship did not allow open discussion of the matter, in 1962 the Committee for Nuclear Disarmament of the Arab-Israeli Region was organized and made its views known; it repeated its call for denuclearization of the Middle East in 1966. The members of the group were all academics and scientists who, through their connections within the elite, were well aware of what was going on (Brecher, 1972). Others recorded the early opposition in 1962: "Many people in Israel believe that the Government is pursuing such a programme at present and it is possible to find much suspicion of the defence authorities" (Beaton and Maddox, 1962, p. 180). As early as 1963, a comprehensive and serious book on nuclear strategy was written in Israel. It—and its popularity—reflected the growing debate within the Israeli elite, as the nuclear option was becoming a reality: Published in Hebrew in 1964, it immediately went into a second printing and was soon published in English (Harkabi, 1966).

There is a possibility that a "bomb of French-Israeli design was tested by the French in their Sahara facility in the early 1960s" (Lefever, 1979, pp. 68–69), and it was "Israel, not India [that] became the sixth nuclear weapons state" (p. 65), after the United States, the Soviet Union, Britain, France, and China. "By 1968 the CIA had informed President Johnson of the existence of Israeli nuclear weapons, and in July of 1970 Richard Helms, director of the CIA, gave this information to the Senate Foreign Relations Committee. These and later disclosures were not followed by censure of Israel or by reductions of assistance to her" (Waltz, 1984, p. 100; Pringle and Spigelman, 1981).

Israel's programs of nuclear research and of nuclear cooperation with South Africa have prompted U.N. General Assembly resolutions since 1978. The two countries have refused to sign the 1968 Nuclear Nonproliferation Treaty, so their nuclear facilities have not been examined by outside observers for many years.

The full history of the Israeli–South African nuclear cooperation may never be known; we can offer only a partial reconstruction. The program was described in some detail on CBS-TV on February 21, 1980. Reporting the contents of a book on Israel's nuclear-weapons program, which had been suppressed by Israeli censorship, CBS described extensive cooperation, dating back to 1955, and including, in recent years, nuclear tests.

Israel and South Africa probably have similar motivations for developing nuclear weapons; they "are more concerned with national survival than with defence proper, but they may also feel the need not only to ensure their survival but, in the last resort, to be able to take revenge on their conquerors. They exist in a hostile environment, they enjoy few friends or allies, and they need at least the reputation of possessing nuclear weapons in order to deter their enemies and to threaten revenge if that deterrent were to fail. They also need to appear to have the ultimate blackmail weapon to seek to ensure that they would not be abandoned by the West if their further existence were threatened" (Wilmshurst, 1984, p. 138).

One thoroughly guarded, academic description of nuclear-weapons development in the two countries concludes, "Analysis shows that when high nuclear propensity converges with technical capability, proliferation decisions follow within a year. . . . In fact, for Israel convergence occurred in the late 1960s, and for South Africa in the mid-1970s. Since neither is recognized as having tested nuclear weapons, however, they continue to be treated as near-nuclear countries. . . . I believe that their governments have already made proliferation decisions" (Meyer, 1983, pp. 232–33).

South Africa's nuclear development paralleled Israel's, with one important difference: South Africa produces enough uranium to export. The South African Atomic Energy Board was founded in 1949, and in 1952 it was already exporting uranium. South Africa was among the eight founders of the International Atomic Energy Agency (IAEA). In 1957, an atomic-energy research and development program was started with a five-year plan (Walters, 1986). Construction on the nuclear research center at Pelindaba was started in 1961, paralleling the Israeli building effort in Dimona.

South Africa, like Israel, has maintained a policy of calculated ambiguity about its intentions in the field of nuclear weapons. It has sought to keep the rest of the world in the dark, while from time to time its leaders have dropped hints, or even boasted, of their nuclear capabilities. The South African decision to develop both a conventional military capability and a nuclear program came in the early 1960s, following the years of rapid decolonization in Africa (Spector, 1984). South Africa sought to develop the technology of uranium enrichment in the 1960s and succeeded in 1970.

The first fuel charge of the Dimona reactor in 1963 contained twenty-four tons of uranium. Of this load, ten tons came from "Israeli domestic production," ten came from South Africa, and only four came from France (Beaton, 1966; Pry, 1984). Even at that early stage South Africa played a major role in Israel's nuclear program. There have been unverified claims that South Africa first shipped uranium to Israel as early as 1957. South Africa reportedly delivered uranium in return for conventional weapons (Peri and Neubach, 1985).

Basic nuclear research in Israel has been fruitful. Two Israeli scientists were granted a West German patent in 1973 for a new way of enriching uranium by the use of laser beams (Gillette, 1974). The two physicists, Yeshayahu Nebenzahl and Menahem Levin, are employed by the Defense Ministry; their work on such projects cannot be explained unless they have been working on nuclear weaponry. And South Africa benefits: "Israel-developed techniques, such as laser separation of uranium isotopes, are believed . . . to have been shared with South Africa, which was apparently preparing to test a bomb in the Kalahari desert in 1977" (Cooley, 1985, p. 40). Many of Israel's nuclear scientists and engineers travel to South Africa quite often (Cervenka and Rogers, 1978).

As for delivery systems, Israel has supplied South Africa with the Jericho missile, which can carry a nuclear warhead (Walters, 1986). Israel and South Africa, together with Taiwan, were reported to be producing a cruise missile intended to carry nuclear warheads (Anderson, 1980). Cruise missiles can be carried on trucks; since there is no need for permanent missile bases or silos, they are mobile and hard to detect.

Since 1977, three incidents that have become public knowledge had to do with possible nuclear tests conducted by South Africa. The first was in August 1977, the second was the widely reported mystery flash off South Africa on September 22, 1979, and the third was another flash on December 16, 1980, in the same area (Walters, 1986).

In August 1977, the Soviet Union reported that South Africa was preparing for a nuclear test in the Kalahari Desert and asked for American intervention. In a TASS message on August 8, 1977, cooperation between South Africa and Israel was mentioned in relation to the development of nuclear weapons. Responding to the Soviet request, the United States indeed put pressure on South Africa, and the test did not take place (Marder and Oberdorfer, 1977).

On September 22, 1979, an American spy satellite recorded a sharp flash of light from the ocean near the southern tip of South Africa. Shortly after the flash, an Israeli delegation, headed by Defense Minister Ezer Weizman, visited South Africa. Experts interpeted the flash as a possible nuclear test, but they could only speculate as to who conducted it. The U.S. government has not revealed any definite conclusions to this day, though there have been speculations that this presumed nuclear test might be related to the Israeli–South African nuclear program.

CBS-TV news reported on February 21, 1980, that the 1979 flash was indeed an Israeli–South African nuclear test. The U.S. Defense Intelligence Agency said on July 14, 1980, only that the flash was probably produced by a nuclear explosion (Walters, 1986). The more specific speculations received some confirmation on December 21, 1980, when Israeli state television carried, without any comment, a British-made program that offered a solution. This program dealt in detail with Israeli–South African nuclear cooperation, and reported that the 1979 flash came from a test of the newly developed naval nuclear shell, part of the joint program. There were no reactions in other Israeli media following the airing of this program. Nor did any public debate arise from the other explosion, earlier that month.

Most reporting and speculation about Israel's nuclear weapons have suffered from being locked into the pattern of generalizing from well-known nuclear-development programs, while ignoring Israel's specific situation. Israel's needs in the nuclear field are different from those of the United States, France, or China. Israeli nuclear weapons are designed to be used only in the Middle East, and they have to fit local conditions. Israel does not need high-yield hydrogen bombs, which would injure its own population if used against its immediate neighbors. One look at the map makes it clear. It needs low-yield

TABLE 3
MAJOR EVENTS
IN THE EARLY HISTORY
OF ISRAEL'S NUCLEAR PROGRAM

1948	Founding of Hemed, the science branch of the Israel Defense Forces.
1949	Geological survey by Hemed indicates potential uranium sources in the Negev.
1952	The Israel Atomic Energy Commission created under the authority of the Defense Ministry (secret—became public two years later). Development of heavy-water technology in Israel. First discussions of nuclear cooperation with France.
1955	First discussions of nuclear cooperation with South Africa. Public U.S.-Israeli nuclear cooperation starts.
1957	First uranium shipment from South Africa? Secret agreement with France on nuclear cooperation, including building research center at Dimona.
1960	Peaceful reactor at Nahal Soreq activated.
1963	Dimona reactor activated. Regular uranium shipments from South Africa start.
1966	Israel Atomic Energy Commission reorganized; Prime Minister Levi Eshkol appoints himself chairman.
1967	Plutonium-separation plant built in Dimona. End of collaboration with France.
1969	Plutonium-separation plant activated. First operational weapons?
1972	Technological breakthroughs in uranium enrichment and tactical weapons. Secret agreements with South Africa on weapons program.
1974	CIA reports that Israel has operational weapons.
1977	South African–Israeli test planned in Kalahari desert; blocked at last minute.
1979	South African–Israeli test of tactical nuclear shell. United States Defense Intelligence Agency states that South Africa, Taiwan, and Israel are collaborating on nuclear weaponry.

weapons, which would be considered tactical (i.e., for use on the battlefield) by the major powers. Israel, like South Africa, needs low-yield, "clean" bombs. This idea has shaped the Israeli nuclear effort since the 1960s.

The solution to this need has been original and stunning, going beyond conventional breakthroughs. The world has been watching Israel, and sometimes South Africa, using the old, conventional notions about nuclear weaponry, as developed by all nuclear nations. What some brilliant minds in Israel have developed is an original Israeli solution to a unique Israeli problem. South Africa has been the partner, and the beneficiary. Both South Africa and Israel realized in the 1960s that what they needed was tactical nuclear weaponry. This led to the development of the nuclear shell, fired from the 155mm howitzer or from a naval gun, which was tested in 1979. This shell contains a low-yield, two-kiloton nuclear device—the ideal nuclear weapon for the two countries (Taylor, 1981).

The real achievements of the joint Israeli–South African nuclear program are possibly beyond anybody's dreams, or nightmares. The program has achieved major technological breakthroughs in response to the specific challenges posed by the two countries' special problems in using nuclear weapons. Such cooperation between two countries in the development of nuclear weapons proves an extremely high level of trust and intimacy in the relations between them. Most nuclear countries jealously guard the secrets of their activities and their technology; for two countries to collaborate on such matters is proof of unusual trust. A nuclear alliance is the height of bilateral relations today. An alliance cemented in plutonium is sealed in blood, and should be taken very seriously.

ECONOMIC TIES

There are three unique aspects to economic relations between South Africa and Israel:

1. The existence of government-to-government agreements on economic cooperation.
2. The involvement of Israeli labor unions and socialist communes in economic contacts with South Africa.

3. The Israeli investment in the Bantustans, the black "homelands."

It is clear that the economic contacts are much more important to Israel than to South Africa. For Israeli entrepreneurs, South Africa has indeed presented a golden opportunity—both cheap labor and a very friendly environment. By 1984, Israel became first (Dishon, 1984a) or second, following Taiwan (Stressler, 1984), in the volume of new investments in South Africa. This did not reflect massive capital; the amount of new Israeli money gambled on apartheid amounted to less than $100 million. It simply reflected the fact that the rest of the world was already pulling out, while Israelis and Taiwanese still showed their confidence in the future of the regime. In 1984, Israel's exports to South Africa (textiles, fashion goods, machinery, furniture, and plastic products) amounted to $104 million, and its imports from South Africa (iron, steel, chemicals, asbestos, sugar, fish meal, and canned foods) amounted to $184 million.

Official Agreements

One aspect of these ties is the existence of official government-to-government economic-cooperation agreements, forged in a long series of visits by finance ministers of both sides. Israel is apparently the only foreign country in which South African citizens are encouraged to invest their money (though an economic-cooperation agreement was also signed with Paraguay in the 1970s); however, total investments have probably not exceeded $100 million.

The general agreement on economic cooperation is renewed every two years; other specific agreements are renegotiated annually. As a result of these agreements, Israel has the exclusive fishing rights to thousands of square miles of ocean off South Africa. The fish, harvested by a private concern, are marketed in Israel by Tnuva, the agricultural marketing arm of the General Labor Union (Histadrut).

A question often raised is the extent to which Israel is being used as a conduit for South African goods that are exported to other parts of the world, or for foreign corporations that may continue business in South Africa through Israeli subsidiaries or fronts.

Israel had such an arrangement in mind: when Simha Ehrlich,

then finance minister, visited South Africa in February 1978, he announced that Israel would serve as a convenient way station for South African goods, which would then be exported (as Israeli-made) to the United States and to the Common Market. In this way higher taxes and political boycotts could be avoided, for the benefit of both countries (Murphy, 1978).

The evidence to date indicates that Israel is not being used as a South African "bridgehead," as Ehrlich suggested—simply because South Africa has not yet needed Israel's good services. So far the world has been very willing to buy South African minerals (gold, diamonds, uranium, manganese, etc.), and boycotts of other South African products have not been a problem. If there is a problem, Israel will be delighted to help. If indeed sanctions and embargoes against South Africa become a serious matter, "Exporters assume that European middlemen and traders in Israel, Taiwan, and South Korea will keep goods flowing to and from South Africa" (Mufson, 1986, p. 38). In at least one reported case the Israeli subsidiary of a U.S. corporation was doing business in South Africa, while the parent company had officially pulled out. Motorola Israel Ltd. is doing business in South Africa, after Motorola won praise for completely divesting its holdings there (Hornung, 1986).

Unions and Kibbutzim Invest in Apartheid

Hevrat Haovdim (the Workers' Corporation), the holding company of the Histadrut (the General Labor Union) in Israel, controls 32 percent of Israeli industrial production, 88 percent of agricultural production, and 33 percent of the banking capital. It also controls civilian trade with South Africa. The near-monopoly of the Histadrut in trade with South Africa has been well documented in the Israeli press. Companies owned by the Histadrut, especially Koor Industries, are heavily involved with business activities in South Africa.

Companies owned by Koor control most of the trade between Israel and South Africa. Koor has a permanent office in South Africa; so do El Al, the Zim Shipping Company, the Dead Sea Chemical Works, Motorola Israel, and others (Levin, 1981). Iscor, the South African state-owned Iron and Steel Corporation, has, together with Koor Industries, founded a steel distributor named Iskoor Steel Services, registered in Israel in August 1973; Iscor owns 49 percent. Iskoor became the largest supplier of steel in Israel, most of it imported from South Africa. Koor created in Johannesburg an affiliated company, Afitra, engaged in promoting exports by industry in the kibbutzim (Langellier, 1984). Koor has invested in the Agbro herbicide factory near East London, with majority holdings by Sentrachem.

Yediot Aharonot (1984) reports on a trip to South Africa by the chairman of the board of the Koor Corporation. The newspaper mentions that it was a routine visit, and asks what exactly was the chairman doing there, while the Histadrut leaders were issuing statements denouncing relations with South Africa. When an Israeli journalist asked the Koor spokeswoman time and again whether its employees in South Africa are treated according to the Sullivan Principles (which promote workplace equality), he received no reply (Alfon, 1986). Since 1971 all three major banks in Israel—Bank Leumi, Israel Discount Bank, and Bank Hapoalim (the Workers' Bank, owned by the Histadrut)—have opened branches in South Africa. When the Israel–South Africa Chamber of Commerce celebrated its tenth anniversary, the happy occasion was marked under the auspices of Bank Hapoalim (Bachar, 1983).

Business dealings of the kibbutzim, the world-famous Israeli socialist communes, with South Africa, deserve special mention here. Here one can find socialist communes, based on the ideas of equality and nonexploitation, involved in making profits from the apartheid system.

One can list numerous kibbutzim that enjoy trading with South Africa, and find its "business climate" quite congenial—Negba, Haogen, Evron, Dan, Dalia, Ramot-Menashe, Merhavia, Ein-Hashofet, Gaash, Ramat-Hashofet, Ein-Dor, Hatzor, Shamir, Eilon, Maabarot, Hazorea, Ein-Shemer, Beit-Zera, and Mishmar-Haemek. What all these kibbutzim have in common, in addition to their South African contacts, is that they all belong to Hakibbutz-Haartzi, the left-wing kibbutz federation, historically Marxist, allied with the Mapam party. Members of these kibbutzim are known in Israel as leftists. While most of them sell civilian products, Mishmar-Haemek, in its TAMA plant, produces helmets for the South African army and police. In July 1986, following three stormy general-membership meetings, Kibbutz Beit-Alpha decided not to sell firefighting equipment to South

Africa. Thus, Beit-Alpha became the exception to the rule in the Hashomer Hatzair kibbutz federation, which consists of almost 100 kibbutzim. The same firefighting equipment has been sold to Chile, where it is used for "crowd control" during demonstrations. When the secretariat of the other kibbutz federation in Israel, TAKAM (with 150 kibbutzim) was asked in July 1986 to declare a boycott on economic and cultural contacts with the apartheid regime, it issued a statement saying that such contacts would continue, as long as there are diplomatic relations between the two nations. So far, only one example has become known of an Israeli plant that imports South African products, only to ship them later to Europe as new products made in Israel. That industrial plant is based in Kibbutz Hanita.

People from all over the world come to visit Israeli kibbutzim and to marvel at this success of voluntary socialism, as indeed they should. But these visitors are happily unaware of the ties between the kibbutzim and South Africa.

Kibbutz Lohamei Hagetaot is known in Israel for its Holocaust museum, visited by tens of thousands every year. The name Lohamei Hagetaot means "fighters of the ghettos"; this kibbutz was founded by individuals who fought the Nazis actively in Eastern European ghettos during the Holocaust. But Lohamei Hagetaot joined a long list of Socialist-Zionist kibbutzim with business ventures in South Africa —it operates the Kama chemical plant in the KwaZulu Bantustan (Dishon, 1984a; Stressler, 1984).

It just seems that members of the kibbutzim, like many other Israelis, have a warm place in their hearts for South Africans. When Major General Neil Webster of the South African General Staff spent several months in Israel during 1976 as a guest of the IDF, he lived in the Socialist-Zionist kibbutz of Sassa.

The Bantustans
and Namibia

The Bantustans are part of the grand scheme of apartheid, which is to make all of South Africa's blacks into foreigners, citizens of their own "homelands." Then, of course, there would be no need to grant them equal rights in South Africa. According to the plan, ten "Bantu homelands" were envisioned: Bophuthatswana, Venda, Transkei, Ciskei, Lebowa, KwaNdebele, Gazankulu, KaNgwane, QwaQwa, and KwaZulu. Of these, the first four have been declared "independent." The rest, according to the South African government, are in various stages of preparation for independence. Since 1984, the Bantustans have become battlegrounds for the struggle against apartheid, and proofs of its nearing end. Reading the Israeli press since 1980, one might get the distinct impression that the "independent homelands" are Israeli colonies, and not South African ones. Names such as KwaNdebele, Lebowa, and KwaZulu are totally unknown to most of the world, but for many Israelis they are part of personal experience.

The official position of the Foreign Ministry in Jerusalem is that the Bantustans are not recognized by Israel as separate states. But Bezek, the government-owned telephone company in Israel, seems to recognize Ciskei, Transkei, and Bophuthatswana as independent states—and they are listed as such in its international phone directory. At the same time, other Israeli government ministries, and many prominent individuals, have been in close contact with the Bantustans. Israeli professors are busy helping set up educational systems, Israeli artists visit to encourage tribal arts, and counterinsurgency experts come to advise on "security." Free trips to the Bantustans have become popular pastimes for members of the Israeli elite. Professors, local politicians, journalists, and members of the Knesset have enjoyed the hospitality offered by the Bantustan leaders, who reciprocate for the treatment they receive in Israel. As the first "independent" Bantustan, Transkei, was being set up in the early 1970s, Israelis were involved in the creation of the new government structure. An Israeli political-science professor, Joseph Ben-Dak (with ties to the South Korean Unification Church), served as a minister in the Transkei government.

In the 1977 elections, Ruth Dayan, the first wife of Moshe Dayan, was a candidate on the peace list. Today she is helping the Bantustans develop their authentic tribal culture by encouraging folk crafts. Israeli artists, typically considered liberals or left-wingers at home, have been working in the Bantustans on such projects. One of them described her work as a way of atoning for the sins of the "evil whites," by reviving authentic tribal cultures (Shimshi, 1985).

Israel is the only foreign country with considerable investments in the Bantustans. Among Israeli businessmen investing are two former finance ministers, Yigal Hurvitz and Yoram Aridor. If you visit Bophuthatswana today, you will see Israeli security guards, soccer coaches, businessmen, and tourists. If you visit one of the casinos in the resort area of Sun City, you are likely to encounter Israeli security guards, who are watching over the fun, and making sure that everything is in order (Egozi, 1985). Support for the Bantustans is a matter of national consensus in Israel. When President Lucas Mangope of Bophuthatswana visited Israel in 1981, he was warmly received by Labor Party chairman Shimon Peres, then in opposition (Karny, 1981a). When the (white South African) commanders of the Bophuthatswana army visited Israel in the next year, they met with Israeli officers and with Defense Minister Ariel Sharon—and Peres, still leader of the opposition, received them at his Knesset office. MK Abraham Melamed is known as the leader of the left wing of the National Religious Party. He supports a variety of unpopular causes, and is a member of the Committee for Improved Relations with the USSR. But this did not stop him from joining the hundreds of Israelis who have visited Bophuthatswana as official guests (Dishon, 1984c).

Despite all the official denials by the Israeli Foreign Ministry, it is easy to demonstrate that there are formal contacts between the Israeli government and the Bantustan rulers. When Ciskei President Lennox Sebe visited Israel in 1983, he was received by government officials, including Deputy Minister Dov Shilansky (Frenkel, 1983a). An innocent-looking item in an Israeli newspaper proves that indeed support for the Bantustans is official Israeli policy, and not just a coincidence of initiatives by private citizens. The director of the sports department in Ramat-Gan (a Tel-Aviv suburb) was absent from his job for a long period. Following complaints to city hall, the mayor of the city, Israel Peled, stated that the sports director was in Bophuthatswana on leave, at the recommendation of the Foreign Ministry in Jerusalem, and that the Foreign Ministry represents state interests, which take precedence over local ones (Dori, 1981b). So much for official denials.

The tie between Israel and Ciskei is truly revealing for anybody who wants to know what the Israel of the 1980s is really like. Ciskei has become a showcase of Israeli activities in the Third World. Among the Bantustans, Ciskei stands out as the worst example of a bloody tyranny. It has become a symbol of the corruption and poverty in the

Bantustans, and has been singled out for attention in the world media. The nature of the Ciskei regime is well known in Israel (Isacowitz, 1984), but this has not daunted the Israelis, from members of Knesset to professors and artists, who flock to the capital of President-for-Life Sebe and enjoy his hospitality.

Five members of Knesset attended the festive opening of the Ciskei parliament in May 1985. Yehezkel Flumin—former deputy finance minister, a member of the Liberal Party in the Likud Bloc— was the star of the show. Flumin, an accountant by profession, praised the Ciskei tax system as "the most progressive in the world," and the government system there as moving closer to true democracy. Flumin's hosts in South Africa were unprepared for his lavish compliments for the Bantustan system, expressed in an interview on South African radio. It seems that he gave them a good idea of what an Israeli liberal was like (Sagir, 1985).

President Lennox Sebe has visited Israel a dozen times since taking office in 1981. It's no wonder, given the royal treatment he gets there, since he is regarded as a stooge and a despot by the rest of the world. During his ninth visit, President Sebe proclaimed that Israel was one of the few nations that still stick to the values of culture and humanity, and that such nations are few and far between (Arkin, 1983).

The situation in Ciskei can only be described by the familiar American euphemism "a good business climate," with most capital provided by the South African government, and all profits kept by the investor. And many well-known Israelis have invested there. The best-known is Yoram Aridor, finance minister under Begin between 1980 and 1983, and MK since then. He has always been a man of vision. One vision had to do with classic cars. Automobile collectors in the First World have an insatiable appetite for "classic" cars, and entrepreneurs have been turning the appetite to profit by manufacturing exact replicas of old models. The Classic Motor Company, devoted to making exact copies of Mercedes-Benz 1929 models, found its natural home in Ciskei, where black workers and government subsidies would make it an easy source of profit. Yoram Aridor promoted the idea and was one of the owners (Yefet, 1986).

General Efraim Poran, military adviser to the Singapore government and a man with good connections in Haiti, is also a happy investor in Ciskei (Levin, 1985). General Poran says: "As of today, in Ciskei people have houses to live in, employment and education for their children, and there is no apartheid" (Shemi, 1986, p. 16). The Tamuz Corporation, which supplied security services to Ferdinand Marcos, has been providing bodyguard services and general security to President Sebe (Lipkin, 1984).

In early 1985, the Israeli investment company Incobe was reported to be building three thousand apartments for government employees in Bisho, the capital of Ciskei (*Yediot Aharonot,* 1985). The Histadrut is represented in Ciskei through its holding company and its subsidiaries. The Koor Trade Division of the Koor Corporation is a partner in Agro-Carmel (financed by the South Africa Development Bank), which won several bids offered by the Ciskei government (Dishon, 1984b). The prospect of using South African government money to reap enormous profits, tax-free, was too hard to resist. Political leaders, businessmen—anybody who could get in—"invested" in the new promised land.

But sooner or later the bubble was bound to burst, and the South African government was kind enough to warn its Israeli friends about it. The end of the party in Ciskei came in the summer of 1985. Even the corrupt Ciskei dictatorship decided that some practices were beyond tolerating—especially when it meant that Lennox Sebe and his cronies were outsmarted by some Israelis with larceny in their hearts. In May 1985, President Sebe accused Dr. Hennie Beukes, his Minister of Health, of corruption. Dr. Beukes, the only white in the Ciskei government, quickly resigned "for reasons of health." An investigation revealed that he had awarded about $150 million worth of contracts to several corporations, mostly Israeli, with results that were quite shoddy and unprofitable for Ciskei, but enormously profitable for the corporations (Isacowitz, 1985c). Several of the Israeli contracts were canceled, but at last report most Israeli business ventures in that corner of South Africa were still going strong.

Venda is another of the "independent" Bantustans. Its president, Chief Patrick Mphephu—together with Minister of Foreign Affairs A. M. Nadzivhandilla, Minister of Economic Affairs F. N. Ravele, Minister of Agriculture and Forestry G. M. Famambulana, and four other officials—spent eight days in Israel in December 1980. The delegation was warmly received in Haifa, where Chief Mphephu received the keys to the city. Chief Mphephu returned to Israel with regularity, and mentioned plans for future visits in a letter to the mayor of Haifa of January 11, 1982. In 1984, the entire thirty-four-member Chamber of Commerce of Venda visited Israel, thanks to the efforts of the Israeli–South African Chamber of Commerce (Streek, 1983).

As of 1987, KwaNdebele was scheduled to become the next "independent" homeland, as far as South Africa was concerned. This meant, among other things, that more and more Israelis have been visiting the small territory east of Pretoria, helping to set up the necessary institutions. Kangwane—a not-yet-independent Bantustan, the planned homeland for South African Swazis—has also had considerable Israeli attention, even though it is totally unknown outside South Africa. Israel is building a teachers'-training college there, budgeted at $25 million. Several Israeli professors of education have been involved in this project.

To invest in a Bantustan is to cast a clear vote of confidence in the future of apartheid—and that is why not many business people have been interested (Joseph, 1987). Very few nations, even those that support apartheid in various ways, have been ready to help support the Bantustans. Several Bantustan leaders have visited Taiwan, including Venda's president Mphephu, and Lebowa's chief minister, Dr. Cedric Phatudi. Numerous Taiwanese corporations have invested in the Bantustans, where their activities have matched those of Israeli corporations (Streek, 1983). Israeli support for the Bantustan states was criticized publicly by Desmond Sixishe, minister of information and broadcasting for Lesotho. Sixishe said that Israel's involvement was of immense propaganda value for South Africa, and added, "One can understand Israel's tilting towards South Africa. But for heaven's sake, what are you doing in the Bantustans? Nobody else is there except you and Taiwan" (Brilliant, 1984, p. 3). By their readiness to legitimize the Bantustans, both Israel and Taiwan indicate their serious support for apartheid, and their understanding of the importance of the Bantustans for the South African regime.

Namibia is not just another African colony struggling for independence. A former German colony, it was assigned to South Africa as a mandate territory by the League of Nations in 1920, and the U.N. General Assembly first voted in 1946 in favor of giving it independence. Officially, since 1966 all responsibility for Namibia has resided with the U.N. Council for Namibia.

The Israeli stance on Namibia parallels its stance on the Bantustans. Officially, the Israeli government has never taken a position on the question. In practice, Israeli officials have visited Namibia, and have offered help to the South African authorities there. The best-known example is the visit by Defense Minister Sharon and his entourage in late 1981, when much time was spent with South African forces in the field, and in operations in Namibia and Angola. As part of Israel's military aid to South Africa in Namibia, Israeli instructors have been training Angolan rebel forces stationed there (*Rand Daily Mail*, 1981).

Israel has demonstrated its support for South African policies in Namibia in other ways. The Israeli ambassador to South Africa, Eliyahu Lankin, paid a visit to Namibia in 1984, and promised Deon Gous, director of development coordination, that Israel would provide Namibia with development aid. (Taiwan has also been aiding South African "development" plans for Namibia.) On April 20, 1985, a "top-level team of officials from Namibian governmental and parastatal organizations left for a twelve-day visit to Israel . . . to study development projects and meet development experts there" (*Windhoek Advertiser*, 1985, p. 1).

FRIENDSHIP AND SOLIDARITY

How can we tell what Israelis feel about South Africa? By listening to their words? Most Israeli "liberals," as well as most Israeli leaders, will say that they are opposed to apartheid. Perhaps we should watch their actions as well. Friendship and solidarity among nations, if they have a serious foundation in common interests and culture, are expressed by ordinary citizens. The citizens of Israel and South Africa have expressed friendship and solidarity in many ways, with little prodding from their leaders, which indicates the degree of normality the alliance has achieved over the years.

Commenting on the situation in South Africa, a liberal Israeli journalist wrote, "It is always good to hear both sides of a story. What we usually hear are one-sided [denunciations] by journalists who also tend to denounce what they call the oppressive policy of Israel in the occupied territories. Since we know how inaccurate these reports are, we must view reports on matters that do not concern us directly [i.e., reports on South Africa] with skepticism" (Golan, 1977, p. 9). Many articles in the Israeli press adopt the South African view of apartheid, and accept the "total onslaught" theory. A good example is an article by Salpeter, a foreign-affairs commentator for the liberal daily *Haaretz*. The article, "The Bastion and the Terror," presents the main problem in South Africa as that of a Soviet takeover, and refers to the campaign against apartheid as "hypocritical" (1980a).

Very few Israelis—only right-wing Zionists—will say publicly that they support apartheid, see it as an example, or admire anything about South Africa. "Liberal" Zionists always try to avoid any association of Zionism with apartheid, despite the obvious similarities. They commonly claim that whereas in South Africa the whites are wrongly oppressing the black majority, in Israel, whatever problems there are stem from the (non-Jewish) minority's refusal to accept the dictates of the (Jewish) majority. What this claim fails to take into account is that, until 1948, Arabs were a majority in Palestine, and turning them into a minority was indeed one aim of Zionism. But when the history of Zionism is examined and remembered, sympathy for apartheid is likely to surface. Thus, a letter to the editor of *Haaretz* in November 1985 reminds the readers of the history of Zionism: "Events in South Africa are constantly in the news. President Botha does not want to hand over control to representatives of the majority. Fifty years ago, in 1935, the British High Commissioner wanted to set up a legislative assembly in Palestine. As far as I remember, Jews were allocated two seats . . . and the Arabs eleven [reflecting the respective sizes of the two communities; the British officials were to have ten seats]. . . . Our representatives turned the idea down out of hand the day it was submitted. Is it so hard to understand President Botha?" (Meyer, 1985).

It is very rare that Israelis' admiration of South Africans is openly expressed, but it happens. Thus, an Israeli visitor to South Africa stated that "while most Israelis sense that something is very wrong with their country, but cannot translate this into political action, in South Africa the government itself is conscious of the need to change policies in order to survive. And the common Afrikaner is sure that his future depends on his actions, and believes that his actions will insure his future. The Israeli visitor regards this self-confidence with envy and nostalgia" (Salpeter, 1980b, p. 13).

In most parts of the world in the 1980s, one could not find department stores promoting special sales devoted to South African products. In Israel, no stigma is attached to South African merchandise, and such promotions are common. Kol-Bo Shalom, the largest department store in Tel-Aviv, had a "South African fortnight" in August 1984. The advertisements presented South Africa as "A land of gold and diamonds. A land of choice meat and superb wine. A land of tropical fruit, beer, and delightful delicacies" (*Jerusalem Post*, August 10, 1984).

In August 1985, while the whole world was watching events in South Africa, a delegation of twenty Israeli Rotarians, headed by District Judge Yitzhak Baraz, went to see things firsthand. The judge produced a sixty-page report, which gives us a chance to see South Africa through the eyes of a member of the Israeli elite: his South Africa is one of the most beautiful countries in the world, with great shopping and entertainment opportunities for Israeli tourists and striking advances in black living standards; apartheid is "separate development," and job discrimination has been eliminated (Edelist, 1986).

Israeli sympathy for South Africans finds expression even in the most unlikely contexts. At an international conference of homosexual-rights organizations in Vienna, the Israeli representative left in protest after the all-white South African delegation was refused admittance (*Haolam Hazeh*, 1983).

Israelis know the realities of life in South Africa much better than Europeans or Americans, because of the large numbers of them who have visited or lived there. Some visit relatives there—either South African Jews or recent emigrants from Israel. They may visit in their official capacities, as government or military officials, visiting scientists, or members of a delegation from an Israeli city to a South African sister city. They may be artists or athletes or simply tourists. So South Africa, for more and more Israelis, is not just a place they hear about in the news. When the name comes up, tens of thousands of Israelis recall their own firsthand experiences and memories. South Africa is mentioned in conversations among Israelis as a place they have visited or plan to visit, as a place where acquaintances are having a good time and making a lot of money, as a place where other acquaintances have visited in an official capacity. It is no longer remote and exotic. As both tourists and immigrants, Israelis seem to find South Africa a congenial place.

The warm glow of the alliance is experienced by people in both nations. Individual Israelis have felt the growing isolation of their country, and growing hostility from various quarters. When visiting Europe—the usual destination for Israelis abroad—this has been increasingly noticeable. In South Africa things are different. Visiting Israelis are welcomed, a pleasant and unusual sensation for Israelis. They are honored and desired visitors, and they bask in the warmth of Afrikaner hospitality. When South Africans visit Israel, the warm welcome there is even more unusual and enjoyable.

South Africa has become a favorite vacation spot for Israelis, who also visit Namibia and the Bantustans. To many Israelis, South Africa is simply a great place to visit, and about 200,000 have done that. Hundreds of articles about South Africa as a beautiful vacation spot, with details about sightseeing highlights, have been published in the Israeli press since 1970. Not a single one has mentioned the political reality of the place. A typical article describes a dance performance offered by black goldminers (Getegno, 1981). The writer comments on the hard work in the mines, which has not managed to "suppress their innate love of dancing" and the "rhythm in their blood," but mentions nothing about the miners' living conditions or political rights.

The airlines of the two countries have been essential to the growing contact. El Al, the Israeli national airline, started flying to Johannesburg in October 1955. Since the early 1960s, it and South African Airways, SAA, have cooperated closely, while most African countries have shunned all air contacts with South Africa. The volume of traffic between Israel and South Africa started growing after 1967, so that El Al had to increase the number of flights to once a week in 1968, and twice a week starting December 12, 1970. The line to Pretoria, operated in consortium with SAA, has been El Al's most profitable (*Business Week,* 1978).

The number of South African tourists to Israel reached 7,000 as early as 1970. Regular package tours to South Africa have been offered by Israeli travel agents since the 1970s. The number of Israeli tourists in South Africa reached 8,300 in 1980, and it passed the

149

10,000 mark the following year (*Davar,* 1981). A branch of Satour, the South African Tourist Company, was opened in Tel-Aviv in 1979, and it started publishing brochures in Hebrew; tourism to South Africa has grown so much that a guidebook was published in 1984. While South Africa was exploding in revolt in the summer of 1985, hundreds of Israelis were enjoying themselves there; the flow of tourists did not stop even that fall, after months of anti-apartheid rioting (Blumenkrantz, 1985a). In the summer of 1986, Israeli tourists continued to make South Africa their favorite vacation spot, and the number grew to 12,000 (Alfon, 1986). The number of Israelis visiting South Africa has not stopped growing; 1987 is expected to be another banner year. This trend is especially conspicuous when viewed against the background of the decline in tourism from Western Europe and the United States (Israeli, 1987).

One rather ceremonial indication of friendship is the number of sister-city arrangements created by mayors and city councils in the two countries. Tel-Aviv is sister city to Johannesburg, Haifa to Cape Town, Acco to Simonstown, Eilat to Durban, and Ashkelon to Port Elizabeth. Ariel, an urban settlement on the West Bank, is, appropriately, sister city to Bisho, the capital of Ciskei. These twinning agreements, initiated by local politicians, usually mean pleasure trips for them and their families, and also mean more informal contacts among individuals in both places. The mayor of Tel-Aviv, Israel's largest city, paid an official visit to Johannesburg in 1984, and was warmly received. A year later, he hosted the mayor of Johannesburg. Mayor Shlomo Lahat is one of the leaders of the Liberal Center Party, founded in Israel in 1986. His warm feelings toward South Africa indeed reflect the ideals of the "liberal" center in Israeli politics.

Immigration:
A Vote of Confidence

One cannot think of a better show of support for the apartheid way of life than the emigration of tens of thousands of Israelis to South Africa since 1970. This phenomenon conveys something quite important about Israelis and their view of the world. To most emigrants searching for a new home in recent years, South Africa would not loom as a very desirable place. To Israelis, the world looks very different, and so Israel has become, in proportion to its population, the leading nation in the world in the number of emigrants it sends to South Africa. These are individuals who presumably decided that Israel did not have much of a future, but apartheid did.

Estimates of the number of Israeli immigrants in South Africa vary, but none is below 20,000. This makes South Africa second only to the United States as a magnet for Israelis looking for a new home. There were reportedly 18,000 Israelis in South Africa by 1978 and 20,000 by 1981; in 1985 Abba Eban, former Israeli foreign minister, put the number at 25,000 (*Business Week,* 1978; Peres, 1981; Margalit, 1985).

Emigration to South Africa has been encouraged by efforts to recruit Israelis to work there. South African corporations, the South African government, and the Bantustan puppet governments have all recruited Israeli workers, including professionals, since 1976. In the summer of 1980 advertisements for positions in South Africa became common in the weekend editions of all Israeli newspapers. They offered positions for engineers, technicians, skilled workers, and medical personnel. A typical ad opens: "Electronic engineering posts in booming South Africa. How would you like to live and work in Cape Town, probably the world's most beautiful coastal city?" It goes on to describe the good life and good working conditions in South Africa, (*Maariv,* June 26, 1981). Another ad proclaims "a land of sunshine —a world of opportunity" and adds, "We are an equal-opportunity employer" (*Maariv,* September 5, 1981). More exotic ads offered work in the South African goldfields, as technicians and mine-ventilation engineers, and others offered jobs in industrial engineering, power-plants, and the garment industry. Perhaps the most intriguing ad so far was published in *Yediot Aharonot* on September 29, 1980. It called for a reserve lieutenant colonel, fluent in English and trained in anti-terrorist operations, for a twelve-month assignment; three weeks later the position was filled and the successful candidate was in South Africa. The South African government has recruited Israeli physicians to work for military field hospitals on the Namibia front; they are paid $15,000 a month and are much in demand (*Haolam Hazeh,* 1985a). It was reported in November 1985 that South Africa was also recruiting Israeli psychiatrists (*Haolam Hazeh,* 1985b).

Science, Sports,
and Culture Exchanges

All Israeli universities have cooperative exchange programs with South African universities, and many Israeli academics spend their sabbatical leaves at South African universities. Especially active are Ben-Gurion University of Beersheba and the University of Haifa, which sent a delegation to South Africa in 1981. The universities are following the lead of the Israel National Council for Research and Development, which has an extensive cooperation program with its South African equivalent and with the Medical Research Council (MRC) in South Africa. This latter connection led to a joint conference on immunology at Israel's Weizmann Institute in February 1981. An exchange program for scientists from all of South Africa's universities and research institutes and the Weizmann Institute was officially established in 1983. An annual Israeli–South African science symposium alternates its locale between the two countries. Israel has cooperation agreements with the South African Council for Scientific and Industrial Research (CSIR), which according to Breytenbach "operates as a think-tank for the Government, and more specifically, for the security forces" (1984, p. 249).

It has become normal practice for Israeli academics and scientists, in fields ranging from nuclear physics to literature and sociology, to visit South African universities and research institutes. Though South Africa is not known as an international center of learning, there are hundreds of Israeli students there, most of them studying for graduate degrees. And while South African academics and scientists may feel unwelcome in most countries today, their Israeli colleagues have nothing but the warmest attitude toward them. Hebrew University awarded an honorary doctorate to Senator Owen Horwood in 1980. On October 1, 1981, the honorable Lucas Mangope, president of Bophuthatswana, presented a scholarly lecture at Bar-Ilan University and received an honorary degree.

Scientific collaboration ranges from archaeology to rainmaking, not to mention nuclear physics. When Israeli archaeologists need validation for their radiocarbon dating, they turn to their colleagues in Pretoria (Reif, 1985). Ben-Gurion University has joint research projects with the University of Pretoria, the University of Cape Town, and the University of the Orange Free State (*Rand Daily Mail,* 1984). Other Israeli universities have not lagged behind; "university personnel are in constant and close touch with one another and teams of scientists and technical specialists are engaged in joint research projects of tremendous political benefits to both peoples" (Arkin, 1981, p. 8). The vice-president of Ben-Gurion University, Yaakov Arnon, was asked whether there was any fear at his university about possible political pressure in reaction to cooperation with the University of Pretoria. He replied, "It never occurred to us" (Abendroth, 1979, p. 13). Arnon was undoubtedly telling the truth; his response reflects Israeli thinking.

The practice of apartheid in sports has led to South Africa's exclusion from all international sports organizations and from the Olympic games. It has also led to a secondary boycott against athletes who compete with South African teams under any circumstances. Israel itself has been the target of numerous boycotts, so Israeli sports associations, concerned about their own international contacts, have paid close attention to these actions. Officially they are on record as avoiding any South African contacts.

Nonetheless, athletic exchanges between South Africa and Israel are simply routine; they are reported often in the media. The reason for the discrepancy is that the boycott is simply not enforced. Violators who have faced disciplinary charges before the sports associations' internal courts have been acquitted or have gotten off lightly (Yehezkeli, 1983).

When South African sports teams visit other countries, riots erupt, but nothing of the sort has even happened in Israel. *Bamerhav* reported on a 1983 visit by a rugby team from Stellenbosch University to Kibbutz Yizreel: "There is no end to the surprises offered us by Israeli reality. The kibbutz, which is supposed to be a socialist society based on justice, equality, and fraternity, hosts a group of South African racists. . . . There is nothing left but to long for the mass demonstrations that took place in New Zealand, during a visit there by a South African rugby team. New Zealand does not have kibbutzim, but on the other hand there are still a few people with principles who think rather naively that a visit by an apartheid rugby team should not pass unnoticed" (1983, p. 9). The rest of the kibbutz movement has not reacted to the visit; Kibbutz Yizreel has hosted other South African teams and, as of mid-1986, was determined to continue these contacts (Hermoni, 1986).

True, athletes from some other countries have ignored the boycott against South Africa, but Israeli athletes have won the distinction of being the only ones in the world to have sports contacts with the Bantustan states. A team from Bophuthatswana visited Israel in March 1981 and played against the Petah-Tikva Hapoel soccer team. Hapoel (Worker) teams, affiliated with the Histadrut, constitute the largest sports association in Israel. The Petah-Tikva team was defeated by the visitors, but did much better in a tour of South Africa a few months later, when they played against teams from both Bophuthatswana and Venda (Porat, 1981). The team was accompanied by the Laborite mayor of Petah-Tikva, Dov Tavori (Dori, 1981a). The romance between Petah-Tikva (which coincidentally was the first Jewish agricultural colony in Palestine, founded in 1878) and Bophuthatswana continued. The Petah-Tikva coach, Amaziah Levkovitz, impressed with the talent of the Bantustan players, moved to South Africa just after the tour to become the coach for the Bophuthatswana national soccer team.

In another kind of competition, a team of Israeli chefs won fifteen gold and silver medals in a 1983 South African cooking contest. In 1981, it had won only third place.

In the United States and around the world, artists who have performed in South Africa have been blacklisted, but no such problems exist in Israel. There, popular artists go to South Africa regularly and enjoy an appreciative audience. When they return, nobody would dream of blacklisting them. Exchanges between the two countries are especially prominent in the fields of music and dance. The Israeli classical-ballet troupe Bat Sheva and the modern-ballet troupe Bat Dor visit South Africa frequently. Israeli musicians have toured South Africa hundreds of times, and the Israeli Philharmonic Orchestra toured the country in 1974. (White) children's choirs from South Africa and Israel exchange visits and sing together regularly. As of 1986, all cultural ties with South Africa were maintained at normal levels; the Israel Chamber Ensemble played in major South African cities in July 1986.

Propaganda War
and Muldergate

Israel has volunteered to help South Africa with its public-relations problems in the West. In the Israeli press, one often encounters the theme that both South Africa and Israel are subject to campaigns of vilification, and that the response to those should be effective dissemination of the right kind of information. The South African propaganda campaign of the 1970s was started and carried out with Israeli help; its origins lie in South Africa's envy of Israel's positive image in the Western media. Despite its openly discriminatory policies, Israel is described in the Western media as a "Western democracy," while South Africa is almost universally condemned. Eschel Rhoodie expressed his envy of Israeli public-relations successes in the West, and compared the merits of apartheid and Zionism, which he found basically similar. It is quite clear from Rhoodie's book (1969) that he not only envies Israeli public-relations efforts but thinks they should be emulated.

The "Muldergate" scandal was inspired by this public-relations gap. It was Israel's suggestion that led to a major covert South African campaign to improve apartheid's media image (de Villiers, 1980). Under C. P. Mulder, the rising star of the National Party, the South African Information Department spent about $160 million between 1968 and 1978 in buying influence by investing in newspapers and magazines. There was an attempt to acquire the London *Observer.* Investments were made in U.S. media. Money was invested in campaigns to defeat political opponents in foreign countries, such as Senator Dick Clark of Iowa—who was indeed defeated.

When the South African Information Department decided to acquire the London-based *West Africa* magazine in 1975, the actual buyer was Mossad man Arnon Milchan (Bloch and Weir, 1982). Milchan was "the key financial figure in the South African scheme that later became known as Muldergate" (Rapoport, 1986, p. 13). In an interview in 1986, he said that he had been recruited for the operation by "a Hebrew University professor, and a Foreign Ministry official" (p. 13). One may wonder who these individuals are. The story does stretch the limits of plausibility, but in itself is suggestive. We are expected to believe that it is only natural for Hebrew

University professors and Israeli Foreign Ministry officials to be involved in covert South African propaganda.

There were other Israeli connections. South African "public relations" in the United States were handled by Sydney S. Baron and Company, management and public-relations consultants in New York. Sydney Baron received this assignment in 1976: "Baron says that he got involved with South Africa at the suggestion of certain personages in Israel, but refuses to elaborate beyond noting significantly that South Africa is Israel's only friend in Africa, with the implication that anything he could do would help Israel" (Stone, 1979, p. 391). It can safely be assumed that Baron was not the only U.S. supporter of Israel who was thus motivated to help South Africa.

Ariel Sharon volunteered to present the South African viewpoint to the American public and did it rather well. In a 1981 interview with Drew Middleton of the *New York Times,* "he said that South Africa is one of the few countries in Africa and southwestern Asia that is trying to resist Soviet military infiltration in the area. He added that there had been a steady flow of increasingly sophisticated Soviet weapons in Angola and other African nations, and that as a result of this, and Moscow's political and economic leverage, the Soviet Union was 'gaining ground daily' throughout the region" (1981, p. A9). This is, of course, the South African point of view, and Sharon carried a message that would be warmly received, at least by some segments of the American elite.

In the 1980s, the Israeli–South African alliance, quite naturally, became an argument in support of apartheid. "Officials in Pretoria and their representatives have recently been able to play on the close economic, political, and military ties between Israel and South Africa as a basis for rethinking attitudes. South Africa, they argue, has become one of the few friends Israel can count on, apart from the United States, and so Israel's supporters here should think about reciprocating" (Ungar, 1985, p. 112).

DESPERATION
AND DEFIANCE

Why are we calling this relationship between the two countries an alliance? Why not refer to the relations as close or friendly? The distinction is quite deliberate, and there are real differences between friendly relations and an alliance, which implies coordination of efforts on the basis of common policy goals. The meaning of the distinction will become clear if we examine the relations between Israel and France during two time periods. Israel in the 1980s could be said to be on friendly terms with France, as indicated by official contacts and visits by foreign ministers, prime ministers, and presidents. But in no way can the relations be construed as being an alliance, because of several basic policy disagreements. France and Israel in 1956 had an alliance, as indicated by their close collaboration, based on shared strategic-policy goals. The relations between Israel and South Africa, since the mid-1960s, give every indication of being superior to the great and glorious French-Israeli alliance in the 1950s. The alliance between Israel and South Africa is more intimate and more extensive than anything similar in Israel's history. If we compare it with the alliance between Israel and France, it becomes clear that the ties with South Africa have held longer, and have been more intense, because Israel and South Africa are in similar historical predicaments. Such a commonality of fate was never shared by Israel and France.

When we discuss Israeli relations with South Africa, and try to assess their significance, we should have some standard of comparison so that we can judge specific actions against some general norm or average. Our norm of comparison should be the behavior of those countries that Israel itself sees as its sisters, the Western democracies that are similar to Israel by general political orientation and living standards. Such a comparison is clear and immediately enlightening.

Many countries conduct business with South Africa, and many countries support the survival of apartheid in various ways, but only Israel's support is so direct and unreserved. Only in Israel are the red carpets rolled out for the visits of South African leaders; only there are they so openly wined and dined. We can safely assume that South

African leaders have been received even more warmly on secret visits. In how many countries in the world can both Israelis and South Africans feel really welcome?

The alliance between Israel and South Africa is a matter of true national consensus. No difference is discernible between Labor Party governments (until 1977) and Likud governments (after 1977) in conducting the business of this alliance. The alliance "drew little public protest from Israelis, who have come to feel themselves increasingly isolated in the United Nations after the massive break of diplomatic reations by virtually all the countries in Africa in late 1973. They also bitterly resented the U.N. General Assembly vote equating Zionism with racism and apartheid" (Legum, 1982, p. 11).

There is a profound and basic difference between the Israeli alliance with South Africa and Israel's relationships with other right-wing Third World regimes. South Africa is a true partner and equal in the alliance. Other Third World regimes are only clients. The ideal ally for Israel "should not be susceptible to American influence, should have shared geopolitical interests with Israel, and above all, should have the resources and technology needed to help build a sophisticated weapons industry" (*Economist,* 1977, p. 90). In the 1950s, France was the country that best fit the bill; in the 1980s, it was South Africa.

If the overall strategy for Israeli survival is based on stopping true decolonization and having a nuclear option, then South Africa plays a major role in both facets of this strategy. Israel aids South Africa's attempt to survive and thus slow decolonization, and South Africa aids Israel's nuclear program (and is, in turn, helped by Israel). Alliances do have their limits, though; between nations, as between individuals, intimacy has its boundaries. Israel's leaders have time and time again been forced to realize that Israel can rely on itself alone, so self-interest dictates that even this intimate alliance cannot lead to a complete sharing. Israel does not share all its intelligence information and military technology with South Africa. Third-party alliances still play a role; military technology granted by the United States to Israel is not transferred to South Africa.

The background for the alliance is described by a spokesman for the Israeli leadership as follows: "Both Israel and South Africa are the targets of hypocritical attacks from the Communist and Afro-Asian world (and it is hard for Israelis not to identify with the South African contempt towards the self-righteousness coming from the U.N. and other international organizations). . . . Israel and South Africa claim that the situation of Arabs in the occupied territories (and blacks in Soweto) is much better than that of farmers in Arab countries (or of blacks in black African countries). . . . Both Israel and South Africa fight a terrorism which relies on sympathy and support from neighboring countries—and in both places there is a merging (on a different scale) of internal and external threat. In both cases, the terrorists murdering women and children, Israeli or South African, are viewed, even by public opinion in enlightened countries, as 'freedom fighters.' . . . The two states carry the burden of extremism growing from a sense of mission—to rule again in the ancestors' land, or to preserve the white man's ideals" (Salpeter, 1980b, p. 12).

In December 1973, General Haim Herzog, former chief of military intelligence and most recently the president of Israel, suggested that Portugal and South Africa, the only two friends whose loyalty was demonstrated in the 1973 war, should be Israel's future allies as well (Herzog, 1973). The end of fascist dictatorship in Portugal, through the coup of April 25, 1974, was a major blow to the remnants of Western colonialism in Africa. It was also a blow to President Herzog's survival strategy and to the Republic of South Africa, a close ally of fascist Portugal.

From the South African side, this is how the alliance looks: "Israel and South Africa are both menaced from without; both have been reviled in the United Nations by what passes as progressive world opinion. Despite the many differences between them, the two countries have been imperceptibly drawn together, with consequences that cannot as yet be easily assessed" (Gann and Duignan, 1981, p.27). *Die Burger,* the Cape Province newspaper of the South African National Party, wrote in an editorial on May 29, 1968: "Israel and South Africa have much in common. Both are engaged in a struggle for existence, and both are in constant clash with the decisive majorities in the United Nations. Both are reliable foci of strength within the region, which would, without them, fall into anti-Western anarchy. It is in South Africa's interest that Israel is successful in containing her enemies, who are among our own most vicious enemies. . . . The anti-Western powers have driven Israel and South Africa into a community of interests which should be utilized rather than denied" (Cervenka and Rogers, 1978, p. 235).

The alliance with Israel breaks through the psychological and practical isolation in which South Africa has found itself trapped. In some areas of activity, such as nuclear development and military planning, Israel is the only real partner South Africa has gained, and in these areas Israeli cooperation is vital. Of course, Israel is not South Africa's only ally in the world, though it is the closest. South Africa has had ties with conservative Arab countries, with Iran under the shah, and with certain Latin American countries (Landau, 1976). The latter are the best known. Moorcraft lists as South Africa's closest allies "Israel and Taiwan, two other garrison states . . . similarly threatened by the capriciousness of the West" (1981, p. 18).

Israel is the only country offering practical aid on several levels —and sometimes ideological-political aid as well, as with the Bantustans and weapon development. No other country is prepared to be involved so intensively. In an interview with an Israeli journalist in August of 1973, General Hendrik van den Bergh, chief of BOSS, said, "I went to Israel recently, and enjoyed every moment there. I told the Prime Minister when I got back that as long as Israel exists we have a hope. If Israel should, God forbid, be destroyed, then South Africa would be in danger of extinction" (Cervenka and Rogers, 1978, p. 187). Karny (1981a) quotes a speech by South Africa's president, who said to an audience of military cadets: "Israel is a source of inspiration to us. We learn from it dedication and faith." Israel has shown South Africans how a small country, surrounded by Third World hostility, can successfully defend itself against a native liberation movement, with the help of sophisticated technology and sophisticated tactics.

The historical similarities between the Afrikaners and the Israelis are portrayed as follows by an American journalist: "To Afrikaners, the parallels are as obvious as they are embarrassing to the Israelis. They and the Israelis are essentially white, Europeanized peoples who have carved their own nations out of a land inhabited by hostile, non-European majorities that would destroy the two nations if the Afrikaners, and the Israelis, listened to the United Nations or world opinions. Their religions are similar, each being a 'chosen people.' Israel, to the Nationalist government, is the other Western outpost in the Third World. The 1967 victory of the outnumbered but technologically superior Israeli forces over the Arabs gave the South African whites a tremendous boost in morale" (Hoagland, 1972b, p. 71).

That victory was inspiring: "Israel's victory was that of quality over quantity, a victory of a developed minority over the developing world. The Six-Day War seemed a decisive proof of the notion that in the confrontation between a developed society and a developing society the technological gap is not narrowing but widening, and this conclusion gave the South Africans confidence as to their ability to counter African nationalism" (Tamarkin, 1980, p. 21).

Traditional Afrikaner anti-Semitism did not stand in the way of the Afrikaners' positive view of Israel as an ally and a model (Hoagland, 1972b.). One can detest Jews and love Israelis, because Israelis somehow are not Jews. Israelis are colonial fighters and settlers, just like the Afrikaners. They are tough and resilient. They know how to dominate. Jews are different. They are, among other qualities, gentle, nonphysical, often passive, intellectual. So one can go on disliking Jews while admiring the Israelis. Breyten Breytenbach, an Afrikaner himself, writes, "What a strange identification the Afrikaners have with Israel. There has always been a strong current of anti-Semitism in the land, after all—the present rulers are the result and the direct descendants of pro-Nazi ideologues. And yet they have the greatest admiration for Israel, which has become . . . White South Africa's political and military partner in 'the alliance of pariah states.' They identify themselves with Israel—as the Biblical chosen people of God, and as a modern embattled state surrounded by a sea of enemies. Which, they believe, justify aggressive foreign military adventures" (1984, p. 47).

Both Israel and South Africa are built on a hierarchy of ethnic groups, and in both cases the state is identified with one of these groups. The official ideology of both countries presents them as doubly victimized, first by European colonialism and oppression, and then by Third World hostility. Both countries share the position of being increasingly isolated in their worldview, which is opposed by more and more nations. Israel's foreign-policy goals, just like South Africa's, are two: legitimacy and survival. Both countries are facing an uphill battle in approaching these goals. The challenges to them have been growing with time. The increase in the power of the Third World is a threat to both.

An enthusiastic supporter of apartheid describes the common fate of Israel and South Africa: "It was with a firm belief in God's guidance that these two people—one in the Middle East and the other in the south of Africa—went forth in confident search of a home of their own. Millennia separated their experience . . . but it was in the same month of the same year that they arrived. In May 1948 the British Mandate in Palestine ended and the state of Israel was established. In May 1948 the long dominance of British influence in South Africa ended, and an all-Afrikaner government under Daniel Malan was formed. . . .

"Through the ages, and for a reason which defies just explanation, the Jews were scorned by the world. . . . In those same years, and again for a reason which defies just explanation . . . the Afrikaners . . . were scorned by the world: and as the Jews were seen as the victims of race oppression, so were the Afrikaners presented as the perpetrators of race oppression. But soon the experience of Israelis and Afrikaners was again to coincide. These were the only two peoples to have established Western nations in predominantly non-white parts of the globe. They were situated moreover at points of crucial strategic significance: and for a power bent upon global domination, such as the Soviet Union, they were marked targets. Accordingly the Kremlin backed the militant Arabs who wanted the elimination of the state of Israel, and they backed the militant Africans who wanted the elimination of white rule in Southern Africa. The United Nations was the main scene of the action, and the Afrikaners were its first scapegoats. But Israel's turn was to come. In 1974 Israel like South Africa was gagged in the General Assembly: in 1975 the resolution was passed equating Zionism with racism: in 1976 Israeli Prime Minister Rabin and South African Prime Minister Vorster met in Jerusalem to sign a pact and set perhaps a new pattern—an association of middle-power states—in international relations" (Steward, 1977, pp. 5–6).

Discussing torture in South African prisons, Breytenbach considered the possibility of using outside pressure to reduce it, and expressed his judgment that foreign powers such as the United States, Britain, West Germany, and possibly Canada and France could be expected to put such pressure on South Africa. Then he adds: "No pressure in that direction could reasonably be expected from South

Africa's allies—Taiwan, Israel, some Latin American countries" (1984, p. 352).

Both Israel and South Africa hold on to occupied territories (the West Bank, Gaza, and the Golan Heights in the case of Israel, Namibia in the case of South Africa) in defiance of U.N. General Assembly resolutions, which represent world opinion, and with the support of the United States. The defiance of the United Nations. in both countries extends to all areas of their international behavior, and especially the Israel–South Africa alliance itself, which has been condemned by the United Nations numerous times. The two countries share an identical pattern of relating to the United Nations. The international organization has regularly condemned them for similar policies, and the reaction has been the same: noncooperation with U.N. committees and a tradition of ignoring most relevant U.N. resolutions.

Israel has been performing an important service for South Africa in several black African nations, by supporting the conservative regimes that South Africa wants to keep in power. In such nations as Malawi, Ivory Coast, Zaire, Liberia, and Kenya, Israeli involvement, either covert or public, plays this role. Diplomatic victories for Israel in black Africa are also victories for South Africa, so it has been ready to fund Israeli efforts, sometimes with large sums of money transferred to the Swiss bank accounts of such leaders as Mobutu or Houphouët-Boigny.

The extent of South Africa's international isolation often tends to be overlooked. The psychological and ideological consequences of such isolation are bound to be quite serious. Israel has been relatively isolated in international organizations, but its situation cannot begin to compare with that of its "big sister." In 1964, South Africa left the International Labor Organization, and then the World Health Organization. It has been banned from all international athletic competitions and from the Olympic movement. It has no official place in UNESCO, the International Civil Aviation Organization, the International Telecommunications Union, and the Universal Postal Union. In 1974, the South African delegation was rejected by the U.N. General Assembly credentials committee; since then, while remaining a U.N. member, it has not taken part in General Assembly deliberations.

South Africa's diplomatic isolation is matched only by Taiwan's. Only twenty-six countries maintain diplomatic relations with South Africa, most of them Western, and only nineteen have embassies there. Only about two hundred foreign diplomats are accredited to Pretoria, and the Israeli contingent is the third largest, after the United States and Britain.

When Israelis contemplate the world's ostracism of South Africa, they do not see it as the result of a rightful indignation at apartheid. Rather they see themselves as another possible target of such treatment, so they oppose any boycotts or sanctions. They identify, naturally, with the South Africans.

South Africa's growing isolation in international politics after 1960 parallels, with a lag of about five years, Israel's situation. While South Africa was a leading member of the United Nations in 1945, and a normal member until the 1960s, the rise of new independent Third World nations made it into a pariah by 1975. It is important to recall that despite the similarities, Israel has enjoyed much more support at the United Nations. But the related declining fortunes of Israel and South Africa at the United Nations were symbolically tied in 1974: on November 12 the General Assembly excluded the South African delegation; on the next day it welcomed Yassir Arafat, the chairman of the Palestine Liberation Organization. Both Israel and South Africa have been losing confidence during the 1970s—Israel since 1973, and South Africa since 1976. There was a panic reaction, a "disaster syndrome," in both countries.

Both countries are struggling to survive in a world increasingly hostile, which will grow even more hostile in the future. The two countries feel deeply suspicious about the rest of the world, including even seemingly friendly countries. For both, the alliance is indispensable. Neither one has anybody else to turn to. Even though the United States has been supporting Israel seemingly without limit, Israeli leaders fear lest this support end in the future, or at least decrease. Many have mentioned the "siege mentality" shared by South Africa and Israel; such a mentality is obvious in both places, and fully justified. The concept of Fortress South Africa, the survival strategy of the apartheid regime, parallels Israel's view of its own situation. The two countries predicate their survival on the achievement of complete military self-sufficiency, and on putting the need for survival above any other consideration.

The two countries have obviously been acting, separately and jointly, out of a growing desperation. The realization that time is not on their side has pushed them toward strategies and acts of nihilistic despair. Both countries publicly deplore the changes in the world—the growing power of the Third World, the decline of the West. They both call for toughness in the face of Third World "terrorism." Following the 1973 Arab-Israeli war and the Angola invasion of 1975, both Israel and South Africa have become more convinced that they have to follow a tough survival strategy, using more desperate means to ensure their existence, avoiding the fate of the Crusaders by using technology and sophistication. The two countries share the same overall strategy, which includes the two elements of resisting decolonization and developing nuclear weapons. The same basic historical situation has, not too surprisingly, led to similar worldviews and strategies. From the South African vantage point, Israel has had two staggering achievements: First, frustrating and subduing a national liberation movement. Second, enjoying much support and legitimacy in Western public opinion and politics. These achievements make the South Africans envious and admiring. They also want to learn some lessons for themselves. How do the Israelis do it?

The example provided by Israel to South Africa and to similar regimes is one of cool defiance. A South African businessman says, "We can be like the Israelis. . . . We can be like the Israelis and tell the world to get stuffed. *Fuck the world!*" (Lelyveld, 1985, p. 358). We can easily imagine Pinochet and Stroessner uttering these words, too. South African leaders regard the United States, and "the West" in general, as soft and nervous in the face of the Third World onslaught. A South African political commentator wrote, "The Western world needs a courageous minority to inspire and to mobilise the convictions of the majority. South Africa and Israel have the potential to be the joint spearhead of a turning point" (*South African Digest,* 1976, p. 11).

The American Connection

While the United States may be described as a spectator in regard to the Israeli alliance with South Africa, it is not completely neutral. In one instance, in fact, the United States asked Israel to support South Africa—in 1975, U.S. secretary of state Henry Kissinger asked Israel to help with the failing South African invasion of Angola. Israel responded by sending military advisers and electronic equipment to the front (*Economist,* 1977). The Kissinger move was apparently part of general policy in which "The Americans may be waiting to use Israel as a clandestine conduit to South Africa" (p. 91). But in 1977, the Carter administration was said to be pressing Israel to limit its support for South Africa. The result was a reduced number of public visits, for a while, but a continuation of all normal contacts (*New York Times,* 1977). It is clear that some aspects of the Israeli–South African alliance remain unknown to the U.S. government, especially details of joint military and nuclear projects.

Israel has come to play the role of intermediary between South Africa and the United States. South Africa has often asked it to use its influence in the United States. Because of their close ties with South Africa, Israeli leaders have been regarded as experts on events and processes there by their American counterparts, and their advice is often sought. Recent events have made the State Department and the CIA ready to listen to Israeli assessments of the future of apartheid.

Israel and the Crisis of Apartheid

Recent events in South Africa, starting in September 1984, are qualitatively different from earlier expressions of revolt and unrest—"a mighty upswelling of black rage, that, over years rather than months, will sap and haemorrhage the white power structure until it falls in on itself" (Uys, 1986, p. 15). Israel and South Africa now defy the censure and pressure of the international community and its U.N. resolutions. They do that because of their military superiority. Their message is clear and simple: You can defy world opinion—as long as you have the military might.

But military might cannot guarantee long-term survival, and the implications of recent events strike terror in the hearts of Israelis and others. The coming of black majority rule in South Africa has implications for Africa, for the Middle East, and for the world almost too momentous to contemplate. The day majority rule is proclaimed in Pretoria will be the start of a new age, in which the Third World will be a giant step closer to true liberation, and in which the United States and its allies will be much weaker. For Israel, the consequences are horrifying. It will remain the last colonizer, the last domino, the last thorn in the flesh of the whole Third World.

Israel's attitude about the end of the apartheid regime was succinctly articulated in a November 1986 lecture by Yitzhak Unna, who was Israel's first ambassador in Pretoria. "We don't want another Mozambique or another Angola. We don't even want another Liberia." Israel's preferences in Africa are clear. Even Liberians are too independent. For Israel, the fall of apartheid will be not only a psychological blow, but also a strategic setback of incalculable dimensions. Meanwhile, Israel's reaction to the apartheid crisis is an offensive on two fronts. On the public one, Israel will try to put more distance between itself and South Africa. On the secret front, Israel will mount a campaign to help apartheid survive by every available means, from helping South Africa with everything from public relations to military and counterinsurgency measures.

When the serious deterioration in the whites' control of South Africa became clear, a series of emergency meetings was held in Jerusalem. Prime Minister Shimon Peres demanded two things from his aides: first, an assessment of the future chances of the apartheid regime, including a timetable; second, a plan for action.

The assessment concluded that the apartheid regime would probably survive at least another ten years.

Countless cables from Israeli diplomats around the globe underlined the government's dilemma. The whole world was denouncing apartheid and closely watching the crisis mount. The professional diplomats at the Foreign Ministry yet again informed the backers of Israel's alliance with South Africa that it was an acute embarrassment to any Israeli official in any international forum. More and more governments were distancing themselves from the South Africans. At the height of the 1985 summer crisis, only seven ambassadors stayed on in Pretoria—those of Switzerland, Austria, Taiwan, Paraguay,

Chile, Malawi, and Israel. Students were demonstrating in cities around the world; only in Israel were no voices raised against apartheid.

The government's problem was how to improve its public image, while still maintaining the alliance and continuing the numerous collaborations with South Africa, including the projects devoted to nuclear arms. The solution was to adopt two policies—a public one, and a covert one that would leave the basics of the alliance unchanged. In public, the Israeli government issued statements critical of apartheid and announced that the new Israeli Ambassador to Pretoria, David Ariel, would not start his duties there until December 1985, instead of September. Ambassador Ariel arrived in Pretoria on November 15, 1985, and a few weeks later presented his credentials to the government.

As we have seen, Israel has been involved for at least fifteen years in attempts to improve South Africa's reputation in the West. Israeli journalists frequently comment that South Africa shares Israel's problem of hostile propaganda, and that Israel could offer advice on countering it. Since the early 1970s, Israeli leaders have persuaded South Africa to invest more money and effort on image-building, since it, like Israel, could not afford to do otherwise. They also offered to help South Africa through Israel's influence in the United States.

For most Israelis, recent events in South Africa have not altered the atmosphere of "business as usual." Israeli corporations continue with projects in Soweto and in the Bantustans. Israeli tourists continue to go there on vacation. And while governments all over the world were debating economic sanctions against South Africa, an Israeli economic delegation headed by Dr. Emanuel Sharon, director-general of the Finance Ministry, went to South Africa in August 1986, to renew economic-cooperation treaties—on more favorable terms. This particular economic delegation had an additional mission—to offer help in getting around economic boycotts and embargoes. The proposal of an official agreement was turned down by the South African side. The Israeli side has not given up, though, and the offer still stands.

When CBS-TV showed a handful of Israelis demonstrating against apartheid, in October 1985, the correspondent said, "You are watching a distinctly rare political phenomenon, an Israeli demonstration against apartheid. Despite the worldwide clamor for action against South Africa, neither the Israeli people nor their government seem anxious to break ties with Pretoria" (October 20, 1985). The largest anti-apartheid demonstration in Israel took place on November 13, 1985—about six hundred people. (All such demonstrations in Israel have drawn very small numbers, often less than ten.) The slogans condemned apartheid—the placards read ISRAELIS AGAINST APARTHEID, BLACK IS BEAUTIFUL, FREE NELSON MANDELA, and APARTHEID = FASCISM—and demanded that the government not send a new ambassador to South Africa, but not did mention the Israeli–South African alliance (Handwerker, 1985).

Israel's Foreign Minister, Yitzhak Shamir, declared at a meeting with American Jewish leaders in September 1985 that Israel would not join other countries in putting pressure on South Africa (Bird, 1985).

In a *Haaretz* article titled "Why South Africa?" political columnist Schweitzer expresses the views of the Israeli elite on the alliance: "From the Israeli side these relations lack any ideological motives. Their connection is a common and weighty interest" (1985a). His prognosis for the future of apartheid is positive, and presumably is based on government evaluations: "It seems that Israel's government, which continues its contacts with South Africa, does have a good idea of the outcome of a contest between white existence in South Africa, and the doom predicted by its domestic critics." And he gives another reason why Israel should support apartheid in its crisis: "The Third World, with Soviet guidance and Arab financing, has been carrying on for years an offensive against two states tied to the West: Israel and South Africa. . . . It should be clear that the fall of one of the two will lead to storming the other one. We will not do ourselves a favor if we hasten to ring the knell for South Africa, or accelerate its decline through our deeds, diplomatic or other. On the contrary, we have to hope that it will overcome the current crisis" (p. 5). A new domino theory is making the rounds in Israel. It states, quite bluntly, that the fall of the Portuguese colonies led to the fall of Rhodesia, which is leading to the fall of South Africa—and the fall of South Africa will lead to the greatest crisis Israel has ever faced. The essential correctness of this domino theory cannot be denied.

Another commentator states that "Israel must follow the South

African struggle" because "success or failure of the blacks in using a warfare technique against South Africa may influence the readiness and energy of the Arabs to use similar methods against Israel. . . . It is easy to imagine that the current situation will spur the Arabs to copy the strategies used against South Africa. . . . Israel must, no less than the Arabs, regard South Africa as a test case and closely follow the successes and failures of strategies used there" (Salpeter, 1986, p. 7).

Israel's readiness to help was demonstrated in August 1985, with the visit to Israel of Chief Gatsha Buthelezi. Milton Friedman has called him "one of the most respected, knowledgeable and able black leaders" (1986, p. 27). He earned Ronald Reagan's stamp of approval when he visited the White House in February 1985 and expressed his support for "constructive engagement" (Weil, 1985). Chief Buthelezi has become the favorite black leader for the U.S. establishment, and "is often compared to Rhodesia's Bishop Abel Muzorewa, the black conservative who was trounced in independent Zimbabwe's first national elections. He is also described as the likely candidate for 'contra'-style support from Washington in the event of a radical change in South Africa" (Connell, 1986, p. 14). Those who don't compare Buthelezi to Muzorewa compare him to Kerensky, the Russian leader deposed by the Bolshevik Revolution.

Mangosuthu Gatsha Buthelezi carries with pride the titles of chief minister of KwaZulu, president of Inkatha, and chairman of the South African Black Alliance. KwaZulu is a black homeland, according to South Africa, on its way to independence. Inkatha is the tribal Zulu movement, fighting against the African National Congress and maintained by the South African government for that purpose. The South African Black Alliance is the black organization opposed to the United Democratic Front, the main political organization fighting apartheid. Chief Buthelezi is a nationalist who believes in a separate Zulu identity and a separate Zulu nation, which is precisely what endears him to the South African government. He is a perfect instrument in its hands: He represents the forces of tribalism and the vision of the homelands, being a hereditary Zulu chief and the chief minister of the homeland of KwaZulu. He proclaims himself opposed to apartheid—but at the same time he is also opposed to the African National Congress (the main threat to apartheid), and to economic sanctions against South Africa. He is exactly the kind of black leader that South Africa will promote, and Israel offers its help in this propaganda campaign.

The Israeli government scored a propaganda coup in August 1985 when Chief Buthelezi visited Israel. The main goal of the visit was to sell Buthelezi to Western public opinion as an acceptable and desirable black leader, since he is accepted and desired by South Africa. But Israel stood to profit, too: "Israel may gain much in terms of public relations when Western television networks bring comments on current events in South Africa from the Zulu leader—live from Jerusalem" (Mann, 1985, p. 13). The chief reiterated his well-known opposition to the ANC and to the UDF, as well as his opposition to economic sanctions against apartheid. Sure enough, only two days after the resulting article appeared in Tel-Aviv, the *New York Times* was quoting Buthelezi's comments on apartheid, datelined Jerusalem (Friedman, 1985b); the major U.S. television networks followed suit.

Israel had been supporting the Inkatha forces and the KwaZulu homeland even before the Buthelezi visit. In 1983, Dr. Oscar Dhlomo, secretary-general of Inkatha and KwaZulu minister of education and culture, visited Israel, together with Mrs. Abbie Mchunu, the chair of Inkatha's Women's Brigade. Buthelezi himself was invited to come to Israel as early as 1978 (Buthelezi, 1985). Israel took upon itself the task of developing KwaZulu and helping other aspects of Buthelezi's political plan, including the Inkatha organization and the trade unions it runs (Isacowitz and Richardson, 1985). The Buthelezi 1985 visit was part of Israel's continued cooperation with South Africa on the propaganda front.

Even Israel's public condemnations of apartheid are milder and more ambiguous than in other places, as was seen in the events following the execution of the poet and African National Congress fighter Benjamin Moloise on October 18, 1985. Most world governments appealed to South Africa not to carry out the death sentence—even the Reagan White House. In Paris, French prime minister Laurent Fabius took the unprecedented step of standing alone in a one-person demonstration in front of the South African embassy. The Thatcher government of Britain protested the intended execution. One government took no such steps—Israel's.

On October 18, Benjamin Moloise went to his death, not just a victim, but a fighter. On October 20, MK Yair Tzaban, of Mapam, the Zionist-Socialist party, presented an urgent motion to the Knesset presidium for debate on the Moloise execution and the lack of reaction to it in Israel. Tzaban's motion never had a chance, since the government and the Knesset presidium were opposed to a debate. Then more opposition MKs and journalists underscored the fact that the event had elicited no voice of protest in Israel. The government felt that something had to be done; finally it showed exactly how events in South Africa are perceived in Israel.

The government reaction came in a form of a letter from Moshe Shahal, the energy minister in the Peres cabinet (and a leading member of the Labor Party), to the Knesset presidium. Why the energy minister was chosen to deliver a protest to a foreign government seems a mystery, but, like other mysteries, it has a solution. The prime minister, Shimon Peres, did not want to touch the matter. The foreign minister, Yitzhak Shamir, saw no reason to protest something he saw as fully justified. The problem before the Israeli government was how to issue a protest—without issuing a protest.

The Solomonic solution was to use Shahal, who happens to be a leading attorney. Among cabinet ministers, Shahal is charged with "liaison with the Knesset," which normally means being the floor manager for government bills. On this occasion, as the liaison, he sent a letter to the Knesset presidium—the Israeli government reaction to the Moloise execution was not delivered to the South African Embassy in Tel-Aviv, or directly to the government in Pretoria. It was delivered, instead, to the Knesset in Jerusalem. Actually, the letter went from Shahal's office on the third floor of the Knesset building to the Speaker's office on the fifth floor. It expressed sympathy with Moloise's family but refused to enter into "the legal questions involved in the execution." Morover, it decried the violence "besetting the South African population"—without mentioning its possible sources. That was not the end of the affair. At least one member of the Knesset publicly expressed dissatisfaction with the letter. Letters to the editors of *Haaretz* also objected to protesting against the execution of a "murderer."

The story of the official Israeli reaction to the Moloise execution is typical of all Israeli statements about the apartheid regime since

1984. The government, while it does respond to outside pressures, will not express direct criticism of South African policies.

Friends are tested and proven in an hour of need; in white South Africa's hour of need, Israel has been proving itself a true friend. Israeli government officials, including cabinet ministers, continued to visit South Africa. Especially close to the South African leadership during this crisis have been the following Israeli leaders: Yitzhak Rabin (IDF chief-of-staff in 1967, prime minister 1974–1977, defense minister since 1984), Shimon Peres (director-general of the Defense Ministry 1953–1958, deputy defense minister 1958–1963, defense minister 1974–1977, prime minister 1984–1986), Moshe Arens (ambassador to Washington 1977–1982, defense minister 1982–1984), and Ariel Sharon (defense minister 1979–1982). The true friends of South Africa encourage the leaders of the South African regime to hang tough; they have been offering such direct encouragement since 1984. As the leaders of white South Africa are getting ready for their final battle, they have the blessings, the practical support, and the moral support of Israel's leaders.

Israel's pivotal role in supporting the apartheid regime was recognized by the *Nation,* when it stated editorially, "Functionally and visibly, Israel is South Africa's only important ally in the world, providing Pretoria with the material, training, technical advice and logistical support that other Western nations have felt obliged to withhold" (1986, p. 748). The state of emergency declared by the South African government on June 12, 1986, resulted from Israeli advice and instigation. Israeli counterinsurgency advisers in Pretoria had been encouraging the government to "get tough" and not pay attention to outside pressures. Some details of the state-of-emergency regulations bear clear Israeli marks, such as the rules about funerals of the victims of apartheid violence. Attendance at such funerals has been limited to two hundred. This is in the spirit of Israeli regulations for funerals of Palestinians killed by Israeli authorities in the occupied territories. The actual number allowed by the IDF is more like thirty.

Another cloud in the darkening skies of the Israel–South Africa alliance was added by the U.S. Congress. The Comprehensive Anti-Apartheid Act, passed in 1986, had an amendment attached to it that required the administration to report to Congress by April 1987 on any countries supplying South Africa with weapons. U.S. military aid to these countries would then be cut off by October 1, 1987. The Israeli embassy in Washington lobbied hard and long against the amendment, but lost. In early 1987, this matter has caused considerable panic in Jerusalem. An official report to Congress naming Israel as South Africa's main military ally would be an acute embarrassment. Of course, it is inconceivable that a U.S. Congress will cut off aid to Israel, but this is a public-relations hot potato for everybody involved.

The solution is to follow the precedent established in the 1977 arms embargo: when pressed to do so, Israel's representatives will deny any dealings with South Africa. On March 19, 1987, the Israeli government announced "limited sanctions" against South Africa, consisting mainly of an official decision not to renew contracts for military cooperation. This was an obvious public-relations move designed to counter the effect of the report scheduled to be submitted to Congress on April 1. But in practice, nothing will change. As one Israeli official said, the message to Washington announcing an end to arms sales is meaningless (Melman, 1987). The one change will be a renewed effort to keep things under wraps, and to get away from those sniffing journalists, who still insist on reporting the continued story of the alliance.

It is important to realize how deeply concerned Israel's leaders are about the survival of apartheid. It is much more than most foreigners feel about apartheid, much more than the concern of foreign corporations worried about their investment. It is a true commitment to something that is vital to the survival of their own country. Israel is fully committed to the survival of apartheid. We can expect this commitment to continue in various forms, most of which will be unpublicized. Israel will also continue to play the role of a middleman between South Africa and the United States. We can predict that at some point Israeli military advisers will leave South Africa and the cooperative projects will be discontinued. That has happened before —in Iran, Algeria, Rhodesia, and other places. And just as in all those other cases, the Israelis will leave South Africa and end their collaborations not because they want to, but because they are forced to.

6

At War
with the
Third World

T he aim of Israel's foreign policy since its founding has been
to achieve legitimacy as a "normal" state, despite its abnor-
mal history, through diplomatic contacts and recognition,
and to deprive the Palestinians of similar legitimacy
(Eytan, 1958). For the first few years, this policy was a
success. On the day of Israel's founding in 1948, the two superpowers
vied for the privilege of being the first to accord it diplomatic recognition, and in its first year it won recognition from fifty-three states. In
1959, Israel was represented in fifty-five countries, and in early 1967,
seventy-eight. But this base of legitimacy has been eroding with the
progress of decolonization and the rise of the Third World, largely in
reaction to the 1967 and 1973 wars.

THE THIRD WORLD

The Third World is a world of struggle, misery, and suffering, the part not included in the First World (the industrialized West and Japan) or the Second World (the Soviet bloc). "It is roughly equivalent to what used to be called the underdeveloped world, or in official U.S. parlance 'LDC' (Less Developed Countries)" (Barnet, 1968, p. 4). "The 'third world' is one result of the process by which, since the late fifteenth century, the previously scattered peoples of the globe have been brought together into what is in many respects a single society, economy and political system. By far the major part of this process has taken place over the last century, while its political aspects . . . are the product of the emergence of third world states which, except in Latin America, have mostly become independent since the Second World War." The Third World is separate from, and subordinate to, "the dominant industrial economies which have developed especially in Europe and North America. . . . They have entered the world economy especially through the supply of primary products such as minerals and cash crops to the industrial economies, and for the most part continue to be primary export producers" (Clapham, 1985, p. 3).

The Third World today consists of about 120 countries. Most of its nations export raw materials at low prices, and pay for processed and manufactured goods, made of the same raw materials. Attempts to change this economic reality are the source of conflicts with the First World (Jouve, 1983).

When we refer to the Third World in this book, we are using some very simple and very basic statistics. Such things as life expectancy, infant mortality (directly tied to life expectancy), per-capita GNP, and literacy are what we call "quality-of-life indicators." The Third World includes those countries of the world where quality-of-life indicators are at their lowest, where life, in Hobbes's phrase, is poor, nasty, brutish, and short.

Life expectancy is still about 55 years, and the annual per-capital income averages $270. According to U.N. data, in 1980 life expectancy for males in the "more developed countries" was 68.1 years (for females, 75.4). In the Third World as a whole, life expectancy for males was 55.2 years (for females 57.7)—but in 1983 there were still eighteen countries where life expectancy was under 50, and four where life expectancy did not even reach 40 years (Brisset, 1983). Most of these countries are ruled by oligarchies whose quality-of-life indicators are vastly different; they enjoy the highest standards of living available to mankind at the end of the twentieth century.

Israel and the Rise of the Third World

The Asian-African Conference at Bandung, Indonesia, in April 1955 was the first step in the emergence of the Third World coalition. The participants represented twenty-nine countries, divided into four regions: the Arab world, Southeast Asia, South Asia, and black Africa. The nine Arab countries were the largest group. There were only three African countries: Liberia, Ethiopia, and not-yet-independent Ghana. The participants were deeply divided in their ideologies and alliances, from Japan to North Vietnam and China, from Ethiopia and the Philippines to Egypt. Israel, South Africa, South Korea, and Taiwan were not invited (Mortimer, 1984). Israeli leaders expressed disappointment and surprise at their exclusion. These professions of surprise might have reflected ignorance or naiveté, but the Bandung Conference made it clear that the emerging coalition was likely to be less than friendly toward Israel.

For many of the Third World nations gaining their independence in the 1950s and the 1960s, the history of the Arab-Israeli conflict was almost unknown, and the setting quite distant. When the details of the conflict did become known, not too surprisingly, attitudes tended to favor the Arab bloc, as a Third World partner in the same struggle against the West. In the various meetings of the Third World coalition after 1955, the Arab-Israeli conflict was often mentioned, but it was only after 1967 that the rights of the Palestinians became a permanent part of the agenda.

Palestine has become a symbolic issue for the whole Third World, matched only by the issue of apartheid in the intensity and frequency with which it has been raised. "The anticolonialist/antiimperialist ideological lens directed the Third World toward a pro-Palestinian Arab and anti-Israel position. This was reinforced by the largely Western bourgeois style of life that developed in Israel, by the treatment of the Arab minority, and by the collusion with Great Britain and France, the arch-imperialists, in the 1956 Suez operation. Since 1967, Israel's heavy reliance upon the United States for military and economic aid eventually sharpened the negative image of Israel among Third World states" (Rivlin and Fomerand, 1976).

Indeed, the Third World's view of Palestine is diametrically opposed to Zionism. It sees the Palestinians as the victims of colonialism, and the Israelis as guilty of colonialist dispossession. Palestine has become a symbol of one more colonialist account to be settled with the West. The Third World coalition is divided on many political issues, and it is far from the automatic, anti-Western voting bloc mentioned so often in the U.S. media. Thus, for example, the Third World is evenly divided on Kampuchea and East Timor, and it overwhelmingly opposes the Soviet Union on the Afghanistan issue. Nevertheless, there is a complete unity on the two remaining colonial issues, namely South Africa and Israel-Palestine. South Africa and Israel have come to play a special symbolic role for the whole Third World. They are regarded as the two last bastions of colonialism. Even right-wing countries that have close relations with Israel, such as Zaire and Honduras, are pro-Palestinian; their leaders do not hesitate to voice support for the Palestinian cause and for the idea of a Palestinian state during official visits to Israel. When Edgardo Paz Bárnica, the Honduran Minister of Foreign Affairs, visited Israel in August 1985, he openly expressed his support for an independent Palestinian state (*Jerusalem Post,* 1985).

A worldwide consensus against Zionism has been developing since the late 1960s, reaching its clearest expressions in repeated condemnations of Zionism by the United Nations in the next decade. Israel's growing isolation has reflected the Arab countries' growing diplomatic power. In the 1950s, the Arabs were militarily weak, but gathered both Soviet and Third World support. After 1967, the diplomatic front changed quickly, with the Arab camp winning more sympathy in the Organization of African Unity (OAU), at the United Nations, and in the nonaligned movement. In the late 1960s, the Palestinians penetrated Third World consciousness, and started forming relations with Third World radical movements.

The military shock of the 1973 war was accompanied by political setbacks. It was during the war and immediately afterwards that many African countries broke off diplomatic relations. In November 1973, the OAU Ministerial Council denounced Israel for its "expansionist designs." During the war, all European countries except Portugal refused to allow the use of their airports and airspace for the U.S. resupply shipments to Israel. On November 6, 1973, the European Economic Community issued a communiqué that called on Israel to end the occupation of 1967, and to recognize the legitimate rights of the Palestinians (Reich, 1985). The years 1973–1975 saw growing isolation and repeated failures, and the experience of those years has become a nightmare that Israeli leaders vowed not to relive.

The process of decolonization also created a Third World majority at the United Nations, which until the 1960s was very much a European club. The U.N. General Assembly voted in the fall of 1974 to suspend South Africa's participation in the General Assembly (the vote was 98–23–14) and to allow the PLO to present its views before the same body (the vote was 105–4–20). Before 1967 the Palestinians were largely absent from world consciousness, and just after 1967 references to them were mostly negative (terrorists, spoilers of Western designs), but after 1973 positive references started to appear even in the West. By the mid-1980s, the Palestinian people and the PLO have gained such wide recognition that Israeli leaders have increasingly felt the panic of growing desertion and isolation.

The historical change in United Nations membership, from 51 states, mostly European, at the first General Assembly, to 159 nations forty years later, was accompanied by a decline in Israel's fortunes. The voting tallies over the past thirty years clearly demonstrate that decolonization is a threat to Israel—it means more and more opponents and less and less diplomatic support. The Partition Resolution of November 29, 1947, which called for dividing Palestine between an Arab state and a Jewish state, could not have passed in the General Assembly in 1985—or any time after the late 1960s, for that matter. The Third World victory at the United Nations was symbolized by the recognition of the Palestine Liberation Organization in 1974, and in the condemnation of Zionism in 1975.

The General Assembly resolution of 1975 equating Zionism with racism was the result of the emerging Third World consensus. While the First World steadfastly considers Zionism a legitimate political ideology, the Third World regards it as a form of colonialism to be relegated to the same class as apartheid. Since 1967, several U.N.

bodies have been set up to deal with the Palestine question and with Israeli-occupied territories. Israel has refused to cooperate with these U.N. bodies, which have initiated many conferences and prompted many U.N. resolutions, again emphasizing Israel's growing isolation. The Special Political Committee votes every year to condemn various Israeli policies toward the Palestinians. On these resolutions, Israel usually casts the only No vote (sometimes joined by the United States) while a Third World coalition of more than a hundred votes Yes. In 1984 the committee passed a resolution confirming the applicability of the Geneva Convention to the occupied territories; the vote was 119 for, Israel against, and even the United States abstained.

The U.N. Security Council has voted on about two hundred anti-Israel resolutions since 1967, which either were adopted or were defeated only by American veto (about 30 times). Most U.N. resolutions condemning Israeli policies are not binding, since they are passed in the General Assembly, and even Security Council resolutions do not lead to action. But for Israel they are writings on the wall, symptoms of a progressive isolation and a growing hostility within the world.

Currently, only 75 countries have diplomatic relations with Israel, as compared to 115 that recognize the PLO. In 1966, the number of countries recognizing Israel was about 110. In an attempt to overcome this isolation, which is clearly in evidence at the United Nations and other international organizations, Israel is always on the lookout for allies, and cannot afford to be choosy. Every nation tries to broaden its base of political support and is ready to enter alliances without regard to seeming ideological and historical constraints. This is true of the Soviet Union, which had close relations with the right-wing generals of Argentina between 1976 and 1983, and of the United States, which has supported Pol Pot of Kampuchea after denouncing him as a mass murderer. Israel's effort to overcome growing isolation by forming as many contacts as possible is not unique.

Israel, by several measures, is the most militarized nation in the world. It spends about 30 percent of its gross national product on defense; the United States spends about 7 percent. No other industrial country has been involved in so much fighting since World War II, except the United States. Israel is not a superpower, so leaders of small countries judge it able to teach them useful lessons in the art of war.

France and Britain cannot offer the kind of military expertise that seems relevant to small countries, and they actually have less experience in modern warfare. Israel offers the world a new kind of warrior: contemptuous of parades and marching drills, but resourceful and efficient; though he may not look impressive, he gets the job done against considerable odds. Israel has achieved a unique reputation for having developed an effective military machine despite limited resources; many small countries and small-time dictators have wanted to learn from Israel's experience and emulate its performance.

Israel is always ready as a military supplier of last resort to desperate regimes, and its competitive advantage, so to speak, in the field of military exports extends to battle-tested and proven military software and counterinsurgency techniques, which enjoy a worldwide reputation among those interested in importing them. Beyond this, Israelis have earned a reputation for excellence in covert operations, and they have been exporting their secret-police experience, which is much in demand all over the world.

And since Israel has been unable "to reverse [its] decline internationally through statecraft" (Klieman, 1984, p. 7), its leaders have become ready to ask for very little overt recognition in return for their aid to foreign governments, especially military aid. Beggars can't be choosers, and in the arena of international relations, Israel—together with Taiwan, South Africa, and Paraguay—is indeed a beggar.

To understand the Israeli leadership and its perplexing decisions, we have to enter its world, share its perceptions and fears. We need not only sympathy, but empathy. The basic Israeli stance toward the world is a conservative one. After 1948, Israel was interested in conserving its achievements, as it was after 1967. After 1973, Israel was interested in conserving the world order, to prevent her precarious position from becoming untenable. A red thread leads from the 1954 Cairo affair, an attempt to stop decolonization in Egypt, to current events in Central America. Stopping decolonization is the only way Israel sees to ensure survival, and in the 1980s it has to be stopped on a global scale: every national liberation movement is a danger and an enemy.

Israel's survival strategy has achieved survival, but not acceptance by either the Arab world or the rest of the Third World. The Israeli involvement in the war with the Third World can only lead to more antagonism. The more Israel acts to stop radicalization in the Third World, the more hostility will result, justifying the Israeli claim that "the whole world is against us."

Such an ardent supporter of Zionism and Israel as Brecher (1972, p. 561) notes that Israel's leaders never used the term "liberation movement" to refer to Zionism. His interpretation is that "it symbolizes the unwillingness of Israel's decision makers to identify their struggle with the anti-colonialist revolt." And indeed, the term "national liberation movement" has taken on positively frightening attributes for most Israelis, and with good reason. "Self-determination," "liberation," "revolution"—these words sound ominous to Israeli leaders, and they should. The expression "self-determination" has been banished from Israeli political discourse because it obviously brings to mind the Palestinians. The connection between Palestinian rights and the rights of other oppressed groups in the Third World is never far from anybody's mind. And so the feeling is that Israel has to commit itself to stemming the tide of radicalism, to trying to reverse the current of decolonization.

A specter is haunting the leadership and the people of Israel— the specter of the Crusaders, who established a kingdom in Jerusalem in the eleventh century, only to be driven away two centuries later. A more recent specter is that of settlers in Algeria, Rhodesia, and South Africa. The parallels with the Crusaders, the Rhodesians, and the South Africans haunt every thinking Israeli, and even those who try not to think. To be or not to be like the lost colonies of Europe, that is the question for Israel. Indeed, Israel's problem, and the problem of the whole Zionist project, is how to avoid the fate of the Crusaders.

Israel's leaders saw only two solutions: either an alliance with a major world power, or the development of nuclear weapons (Perlmutter et al., 1982). Apparently, Israel has chosen both—because even a foreign power cannot ever be fully trusted, while an independent nuclear capacity seems like long-term insurance. But though it is true that nuclear weapons can serve as a deterrent against conventional attacks by Israel's neighbors, they do not address Israel's most serious problem: the Palestinians. For both Israel and South Africa, nuclear weapons are an illusory solution.

When Israel's master plan for survival was conceived and developed in the 1950s, what the planners had in mind was a conventional (or unconventional) war with the Arab countries surrounding Israel. The aim then was to keep these countries from becoming independent and radical, and then to develop the ultimate weapon to subdue them if they did turn that way. In the 1950s, no thought was given to a truly radical challenge in the form of a Palestinian national movement rising from the ashes of war. No one would have advocated nuclear weapons to answer that challenge, since they are obviously irrelevant when you are trying to fight against guerrillas (or against Soweto). Even tactical nuclear weapons could not help Israel in Southern Lebanon and cannot help Israel on the West Bank.

The 1956 Suez War demonstrated Israel's short-term military effectiveness and long-term historical weaknesses. Israel easily conquered the Sinai peninsula, but was defeated just as easily on the political front. It allied itself with the declining colonial powers, which were decisively humiliated and forced to leave the Middle East. While the French and the British packed up and went home, Israel was left behind in the Middle East, right in the midst of resurgent Arab radicalism, which did not go away. Already in 1956, Israel's historical problem was clear.

In the 1950s, an independent Third World was a distant dream —or a distant worry, depending on one's point of view. For Israel, the threat was a unified Arab world. Israel's strategy was to check the development of Arab unity and power. The Israeli victory in the 1967 war was a victory over the Pan-Arabist dreams of Nasserism, and the beginning of a new stability, from Israel's point of view. Israel's basic insecurity about its future survival was somewhat relieved by the 1967 victory, but the 1973 war heightened it to an unprecedented level.

What seems unique about the Israeli enterprise in the Third World is the readiness of the Israelis—government and individuals—to get involved "on the ground" in the armed struggle, on the side of a government as military or counterinsurgency advisers. Israel makes its mark in the Third World "trouble spots" through direct involvement, by getting Israeli hands dirty, and sometimes bloody. This is what we have observed in South Africa, Sri Lanka, Zaire, and Nicaragua. This readiness is unique because, unlike other cases, it is not officially acknowledged. When the United States, the Soviet Union, or Cuba have military advisers in the Third World, it is usually officially admitted. With Israel it is always denied. The nature of some of the governments Israelis work with so directly makes them singular. Several are regimes that no one would want to have anything to do with, regimes abhorrent to most of the world.

The result of all these activities is that the popular perception of Israel in many Third World countries is negative. While right-wingers all over the world have become Israel's ardent admirers, those who fight them and suffer under them have begun to see Israel and Israelis as diabolical, omnipotent forces. Some of the fantastic stories one hears and reads about Israeli activities in the Third World grow out of this perception, born of frustration and weakness. One consequence of Israel's policies is that the hated local regime is associated with the hated foreign powers in the minds of millions, of hundreds of millions in the Third World. Israel has been associated with the late shah of Iran, with the Portuguese colonial regime in Africa, with Somoza in Nicaragua, and with the apartheid regime in South Africa.

We may speak of a new anti-Semitism, something that was not very common before: "Slowly but surely, the Israeli—and his permanent ally, the local Jew—becomes as diabolical a symbol as the Yankee in the eyes of the oppressed and tortured populaces of the teeming Third World" (Ghilan, 1984, p. 1). It is hard to tell whether Israeli leaders have given any thought to this, but judging from their behavior, it does not seem to affect them.

THE U.S. CONNECTION

Since World War II, the United States has been at war, at some place or another, with much of the rest of humanity. As World War II unfolded, it became clear that the old colonial empires were doomed, and that the United States would emerge as the dominant world power. Henry Luce wrote in 1941 about the coming "American Century," and the vision of an orderly world under U.S. control is what U.S. foreign policy has sought to maintain since 1945, with diminishing success. In 1945, when the United States was at the height of its power and on top of the world, it wanted the world to freeze in place. But the world didn't.

The result has been a war against the Third World, what Johan Galtung calls the Third World War. He refers not to the one that will end the world as we know it, the suicide of a civilized humanity, but to a war that has been going on since 1945. This is the war of decolonization, and it is being fought between the First World, led by the United States, which seeks to maintain its domination, and the Third World, which seeks independence from that domination. This may sound a bit simplistic, but it covers most "conventional" wars since 1945 quite well. All of Israel's involvements in the Third World can readily be seen as part of this Third World War.

While the United States' opposition to the Second World, the Soviet Union and its satellites, is being expressed through a "cold war," American efforts to maintain control over the Third World take the form of real fighting, in which more and more violent means are used. Since World War II, there have been no fights between superpowers, and most wars have been in the Third World. The Vietnam War is a good example, as are many conflicts in Asia and Latin America. Angola is another.

"America's 'problem' in the Third World has revolved around the issue of order. Democratic rule and capitalist economic development have always been the stated U.S. goals; but these have been qualified with the stipulation that 'stability' and 'orderly transition' must first be established. Hence, the cozy U.S. relationships with Third World juntas and military establishments—the most reliable instruments for attaining stability and order—and with strong-armed dictators who support or at least tolerate such relationships. One thinks . . . of Mobutu in Zaire, Chiang Kai-shek and his son Chiang Ching-kuo in Taiwan, Marcos in the Philippines, and a long list of right-wing regimes in Central America. Nationalist leaders who have rejected dependent ties with the capitalist world, such as Arbenz in Guatemala (1954), Goulart in Brazil (1964), Allende in Chile (1971), Neto in Angola (1975), and the Sandinistas in Nicaragua today often have had to face U.S.-backed military forces in counterrevolutions and coups" (Gurtov and Maghroori, 1984, pp. 44–45).

Since 1945, the United States has suffered some major failures in the Third World, as revolutionary, independent regimes have taken power. China, Cuba, and Vietnam have become the symbols of American losses and retreats. Since World War II, "American power in the world has clearly declined as measured by reduced ability to influence events far from our own borders, but this was largely an inevitable development. The United States was the only true world power immediately after the Second World War, a situation that could not last" (Wrong, 1980, p. 135). The position of the U.S. in the Third World War was eloquently described by George Kennan, in February 1948: "We have about 50 percent of the world's wealth, but only 6.3 percent of its population. . . . In this situation, we cannot fail to be the object of envy and resentment. Our real task in the coming period is to devise a pattern of relationships which will permit us to maintain this position of disparity" (Chomsky, 1986, p. 48). And this is indeed what the United States has been doing: trying to maintain this position of disparity.

The American Century of sunshine, prosperity, and peace under friendly U.S. guidance did not last long. Soon after 1945, American political discourse became riddled with references to "the loss of China"—or of Cuba, Vietnam, Iran, Angola, or Nicaragua.

The age of colonialism is ending, but the First World refuses to accept the full consequences. The struggle is continuing, and the issue is the division of the world's natural resources and unnatural wealth. The balance of power is changing, and if it is not going to change peacefully, it will change violently. The First World is losing some of its superiority to the Second World, headed by the Soviet Union, and to the Third World, which has only numbers on its side. "Essentially, contemporary wars have been fights for the rights of various political groups within the former political colonial appendages of Europe to take political power and to exercise it on their own terms" (Barnet, 1968, p. 4).

The First World retreat from a complete dominion over the Third World has been only relative, of course. This relative decline in U.S. power is evident when we compare how much more support the United States had during the Korean War (early 1950s) than during the Vietnam War (1960s and 1970s), or when we compare its ability to impose its will in Latin America in the 1950s and in the 1980s. Even if the decline is only relative, any change in the status quo appears precipitous to the United States leadership, and clearly unacceptable. The limited victories of the Third World, as viewed from Washington (and from Jerusalem) seem like a slippery slope, and have to be countered by toughness.

The U.S. claim is that any gains by the Third World constitute "Soviet expansionism." The United States is at war with a diabolical enemy, capable of pulling hidden strings all over the world. A prevailing American view is that there isn't really a Third World. There are only two players in the Global Game: the United States and the Soviet Union. If it weren't for Soviet subversion around the world, peace and quiet would naturally dominate. The problem is, of course, that the frustrating Third World existed even before the Bolshevik Revolution, as any history of American involvement in Central America suggests. The denial of Third World independent initiative and Third World grievances is an attempt to deny the reality of exploitation and oppression around the globe. The ideology of the war against the Third World does more than dehumanize the victims and blame the victims. It sometimes even denies the existence of the victims.

In the 1960s, a new term entered political discussions in the United States: "counterinsurgency." The United States would, from now on, develop "conventional" means of dealing with emerging revolutionary movements. The old policy of sending in the marines was not enough. The United States would support existing regimes by offering technology, manipulation, and other "covert" means. New military units, "special forces" would be created to handle "brushfires" around the globe. An essential component of the 1960s strategy was to equip local friendly governments to handle local insurrection by offering them "counterinsurgency" training and technology.

The war between the First World and the Third World is echoed at the United Nations. There, a world order was created at the end of the Second World War, which reflected the then-existing dominance of the United States and its allies. Between 1945 and 1960, the United States enjoyed favorable majorities at the United Nations, which seemed to be simply another American instrument (Franck, 1985). But decolonization meant that this happy period (happy for the United States) came to an end, and the majority is now supporting another point of view. The problem with the United Nations today is that it represents the world today—which means a Third World majority. While the United States cannot be easily defeated on the battlefield, it can be at the United Nations, where the weak can unite, and where each nation—large or small, rich or poor—has only one vote. At the United Nations the Third World constitutes a majority of over a hundred nations. In 1984, the United States voted with the majority only 4 percent of the time.

And the majority is becoming radical. Efforts to stop the radicalization of the Third World takes two forms: first, attacking existing radical regimes through direct suppression, cooptation, control, and containment, and second, supporting conservative regimes in the Third World. Other nations join the United States in this effort. One might say that the one consistent strategy common to both the United States and Israel in the Third World is that of supporting small minorities, each opposed by the majority in its own country. In this way the Somozas, the Gemayels, the Marcoses, and the whites of South Africa have been supported.

The History of
A "Special Relationship"

Abba Eban, former Israeli ambassador to Washington and foreign minister, has described U.S. support for Israel as follows: "In all of modern history no other small nation has received so much of its power and viability from another nation, as Israel has received from the United States. We are talking about triple backing: Only the United States made it possible for Israel to acquire its military superiority. . . . Only the United States enabled the Israeli economy to develop as it has, within one generation. Only the United States defends Israel against the termination of its legitimacy in international bodies. It is true that the United States receives some support from Israel, but while Israel could not exist with any degree of power, sovereignty, or prosperity without the United States, the United States can survive a breakup with Israel, and millions of Americans will not even notice it" (Barabash, 1982, p. 15).

On March 8, 1949, the Israel government announced that its foreign policy was based on "loyalty to the principles of the United Nations Charter and friendship with all freedom-loving states, and in particular with the United States and the Soviet Union" (Brecher, 1972, p. 40). Israel in the early years followed an official policy of nonidentification with the superpowers, and on January 9, 1950, recognized the People's Republic of China; but by July 2, 1950, it supported United States actions in Korea. The events of the early 1950s were "absorbed into an essentially Western, anti-communist view of the world" (Brecher, 1974, p. 530).

After June 1950 Israel "appeared to be offering itself to the West as an ally in the Cold War . . . repeatedly demanding admission into either NATO or into a bilateral treaty relationship with the United States" (Sachar, 1981, p. 78). As early as 1951 Gershom Schocken, editor-in-chief of the liberal Tel-Aviv daily *Haaretz*, could write: "Israel has proven its military prowess in the 1948 war against the Arab countries, and so a certain strengthening of Israel is a convenient way for the Western powers to create a political equilibrium in the Middle East. According to this conception, Israel is destined for the role of a watch-dog. There is no reason to fear that it will follow an aggressive policy against the Arab countries, if that will run clearly counter to the wishes of the United States or Britain. But if the Western powers will prefer, once, for whatever reason, to close their eyes, you can rely on it that Israel will be capable of sufficiently punishing one or more of the neighboring countries, whose lack of courtesy towards the West has gone beyond the permissible limits" (Frenkel, 1980, p. 46).

Starting as far back as 1949 (Bialer, 1985), Israel's leaders tried to convince the United States that it is a valuable ally, that it should be formally recognized as America's "leading strategic partner in the Middle East" (Klare, 1984, p. 140). As such, Israel sought security guarantees as early as 1948 (Crosbie, 1974); a formal and public defense treaty with the United States was a foremost goal of Israeli policy in the 1950s (Brecher, 1972).

Israel was developing its "periphery strategy" in an attempt to form a pro-American group in the area. The strategy was initiated in 1949 with the aim of showing the United States that Israel was a significant regional power (Bialer, 1985). According to David Ben-Gurion, "Should America take over the idea—the connection between Iran, Turkey, Israel, and, we must add, Ethiopia as well—there is a chance that something important might come of it" (Bar-Zohar, 1977, p. 1322). He connected these efforts in the Middle East with others in the Third World: "Together with the budding signs in Ghana, Liberia, Nigeria, Burma, these relations are of great significance and may provide many opportunities. The good will of the United States will move things forward" (p. 1323). Ben-Gurion sent messages to that effect to President Eisenhower and to the prime minister of France, saying in part, "We are capable of carrying out our mission, which is a vital need for us and also a source of tangible might for the West in this part of the world" (p. 1325). But he saw a treaty with the United States as being more important for Israel than one with France, and tried to obtain it (Eshed, 1979). As early as March 1952, Israel's ambassador to Washington, Abba Eban, met with the chairman of the joint chiefs of staff, General Omar Bradley. Eban proposed having Israel in any Western Middle East defense treaty, and asked for U.S. military aid. Both requests were denied.

The visit by John Foster Dulles to Israel in 1953 contains in its few hours the whole history of the basic Israeli stance toward the United States. Israel's new elite unit, the paratroopers, formed the honor guard for Dulles at the airport, with their red berets and new Uzi submachine guns. Israel was interested in a formal alliance, but "while the United States certainly viewed Israel as the most stable and reliable U.S. ally in the Middle East, American strategy called for the integration of the moderate Arab states into a regional security system of some sort, and this plan clearly precluded any sort of formal military alliance with Israel" (Klare, 1984, p. 140). It was the failure to obtain a formal defense treaty with the United States in the 1950s that led to the 1956 Suez war, Israel's attempt to break its diplomatic isolation and forge an alliance with France and Britain (Zak, 1980). By 1962, President John F. Kennedy defined the relationship (in a private meeting with Israeli foreign minister Golda Meir) as follows: "The United States . . . has a special relationship with Israel in the Middle East really comparable only to that which it has with Britain over a wide range of world affairs. But for us to play properly the role we are called upon to play, we cannot afford the luxury of identifying Israel—or Pakistan, or certain other countries—as our exclusive friends" (Green, 1984, p. 181).

Nevertheless, Israel did not give any practical support to the U.S. war effort in Korea in the early 1950s, unlike such allies as Turkey, Iran, South Africa, and Australia. And Israel was able to resist American pressures for support during the Vietnam War (Neff, 1984), refusing the many explicit requests in 1965 and 1966 for diplomatic recognition for South Vietnam and civilian aid to the Saigon regime. In the summer of 1966, Israel finally agreed to accept eight Vietnamese farming trainees, on condition that the matter be kept secret (Green, 1984). Only on December 21, 1972, was Israel drawn into the American war in Indochina by recognizing the doomed Republic of Vietnam.

Until the 1960s, the United States did not supply Israel with arms directly—but U.S. arms were delivered to Israel by the Germans, so that the United States could claim no direct involvement. Similarly, it knew and approved French sales in the 1950s (Crosbie, 1974). It was only after the 1967 war (when France withdrew its aid) that the United States began to supply major weapons to Israel, starting with Skyhawk jets in December 1967, and Phantom jets in September 1969. This marked a major change in Israel's military arsenal, from French to American technology, and was to lead to a growing dependence on the United States, both military and economic.

Despite many attempts to bring about a formal and public defense treaty with the United States, this cherished goal has remained elusive. In the spring of 1984, Israeli officials were hailing the coming pact as a watershed in Israel's history—which it would have been, but at the last minute, opposing views prevailed in the U.S. administration, to Israel's great disappointment (Goodman, 1984b). Israeli efforts were only partly rewarded in 1981, with the Memorandum of Understanding on Strategic Cooperation, granted for the first time by President Ronald Reagan. The memorandum, signed in Washington on November 30, 1981, by Defense Secretary Caspar Weinberger and Defense Minister Ariel Sharon, was designed to counter "the threat to peace and security of the region caused by the Soviet Union or Soviet-controlled forces from outside the region introduced into the region." In 1983, discussions of a possible Israeli role in overall U.S. strategy against the Soviet Union became public with reports on "a basically new American-Israeli defence alliance. It is a partnership that is most likely to eventually result in Israel's playing an increasingly more important strategic role for the U.S. . . . Israel is becoming integrated into the U.S. global defence system, much like Italy, Turkey and South Korea" (Blitzer, 1984c, p. 2) This was a significant change in Israeli strategic thinking, which had concentrated until then on radical Arab states; the change resulted from American pressure.

In November 1984, a new U.S.-Israeli committee was created—a further step in formalizing a military alliance. This Joint Military and Political Group has held regular semiannual meetings, some secret; according to one participant, the subjects raised included "delicate matters" not normally discussed even with NATO allies (Blitzer, 1984b, c).

Israel's status as a trusted U.S. ally was demonstrated again in March 1985, when it was invited to take part in the U.S. Strategic Defense Initiative. The unexpected invitation to join in Star Wars research gave Israel the same status as NATO members, Japan, and Australia—all formal U.S. allies. It certified Israel's role not just as an ally, but as a strategic ally, on a global (or even galactic) scale. Israel agreed to cooperate, with enthusiasm rare among the eighteen nations invited to join, showing again how deeply Israel is, and wants to be, in the American orbit.

U.S. Financial Aid
To Israel

"In the 1980s, the American connection is the clear centerpiece of the Israeli political, economic and strategic outlook. It is the attitudes in Washington and among the American public that do the most to assure the security and well-being of the people and land of Israel" (Grose, 1985, p. 111). It would be impossible to exaggerate the extent of Israeli dependence on the United States as of 1987.

U.S. support for Israel has been clearly expressed in the form of financial support. Table 4 shows the official figures on American financial aid to Israel (to which we might add 10 percent to account for aid given over the years through budget items other than foreign aid). It is illuminating to observe how high the levels of support have risen in the 1980s. The bottom line, is that without U.S. money, Israel would simply collapse, lacking any economic base of its own.

The total of U.S. assistance to Israel since 1948 is a little over $38 billion, and over the years, Israel has become the number-one recipient of both civilian and military aid from the United States (USGAO, 1983). In the first twenty-five years, the aid totaled only $1.3 billion; since 1973, Israel has received over $36 billion. Through 1965, direct U.S. financial aid to Israel was only $764.7 million, including only

$313.9 million in grants. During the same years, financial support from world Jewry amounted to $3.5 billion, and from the West German government to $1.7 billion (Halevi and Klinov-Malul, 1968). Even in 1967, American aid to Israel totaled only $13.1 million. Military aid to Israel before 1970 was negligible; even in 1970 it amounted to only $30 million. It started growing in 1971, and then grew enormously after the 1973 war. (The increase was due largely to Henry Kissinger's ideas about giving Israel a more central role in the Pax Americana emerging in the Middle East in the period.)

Non-military aid was quite limited until 1972. In 1970, Israel received only $41.7 million in loans and grants—sums that look insignificant today. In the mid-1970s Israel became the major recipient of U.S. foreign aid, which it remained for the following ten years. By way of comparison, the Marshall Plan for Europe, carried out between 1948 and 1951, one of the largest economic support programs in history, cost the United States $10.2 billion. Even with a generous allowance for the decline in the value of the dollar since 1950, total U.S. economic aid to Israel between 1950 and 1985 is comparable to the Marshall Plan.

The dramatic rise since 1973 reflects a new reality on both sides. On the U.S. side, it was a willingness to support a "strategic asset." On the Israeli side, it was a growing dependence on a superpower. The extent of Israel's almost total dependence on the influx of foreign capital grants, and its lack of any real economic base, is indicated by the fact that Israel received a total of $38 billion in grants between 1952 and 1984, while only $2 billion were invested by foreign corporations (Temkin, 1985).

One could legitimately argue that there is indeed a direct correlation between increases in U.S. financial aid to Israel since 1973 and the increase in Israel's involvement in the Third World on the side of the United States. Can Israel be thought of as a "mercenary state"? Yes, in the sense of being kept by the United States in return for services provided. But because Israel does have its own motives for Third World activities, this is not the only explanation for what Israel has been doing. The relationship is clearly not just a matter of payment for services.

TABLE 4
U.S. FINANCIAL AID
TO ISRAEL 1951–1985
(IN $ MILLIONS)

Year	Economic Aid	Military Aid	Total
1951	0.1	—	0.1
1952	86.4	—	86.4
1953	73.6	—	73.6
1954	74.7	—	74.7
1955	52.7	—	52.7
1956	50.8	—	50.8
1957	40.9	—	40.9
1958	61.2	—	61.2
1959	49.9	0.4	50.3
1960	55.2	0.5	55.7
1961	48.1	—	48.1
1962	70.7	13.2	83.9
1963	63.4	13.3	76.7
1964	37.0	—	37.0
1965	48.8	12.9	61.7
1966	36.8	90.0	126.8
1967	6.1	7.0	13.1
1968	51.8	25.0	76.8
1969	36.7	85.0	121.7
1970	41.7	30.0	71.7
1971	55.8	545.0	600.8
1972	104.2	300.0	404.2
1973	159.8	307.5	467.3
1974	88.0	2,482.7	2,570.7
1975	393.1	300.0	693.1
1976	808.0	1,700.0	2,508.0
1977	757.0	1,000.0	1,757.0
1978	811.8	1,000.0	1,811.8
1979	815.1	4,000.0	4,815.1
1980	811.0	1,000.0	1,811.0

Year	Economic Aid	Military Aid	Total
1981	789.0	1,400.0	2,189.0
1982	819.0	1,400.0	2,219.0
1983	798.0	1,700.0	2,498.0
1984	1,200.0	1,431.0	2,631.0
1985	2,700.0	1,250.0	3,950.0
1986	1,180.0	1,700.0	2,880.0
1987 (projected)	1,200.0	1,800.0	3,000.0
Total	14,476.3	23,593.5	38,069.8

ISRAEL AS "STRATEGIC ASSET" AND INVESTMENT

Israel has been regarded by U.S. strategic planners as a regional superpower. As one writer put it, "Regionally dominant powers or 'local Leviathans' have begun to emerge: Brazil in South America, South Africa in Southern Africa, Israel in the Middle East, Iran in the Persian Gulf, India on the subcontinent, North Vietnam in Indochina" (Huntington, 1973, p. 5). That was written before the 1973 war, and between 1967 and 1973 Israel was indeed the local Leviathan. But the 1973 war changed that. Since then, Israel has become a regional superpower manqué, obsessed with proving its worth to the United States—which, duly concerned about the loss of a regional superpower, supported its efforts to regain its superiority in the region.

After the fall of the shah, Israel presented itself time and again as the most reliable U.S. ally in the Middle East, which it clearly is. "In the Iranian and Afghan crises, Israel sees itself as strategically valuable to the United States" (Shipler, 1980, p. 7). The "strategic asset" argument is a matter of a national consensus in Israel. Shimon Peres wrote that "Israel contributed more than any other country to the fact that the West in general and the U.S. in particular have such an impressive bargaining power in our region" (1979). Another commentator said, "We will be sort of another American aircraft carrier out here, a platform from which the Americans can operate" (Goodman, 1984a, p. 7).

And Israel is far from being a passive partner. "Israel today

195

provides at least as much regional intelligence as it receives from the United States. It has contributed important information on the capabilities of captured Soviet weapons systems and has become a leading source on world terrorism. F-15 and F-16 planes were first tested in combat by Israeli pilots. Israel has funneled spare U.S. parts to Iran at U.S. urging and has trained some Central and South American security units the U.S. would rather not have dealt with" (Zelnick, 1985, p. 20).

As a regional "strategic asset" Israel can offer the United States a reliable ally, with a stable regime, very close to strategic oilfields. Israel's importance as a regional power has been discussed in connection with American access to Middle East oilfields ever since the 1973 oil embargo, and especially since the fall of the shah in 1979.

The related claim that Israel is a barrier against "Soviet expansionism" has been heard since the 1950s. It has also been regarded as a barrier against indigenous radical nationalism in the Middle East, such as the Palestinian movement; on American instructions, Israel mobilized in September 1970, to avert a Syrian attack on Jordan while Jordan was extinguishing a Palestinian revolt. Ariel Sharon declared in December 1981 that the role of the Israeli Defense Force was to defend "the area between Pakistan, Libya, and Somalia against Soviet penetration" (Peri, 1983, p. 29); the next year Yaakov Meridor declared that "Israel is doing the dirty work of the United States in the Middle East" (p. 30).

As an official U.S. report says, "The continuity of the U.S.-Israeli relationship is a key tenet of U.S. policy in the Middle East. Towards that end, Israel as a stable democracy and the region's strongest military power is considered by the United States to be a strategic asset" (USGAO, 1983, p. 6). The belief in a "strong Israel" as a bulwark against all possible evils in the Middle East is simply an article of faith for the American establishment. Even those otherwise critical of Israel share it enthusiastically.

Justifying the largest foreign-aid program in the history of the United States in terms of an American strategic investment has not been difficult for leaders on either side. Israeli leaders have rightly pointed out that the U.S. is getting a real bargain; as Yaakov Meridor said, "Even if we consider only Israeli air power, we are a very cheap investment for the Americans. We have six hundred jet fighters, and to keep this number of planes, the United States would have needed a dozen aircraft carriers" (Erez, 1984, p. 39).

Most Israeli leaders, and many Americans, accept the *Jerusalem Post*'s view that "the U.S. is actually paying a bargain price for Israel's services in the region as a superior Western military force that can operate at long range . . . since the U.S. annually spends some $130 billion on its NATO forces and about $40 billion on its military commitments in the Pacific, its military and civilian aid payments to Israel are absurdly small in comparison; especially when considering them as an investment for protecting America's interests in the region" (Maoz, 1986, p. 11). Another writer in the same paper stated that "military assistance to Israel from the United States has not been charity; it has been an investment in building up an ally that can be trusted and counted upon to act when asked to do so and, in acting, can be considered as a credible block to Soviet designs in this region" (Goodman, 1984a, p. 6).

Israel's President Haim Herzog said in a *60 Minutes* interview of Israel's request for $5 billion more aid, "It's a bargain. You get for it the equivalent of American forces in Western Europe. It's good for the defense of the U.S." (CBS-TV, March 10, 1985). Ariel Sharon is reported to have said in 1984 that Israel had served American interests since 1948, and this service was worth $100 billion; since all Israel had received as of 1984 was $30 billion, Israel did not owe the United States anything; the United States owed Israel $70 billion (Kenan, 1984). MK Yitzhak Zeiger expressed Israel's true value this way: "Who will count the tens, or perhaps hundreds, of billions of dollars that the U.S. would pay to create another Israel in the Persian Gulf, in Central America, in Southeast Asia, and in other places?" (Zeiger, 1984a, p. 13). "Israel exports security. To control the Middle East, for a few pennies—the two, three billions Israel receives—it does not have to thank anybody; just the opposite" (1984b, p. 7).

Responding to questions about the American investment in Israel, Prime Minister Shimon Peres said, "Are you ready to invest in the American posture in the Middle East? . . . Imagine the Middle East without Israel" (Goshko, 1984b, p. A14). Senator Richard Lugar, chairman of the Senate Foreign Relations Committee in 1985, re-

197

sponded, "Shimon Peres's argument—that Israel provides an extension of our foreign policy there less expensively than we could provide it ourselves—makes sense" (Lindsay, 1985, p. 56).

An American military expert—Major General George Keegan, a former air-force intelligence officer—has been quoted as saying that it would cost U.S. taxpayers $125 billion to maintain an armed force equal to Israel's in the Middle East, and that the U.S.-Israel military relationship was worth "five CIAs" (Winston, 1985). There can be no doubt that from the U.S. point of view, the investment in Israel is a bargain, and the money well spent (but see Rubenberg, 1986).

FIGHTING THE THIRD WORLD
IN THE 1980s

"The apparent renewal of the Cold War should put an end to querulous talk about the 'failure of nerve' of American leadership and its 'guilt complex' toward poor, non-Western societies allegedly fostered by leftist ideologues" (Wrong, 1980, p. 136). Thus spake an American liberal just before the Reagan era. And the renewed Cold War meant mostly a hot war against the Third World. This is the essence of the Reagan administration's foreign policy, apparently guiltless about exploitation and brutality. The aim becomes the containment and control of the Third World. As of 1987 it has been fairly successful—but the relative success does not mean that future domination is assured, and the leaders of the First World are uneasy. The question before American policymakers in the 1980s is: Can you stop the decline of the empire?

The 1970s were a decade of setbacks to U.S. domination in the world. Six major defeats stand out: Portugal, Rhodesia, Ethiopia, Iran, Indochina, and Nicaragua. There was also a setback in Greece, where in 1974 the military regime headed by Colonel George Papadopoulos was replaced by a civilian government, later increasingly independent of American domination.

In 1974, the revolution in Portugal that ousted the regime of Marcello Caetano, and ended the days of a fascist dictatorship that ruled since 1932, was a major setback, especially because it precipitated the independence of Angola and Mozambique in 1975. This reversal the United States has refused to accept and is still fighting.

The revolution in Ethiopia in 1974, which ended the history of medieval monarchy, was a major setback. The American defeat in Indochina was, of course, the most important event of the decade, in terms of its impact on future American policy. After attempting to control Indochina since the defeat of the French in 1954, the United States had to accept a humiliation that would not be soon forgotten. Vietnam, Laos, and Kampuchea became communist countries, despite the efforts of the most sophisticated war machine ever assembled, despite the millions of human lives lost. The fall of the shah of Iran was another major shock. It was not just a blow; it was a nightmare for those who had envisioned an American Century of law, order, and profits around the globe. The Sandinista victory in Nicaragua and the black-majority victory in Rhodesia constituted wounds which, while not mortal, were and still are traumatic. The Sandinista victory became, for the U.S. foreign-policy establishment, a warning and a nightmare.

U.S. strategy in the 1980s is a reaction to the defeats of the 1970s, an attempt to stem the tide of radical Third World movements. South Africa is now the arena for the next major confrontation.

Israel's leaders shared the basic American response. In addition to the major and direct disaster of the 1973 war, Israeli leaders mourned the loss of Portugal, an ally; Haile Selassie of Ethiopia, another ally; the shah of Iran, a close ally; Anastasio Somoza, a longtime friend; Ian Smith, an ally; and the Saigon regime, which was neither a friend nor an ally, but whose fate brought about persistent and depressing thoughts.

All in all the 1970s were bad years for both Israel and the United States. The more aggressive policies of both countries in the 1980s are the outcome of the traumas of the 1970s. The Reaganite policy toward the Third World reflects the wish of those who, to paraphrase Churchill, do not wish to preside over the dismantling of the American empire. To stop this dismantling, the United States will be more aggressive in pursuing its war against the Third World—but if at all possible, the actual fighting is to be done by non-Americans. Thus, proxies like Israel, of which there are not too many, are going to be used, together with indigenous, CIA-supported contra groups, wherever they can be developed. This is the new wave of the late 1980s.

Israel as a Global Partner
and Proxy

One explanation for Israel's involvement in the Third World is that
it is a reflection of U.S.-Israeli relations. According to this argument,
Israel is so dependent on the United States that it cannot resist requests or pressure to help the United States in achieving its foreign-
policy goals anywhere in the world. This explanation may be true in
cases where there *is* U.S. pressure or initiative for Israeli action, but
not in other cases. Another version of this explanation sees Israel as
a U.S. proxy, acting for the superpower where the latter cannot operate directly. "Israel operates worldwide as a sub-contractor of the
United States in countries where the United States cannot operate
freely" (*Haolam Hazeh,* 1986, p. 8). This explanation has some merit,
but U.S. initiatives and pressures on Israel have to be examined within
the context of Israel's own global strategy and Israel's ideology of
being a partner of the United States.

It is clear that Israel has been acting as a U.S. proxy, but is this
situation the result of American pressure? Or is it the result of perceived self-interest? Or of both factors? According to some observers,
"as a U.S. dependent, Israel can't help but be a willing partner in the
superpower's strategic plans" (Marshall, 1984). When Israelis claim
that they are equal partners of the United States on a global scale,
Americans are likely to regard these claims as pompous, exaggerated,
or at least unwarranted, but they deserve to be taken seriously. Yet
Israeli activities to further American interests around the globe do not
imply orders coming down from Washington to Jerusalem, or American ideas being carried out by Israelis. This does happen, rarely, but
global cooperation does not require such a hierarchy. There is little
need for a detailed coordination of day-to-day activities between the
United States and Israel. The cooperation between the two countries
is based on shared perceptions of the world: Israelis and Americans
see the same friends and same enemies almost everywhere. If the basic
perception of world events is shared, there is less need for tactical
coordination. Frictions between the United States and Israel do appear in local cases, especially around such issues as arms sales, but
they do not stop global cooperation.

The best articulation of the proxy role for Israel was given in

August 1981 by Yaakov Meridor, then the minister of economic coordination: "We are going to ask you, the United States government, not to compete with us in Taiwan. Don't compete with us in South Africa. Don't compete with us in the Caribbean or in other countries where you couldn't directly do it. . . . Let us do it. I even use the expression, 'You sell the ammunition and equipment by proxy.' Israel will be your proxy. And this could be worked out with a certain agreement with the United States where we will have certain markets . . . which will be left for us" (UPI, 1981).

An Israeli journalist wrote about arms deals in the Third World: "Israel has the blessing of the Reagan administration in these deals, and does the dirty work for the United States" (Lichtman, 1983, p. 56). In response to criticism from "liberal circles," "Israeli officials have countered by pointing out that most of these sales have had the blessings of the Reagan administration, which often has been frustrated in its arms transfer policies by Congress. Israel, therefore, could legitimately argue that it was doing America's dirty work—and making a nice profit in the process" (Blitzer, 1983, p. 13). Yehuda Ben-Meir, deputy foreign minister, said in November 1983: "It is no secret that there are agreements for U.S.-Israeli cooperation, in Asian countries, Africa, Latin America and Central America. The United States, as a world power, has interests throughout the world. Israel has its own interests in foreign countries. In some places these interests overlap and the two countries cooperate" (*Israeli Foreign Affairs,* 1985c).

Israeli leaders may not completely share the U.S. point of view in every case, but nonetheless be ready to serve U.S. goals; if Israel can thus help the United States with pursuing its strategic goals, then it is no longer a simple client state, and it can make more demands on the United States. Thus the two sides can benefit from this cooperation, without necessarily sharing the same goals. The Israeli goal in furthering U.S. interests seems to be to extend its value as a "strategic asset" in the Middle East. Thus, Israelis (leaders and public) are quite serious when they assert that Israel is a U.S. global strategic partner. The American foreign-policy establishment does not have to accept these views completely, but the reality of Israel's valuable services in the Third World cannot be ignored. While "moderate" Arab states may contribute to the American concept of "Middle Eastern security," not much can be expected of them in other parts of the world (beyond the financial contributions of Saudi Arabia, which are certainly appreciated). The spirit of Meridor's August 1981 speech is said to have been reflected in the Memorandum of Understanding on Strategic Cooperation that November. When the "strategic alliance" between the two countries was officially documented in the memorandum, the substance of the recognition had much to do with global concerns, and less to do with the Middle East.

The first point of the memorandum dealt with military cooperation between the United States and Israel in areas "outside the east Mediterranean zone," and the third point called for arms sales to third parties. The memorandum was suspended on December 18, 1981, and reinstated on May 17, 1983, as part of the deals around the now-forgotten peace treaty between Israel and Lebanon. At that point, the Israeli establishment felt that "the revival of the agreement now will have its most practical implications not in the Middle East, but in Central America and in Africa . . . largely due to the advantages of U.S.-Israeli cooperation in the Third World" (Samet, 1983b, p. 5). David Kimche, the director-general of Israel's Foreign Office (and former ranking Mossad agent in Africa), concentrated on this subject in most of his talks in Washington that summer. "The Americans need Israel in Africa and Latin America also because of the problems experienced by the U.S. Administration when it comes to getting Congress to ratify all its far-reaching aid programs and, of course, its military activities. According to the foreign press . . . the Americans have been helped by Israel, through its links with Zaire, during the war in Chad. In Central America, which is now the main focus of U.S. activities, the U.S. Administration has long wanted to use Israel as a conduit for military and other aid. One of the secret aspects of U.S.-Israeli contacts over Central America concerns the intention of the U.S. Administration to get Israel to supply the armies of the pro-U.S. regimes there. The financial value of this aid, which the U.S. cannot directly transfer to its allies in the region, will be paid to Israel directly from the United States. As the White House becomes more daring—as, for instance, in Grenada—it becomes more dependent upon support from the liberal circles in which Jewish members of Congress are conspicuous. American cooperation with Israel can, during any U.S. military activities in the Caribbean, make the difference between success and failure in the House of Representatives. Washington's new need for the benefits of the Israeli connection, which it preferred to ignore during better times, now enables Israel to ask for an appropriate reward."

Understandably, Israel has wanted clear recognition of the services provided, and a reward for providing them. During his first visit to the United States as prime minister, Menahem Begin puzzled his hosts by reminding them of the vital role Israel played on the American side during the Vietnam War. Begin's logic was this: The Suez Canal was closed to traffic between 1967 and 1975 because of Israel's military actions, which made the route for Soviet ships supplying Vietnam longer and costlier.

Since 1977, the topic of recognition and reward has often been brought up by Israelis visiting Washington. David Kimche has been especially persistent.

In some cases, Israel is the party that proposes activities in Third World "trouble spots"; such a plan makes sense for Israel, which gains contacts in the Third World and becomes a more valuable ally for the United States. In 1982, Foreign Minister Yitzhak Shamir met with Secretary of State George Shultz and reportedly suggested cooperation in Costa Rica and elsewhere in Central America, "where the United States is trying to stop the spread of Communist revolutionary movements." The Americans were cool to the idea for financial reasons (Mann, 1982).

In April 1983, Kimche went to Washington with a grand plan for an Israeli "assistance program" in Africa, Asia, and Latin America—all financed by the United States. "Coordination with the U.S. regarding Israeli contacts in Africa, South America and Asia" was what Kimche hoped (in vain) to discuss in Washington in June 1983 (Samet, 1983a). "American financing of Israeli technical aid projects to United States allies in Central America and Africa" was mentioned as a topic for Israeli-U.S. discussions in November 1983 (Smith, 1983).

In 1983 it was reported that "Begin's government has for some time sought to play a security role in Central America in cooperation with the United States. Israeli officials have been quoted as saying they would be willing to act as a U.S. proxy in areas where congressional restraints or human rights concerns raise obstacles to direct U.S. aid" (Cody, 1983; so far Shamir and Peres have had the same ideas). In

1984 Kimche again proposed funding for Israeli projects in Central America and Africa—including "military training, personal protection of leaders, and agricultural training." The idea was to be discussed with Lawrence Eagleburger and with Langley Motley, both of the State Department (Benziman, 1984a, b).

In 1981 Ariel Sharon linked Israel's plans in Africa with the Memorandum of Understanding on Strategic Cooperation (Silver, 1981), and in 1982 he described the renewed Israeli involvement in Africa as part of a joint U.S.-Israeli effort to block "Soviet expansionism" (Benziman, 1986). After Sharon visited Zaire in January 1983, the director of the African desk at the Israeli Foreign Ministry, Avi Primor, went to Washington to meet with Lawrence Eagleburger, assistant secretary of state, and with members of Congress to discuss Israeli activities in Africa. In 1984, American and Israeli representatives discussed further cooperation in the Third World, in the guise of technical assistance (Goshko, 1984a). In May 1984, Kimche once again announced that the United States and Israel were moving closer to planning joint economic-aid projects in the Third World (Blitzer, 1984a), though no details were ever announced. A meeting between the Israeli ambassor to Washington, Meir Rosenne, and administrators of the Agency for International Development (AID) in November 1984 continued Kimche's discussions at the State Department about integrating Israeli experts and programs into AID projects (Granot, 1984). Clearly Israeli enthusiasm for this idea is greater than U.S. willingness to embrace it.

One active joint U.S.-Israeli project involves covert deliveries of arms around the world. The CIA and the Mossad have been collaborating on a scheme to deliver Soviet weapons (of which Israel has considerable stocks, captured in the Middle East over three decades) to groups that are fighting forces equipped with Soviet weapons. The logic of the scheme is clear. When Soviet-made weapons are used, they cannot easily be traced to their real sources. The claim is always that they have been captured locally. Five groups enjoying Soviet weapons delivered by Israel, and paid for by the CIA, are the *mujahedeen* in Afghanistan, the contras in Central America, the UNITA forces in Angola, the Habré forces in Chad, and the MNR forces in Mozambique.

The Iran-contra scandal of 1986–1987 was an American problem, not an Israeli one. Paradoxically, the crisis again demonstrated Israel's value for the United States: Israel can be counted on to provide useful services around the globe, with efficiency and sang-froid—and without domestic opposition or commissions of inquiry. As far as the Israeli political system was concerned, there was no real crisis, and business went on as usual.

The affair showed again that Israel was not just a totally dependent client, but a partner that initiates joint U.S.-Israeli operations in the Third World. It was Israel's idea that a "more moderate government in Iran" could be brought to power through U.S. and Israeli moves (Poindexter, 1986). This idea was adopted by the United States and the proposed moves were carried out. Israel has been initiating joint projects with the United States out of confidence in its ability to carry them out, and out of its desire to prove its value as a global partner, and to obtain the well-earned rewards of such a role.

ISRAEL AND U.S. IDEOLOGY IN THE THIRD WORLD WAR

Is it possible that Israelis really identify with U.S. policies? Do they really see the world as the United States sees it? Yes, very nearly. The view of the Third World from Jerusalem is almost identical to the view from Washington. The goal of U.S. strategy since World War II has been to contain Soviet influence and power, and to contain Third World radicalism. It is mostly on the latter point that Israel has supported U.S. policies and offered itself as an ally, but also on the former. Israel's own concern for regaining its superiority against the Arabs has come to coincide with the American goal of halting imperial decline. In the early 1980s, the two agendas became almost identical.

Israel has moved from being the cop on the beat to being a global policeman, distinguished by efficiency and dedication. The Israelis have been able to do in the Third World what other Western powers have often failed to do, which is to blunt the edge of native radicalism. And they do it with aplomb, enthusiasm, and grace—at least as things are seen from the United States. In many of those places, the United States cannot be directly involved, which is why Israeli assistance is so much in demand. The Reagan administration cannot send military advisers to Zaire, Guatemala, South Africa, or Haiti. Even the European governments that are closely allied with U.S. global policies are not always ready to associate publicly with Chile, for example. What others regard as "dirty work" Israelis regard as a defensible duty, and sometimes as an exalted calling. And Israeli involvement lends Third World regimes a measure of special legitimacy, due to Israeli influence on public opinion in the United States. Such considerations have been discussed openly in the case of Israeli support for the Mobutu regime in Zaire, and the apartheid regime in South Africa. Thus Israel, in the view of some of its leaders, is more than just an equal partner—it is an indispensable one.

In recent years, Israel's leaders have increasingly accepted the U.S. view of the bipolar nature of global politics. The expression "the Free World" was seldom heard in Israeli political discourse in the 1950s or the 1960s; in the 1980s it is heard quite often. Since 1973, Israeli political leaders have used anti-Soviet rhetoric more often. Do they sincerely believe in the Soviet threat? Or are they just using this language to ingratiate themselves with the United States? It is hard to tell, but clearly they do use the rhetoric.

Over the past few years at the United Nations, Israel has distinguished itself as the country with the highest percentage of votes supporting the United States. In 1985, it was 91.5 percent, followed by Britain (86.6 percent), West Germany (84.4 percent), and France (82.7 percent). This record indicates not only Israel's agreement with U.S. global policies, but also the frequent isolation of both countries. The United States votes alone, or with Israel, on U.N. General Assembly resolutions on South Africa, Namibia, and the Middle East. A report issued by the U.S. Mission to the United Nations listed Israel alone, under the heading "No affiliation," while the rest of the world's nations were listed by five geographical regions. This classification underscored Israel's not-so-splendid isolation (Sciolino, 1986b). Erstwhile friends of both are recently less likely to support them in U.N. votes, while they both find themselves voting against the whole world, especially on such issues as Palestinian rights.

In the wake of the United States invasion of Grenada, the General Assembly passed a resolution condemning the invasion by a vote of 108 to 9, with 40 abstentions. All the traditional U.S. allies, including Britain, abstained. Those that opposed the resolution were the

United States, the six Caribbean countries that took part in the invasion, El Salvador, and Israel (McMahan, 1984).

Israeli leaders perceive any victory of a Third World radical movement as a long-term threat to Israel—first because it weakens the United States; second because it adds to the radicalization of the Third World, which is opposed to Israel and allied with the Arabs. Any threat to the dominance of the United States is a threat to Israel. If American power declines, so does the power of its dependents. Israeli leaders act as if they indeed believe that there is only one war going on in this world, and that there is really one front.

7

Israel as Pariah and as Model

66"There is a small group of nations that can be characterized as international pariahs, or outcasts. These are countries that for one reason or another have been shunned by their regional neighbors, if not by the international community in general" (Meyer, 1984, p. 55). South Africa, Israel, and a couple of others make up the pariah club, also called the outlaw club and the league of the desperate. Members of the club have been referred to as the fifth or the sixth world, depending on how many other worlds you count. What they all have in common is extreme diplomatic isolation and the fear of being abandoned by their few allies. This anxiety about survival leads to strategies and acts of desperation. One explanation for what we have observed in Israel's behavior is its position as a pariah state. Its history is similar in many ways to South Africa's and Taiwan's; so are its survival strategy and its actions around the world. Not only are these countries isolated; their very legitimacy is challenged by the majority of the international community.

The Pariah Club

Members of the pariah club feel that they can trust each other in certain areas much more than they can trust the United States. The Western allies, such as Britain, West Germany, France, and Japan, generally accept U.S. policy, but there is a common strategy among the pariahs that goes further than the common Western strategy. Israel, South Africa, Taiwan, and other pariahs have their own ideas, strategies, and policies, because in the final analysis they do not really trust the United States or other Western allies: no nonpariah can really understand their predicament.

There is a big difference between the way Americans are involved in war in the Third World, which is never close to home, and the way Israelis and South Africans participate—they are fighting not only close to home, but *for* their home. The United States and other imperial powers can pack up and go home when they are defeated in the Third World, but the Israelis, the South Africans, and the Taiwanese cannot do that, and will not, as long as they can help it. Understanding the depths of despair and desperation reached by leaders of the pariah states is the only way to appreciate their strategies. The problem from their point of view is that the United States is given to unpredictable faint-heartedness, and is often too liberal. It is simply not as ruthless as it should be—at least not in public—and there is always the danger of a "liberal" administration (remember Carter!). Thus, an alliance with the United States, however desirable, is not insurance enough. Self-reliance and the pariah alliance are therefore necessary. So much effort will go into these two strategies.

Cooperation among the pariah states in the nuclear field has been widely noted. South Africa has become the main supplier of uranium to both Israel and Taiwan, and the three countries have been reported as working on a cruise missile to deliver nuclear weapons. But "nuclear cooperation is only part of an intensive pattern of exchanges of conventional military and economic ties among Israel, Taiwan and South Africa, which, officials say, complicate intelligence organizations' efforts to monitor the contacts. The contacts reflect the three countries' perception that their political isolation is increasing" (Miller, 1981, p. 7). This perception is indeed correct.

Israelis see that they share with other pariah nations the fate of

209

being attacked and criticized by the same groups—the Third World and the Left. This leads them to identify and side with the other pariahs. The logic is direct: those that criticize South Africa for apartheid also criticize Israel for its treatment of Palestinians. Since the latter criticism is wrong, the Israelis say, we must be suspicious of the former; we must support our fellow victims, the South Africans, against radical attacks (Golan, 1977).

The major and permanent partners in the worldwide network of right-wing regimes are the pariahs: South Africa, Israel, and Taiwan, along with South Korea, whose insecurity has a different history. These are all garrison states on the margins of the rising Third World, which threatens their continuing existence. According to two pro-apartheid writers, "South Africa may increasingly be called a member of what might be called the international outcasts' league, comprising also Israel, South Korea, Taiwan. . . . All these countries have vigorous enemies that have advanced at an unprecedented pace, . . . are physically threatened from without, and are exceptionally strong militarily in relation to their size. Their respective regimes have lost international legitimacy. . . . There are indications that they might become increasingly linked in a variety of ways through trade, weapons development, or even nuclear engineering and weaponry" (Gann and Duignan, 1981, pp. 181, 184).

The Associate Members

There are internal divisions within the "Western" bloc, just as there are divisions within the U.S. foreign-policy elite. The pariah club forms the extreme right wing of this bloc; the pariahs are part of a looser right-wing network of regimes that find themselves on the margins of historical developments and international alliances for longer or shorter periods.

One goal of the wider international right-wing network is to pull the U.S. government in the direction of a more aggressive global policy. A view of U.S. policies in the 1980s—which could as easily have come from Taiwan, South Korea, or South Africa—came from an Israeli diplomat pleased with what he called "the Beginization of Reagan" (Hadar, 1983). He then compared the invasion of Grenada

TABLE 5

THE INTERNATIONAL RIGHT-WING NETWORK

The Pariah Club:	Israel South Africa South Korea Taiwan
Associate (and Former) Members:	Argentina (under military) Bolivia (under military) Brazil (under military) Brunei Chile Iran (under the shah) Morocco Paraguay Philippines (under Marcos) Saudi Arabia Singapore Thailand

with the invasion of Lebanon, and said that in both cases the invaders "acted in order to destroy an extremist pro-Soviet force which threatened them at a short range." He added, "The very fact that the United States is prepared to use its force in order to protect its global interests is, from Israel's point of view, encouraging" (p. 12). Any detente or accommodation between the superpowers is a threat and a danger to the pariah nations. It means less support for them on every level, and less need for their help to the United States. For the international right-wing network, detente with the Soviet Union is almost always threatening; Israel in particular loses its value as "strategic asset" in the superpower conflict.

There have been numerous reports of a South Atlantic Treaty Organization (SATO)—made up of Argentina, Brazil, Paraguay, Uruguay, South Africa, Israel, and Taiwan—the brainchild of General Vernon Walters of the CIA. SATO is said to have been started in the early 1970s, and Argentina, Brazil, and Uruguay are said to have dropped out since they returned to civilian rule. But South Africa has openly expressed its interest in an "emergent Middle Power bloc in the international arena," including "countries such as Israel and Iran as well as Third World countries which are increasingly moving out of the smaller Third World league into the Middle Power league" (Metrowich, 1977, p. 128).

Since the early 1970s, South Africa has developed what is now known as "the South Atlantic Link" (Metrowich, 1977). Ambassadorial relations with Chile started in 1976. In 1973, Argentina, then under Juan Perón, took steps to indicate support for South Africa, such as hosting the South African foreign minister, Mr. Hilgard Muller. South Africa also developed "particularly close ties" with Paraguay (p. 147); only Israel is closer. General Alfredo Stroessner and John Vorster traded visits in 1974, and numerous cooperation agreements between Paraguay and South Africa are in force today, covering cultural, scientific, and economic affairs. Breyten Breytenbach has predicted that the leaders of white South Africa will escape to South America or Taiwan when the apartheid regime collapses (1984).

After his visit to Israel, Prime Minister John Vorster spoke to the South African parliament about "an economic alliance comprising a dozen countries or more" (*Star*, 1976, p. 1). He refused to name the countries involved, but referred to "middle-rank countries." He said that the "new and closer understanding with Israel would be of great mutual benefit," but made it clear that he had his sights on the broader alliance.

The states of the right-wing network are allies of the United States; though they are insecure, they are not as insecure as the pariah states. Saudi Arabia is a good example; it has supported contra movements around the world (Central America, UNITA in Angola, MNR in Mozambique) and has unofficial contacts with South Africa. Military regimes in Latin America have been temporary members of the network—for instance, Argentina under the generals (1976–1983); during the Malvinas war of 1982, it received aid from both Israel and South Africa. Between the military coup of 1964 and the return of civilian rule in March 1985, the junta in Brazil was a member of the network, offering support in some common ventures, collaborating with South Africa and Taiwan on numerous occasions. Relations between these nations are reflected in the patterns of official state visits. Leaders of these countries are not invited very often to visit other nations beyond the confines of the network.

The international right-wing network can be observed in the same regions where Israel has been involved, supporting the same side. Taiwan, South Africa, South Korea, Brazil, and Argentina have been active in Central America, whether in helping military regimes there or helping the contras (Parry, 1985). Both Israel and South Africa supplied arms to the military regimes in Guatemala. Somoza was also helped by Argentina, Chile, South Korea and South Vietnam. Under the military regime (1976–1984), Argentina sent military advisers to El Salvador and Guatemala, and trained officers from these countries in Argentina (all this has changed, of course, under the Alfonsín administration).

When the ambassadors of South Africa and Israel in Bolivia expressed their readiness to cooperate with the military regime of General Luis García Meza, they were merely fulfilling their responsibilities as pariahs. These responsibilities go beyond a country's immediate areas of strategic concern (Southern Africa and the Middle East, respectively) and extend worldwide. South Africa, Israel, Taiwan, Chile, and other countries of similar persuasions have to be concerned about the global situation and global historical trends. They have to see the whole world as the "strategic sphere of direct interest." Growing historical forces present direct threats to their survival, and they should be concerned and vigilant about them.

The aid offered by the international right-wing network to the contras is another case in point. The same predictable group of countries rushed to help the CIA operation against the Nicaraguan government. In addition to Israel, it included right-wing regimes in Central America, Taiwan, Paraguay, South Korea (through the Moonies), Chile, and Argentina (until 1982). The Argentines were active in the training of the contras in 1981–1982, but pulled out after the Malvinas debacle. One Nicaraguan official said then, "It seems reasonable to presume that Israel will take over Argentina's role" (Riding, 1982). When the United States was recruiting more helpers for the contras, it called on Taiwan, South Korea, Saudi Arabia, and two less-prominent associate members of the club, Singapore and Brunei (Gwertzman, 1987).

In the 1980s, the United States has adopted a strategy of training and financing guerrilla forces to fight against radical regimes in the Third World, thus avoiding more direct involvement. The best exemplars are the contras in Nicaragua; such others as UNITA (Angola) and MNR (Mozambique) are supported not only by the United States, but also by members of the international right-wing network. The unity of right-wing guerrilla movements in the Third World, and their ties to the United States, were expressed in the summer of 1985, with a "summit meeting of Contras from UNITA, Nicaraguan Contras, and Afghanistan in Southern Angola. The meeting was organized by the United States and South Africa" (Cowell, 1985), and it was well covered in the Western media.

The pariah states and the contra movements have a lot in common, so their alliances are natural. They are all fighting the same fight —trying to stem, or reverse, the tide of radicalism in the Third World. All members of the pariah club are committed to the support of contra movements around the world and to the struggle against radical movements everywhere. Isreal is no exception.

Taiwan

The 1970s have seen the increasing isolation of Taiwan, the country that still proclaims itself to be the Republic of China (ROC), the legal government of all of China. The United States accepted this claim from 1949, when the Kuomintang leaders fled to the island of Taiwan, to 1978, when the United States recognized the People's Republic of China (PRC) as China's legitimate and only government. The diplomatic successes of the PRC, its assumption of United Nations representation in place of the ROC, and its growing relations with the United States have sounded the death knell for Taiwan's continuing claims for independence, and its chances of survival. The future, for Taiwan, can only look bleak.

Like other outcast nations, Taiwan has struggled hard to forge alliances and gain diplomatic support. By 1966, Taiwan had technical cooperation agreements with twenty countries, sixteen of them in Africa. The first were agricultural-training programs in Liberia, Togo, Senegal, Cameroon, and the Malagasy Republic. Later on, numerous (up to 160) teams of Taiwanese experts were sent to Libya, Dahomey, Gabon, Rwanda, Sierra Leone, Niger, Upper Volta, Chad, and the Ivory Coast (Laufer, 1967; McDonald et al., 1971). The Taiwan foreign-aid program has been financed by the United States (Anderson and Anderson, 1986). Taiwan has also been generous with financial aid and with invitations to trainees from Third World countries to attend courses on Taiwan. These efforts, like Israel's, were rewarded by some diplomatic support at the United Nations until the early 1970s.

A major effort has been directed at Central America, where Taiwan has embassies in Guatemala, El Salvador, Honduras, Costa Rica, and Panama. Taiwan even kept contacts with the Sandinista government in Nicaragua as long as it could. This was possible because of Nicaragua's close ties with the Soviet Union, which preferred a Taiwanese presence in Nicaragua to a Chinese one (Kinzer, 1985).

South Korea

South Korea has played a unique role not only in its region but much further afield. It has played a central role in the American scheme of things, as indicated by the amount of aid it has received—"more direct aid and concessional loans from the United States than any other country in the world save Israel and South Vietnam" (Gregor and Chang, 1984, p. 59).

South Korea has used an unusual front in its worldwide covert operations. Anyone who has observed the public political activities of Reverend Moon's Unification Church since 1970 will have concluded that the church is an instrument of the South Korean government, an integral part of the international right-wing network. One can find Moonie tracks wherever the pariah club is involved in defending the established order and countering revolutions in the Third World. From Asia to South Africa to Central America, the Moonies are in action.

The Unification Church was scrutinized by the U.S. Congress in 1978 as part of a wider investigation of the activities of Korean agents in the United States. Much interesting material about Moonie beliefs and activities came to light (U.S. House of Representatives, 1978). What emerges is a picture of a religious organization involved in many political activities, clearly working together with the South Korean government in a global right-wing crusade. The Unification Church has been active in various "trouble spots" in the Third World; it owns a newspaper in Uruguay and has tried to buy others in Latin America (Rothmyer, 1984).

The Unification Church uses its many front organizations to promote the causes dear to the hearts of the pariah club and the international right-wing network. The range of Moonie political activities in the United States and around the world is staggering. The French branch of CAUSA, the Moonie political arm, is headed by Pierre Ceyrac, elected to the French National Assembly in 1986 on the fascist National Front ticket. The Moonies collaborate with other right-wing groups, such as the Heritage Foundation, in organizing symposia, publishing pamphlets, and issuing seriously worded statements to the press, often published only as advertisements.

In the United States, the Unification Church publishes two daily newspapers, the *Washington Times* and the *New York City Tribune*. The *Washington Times* has earned a reputation as the first thing Ronald Reagan reads every morning (Jones, 1985); its editor is Arnaud de Borchgrave, known for his outspoken anti–Third World views. The church has carried out political and proselytizing activities on U.S. college campuses under the cover of the Collegiate Association for the Research of Principles (CARP). In the fall of 1985, CARP joined other Moonie organizations in promoting the cause of the contras, and has shown anti-Sandinista films on various campuses and on television.

The Moonie front for the Middle East is the International Middle East Alliance, based at Unification headquarters in New York City. The alliance has organized meetings and symposia on the prospects of Middle East peace and on Moon's philosophy of "Godism."

Another Moonie front, based in the United States but global in scope, is the International Security Council, headed by Joseph Churba, a well-known right-wing "defense analyst" (Churba, 1984). In January 1986, the council held a conference in Tel-Aviv called "State Terrorism and the International System." The participants issued a concluding statement, the Tel-Aviv Declaration, published as a full-page ad in the *New York Times* on February 9, 1986. The Tel-Aviv conference was attended by Israeli officers in uniform and by right-wing Knesset members. The International Security Council is represented in Israel by Shaul Ramati, who was relieved of his duties as Israel's ambassador to Brazil because of financial irregularities.

The Unification Church propaganda efforts, bizarre as they may seem, are reminiscent of the South African–Israeli propaganda campaign of the 1970s. Through the use of fronts and more fronts, various causes, some apparently remote from South Korean interests, are promoted. But everything comes clear once we realize that the South Koreans have a long-range global strategy of promoting right-wing causes wherever they are, no matter how remote they may seem.

The Unification Church was very much in evidence in Bolivia in 1980, expressing its support for the cocaine generals, led by Luis García Meza. Colonel Bo Hi Pak, second-in-command to Reverend Moon himself, stated in a public meeting with García Meza that "God has chosen the Bolivian people in the heart of South America as the ones to conquer communism" (Hermann, 1986, p. 19). The Moonies were also involved in training an anticommunist "people's army" there.

And they were noticeable in a conservative U.S. campaign to defend the apartheid regime against sanctions. John Lofton, a columnist for the *Washington Times,* was allowed to interview Nelson Mandela in his prison cell, a privilege not readily granted by the South African government. The interview was used to prove to *Washington Times* readers and the U.S. public that Mandela was a supporter of violence and communism (Watson, 1985).

The World Anti-Communist League (WACL), a global right-wing organization, was founded in 1966 in South Korea as a joint venture with Taiwan (Anderson and Anderson, 1986). It collaborates with the Unification Church and with a variety of fascist organizations.

Morocco

Morocco's conservative regime, finding itself threatened and marginal, has been active in the defense of similar regimes and movements, especially in Africa. Since the late 1960s, it has had a secret relationship with South Africa (*Newsweek,* 1984), which has sold arms and sent military advisers to Morocco. It has supported the

Mobutu regime in Zaire, sending troops to defend him in 1977 and 1978. In 1985, it was mentioned as a supporter of contra movements in Africa, such as UNITA in Angola.

Saudi Arabia

This medieval Arab monarchy—already mentioned several times in this chapter—is a member in good standing of the international right-wing network. It has been involved in supporting contra groups in Afghanistan, Angola, and Mozambique, together with the original contras in Central America.

ISRAEL AS INSPIRATION

Israel plays a special role in the pariah club as an inspiration for those worried about the decline of the West, American power, and the existing world order. Israel has become an inspiration to many—to Ronald Reagan, to many military men in Central America, to many in South Africa, to right-wing intellectuals in many places.

We find that, unlike many other small countries, Israel not only has friends, but also has admirers and would-be imitators. There is a worldwide fraternity of fighting men, in which Israelis are regular members. It includes the aging veterans of France's wars in Indochina and Algeria, South African counterinsurgency experts, officers in Thailand, secret-police commanders in Chile, and former Argentine generals, now in prison.

In 1983, the first Congress of the Free World's Paratroopers took place in Israel. The congress, hosted by the Israeli Defense Force (IDF), included an assortment of right-wing officers, both retired and active. French veterans, Taiwanese officers, Polish expatriates, Spanish Francoists, Israeli generals, and the commanding officers of South Africa's paratroopers swapped stories and parachuted together from Israeli air force planes.

In this fraternity of military, secret-police, and intelligence men from Chile to Taiwan, Israelis are not only respected but adulated. Admiration for Israel and its policies has been the hallmark of the international right wing, from William Safire on the pages of the *New York Times* through Pinochet and Stroessner in South America to the

Marcos family in the Philippines. (Of course, Israel does have left-wing admirers as well, but for totally different reasons.)

An alliance between Israel and right-wingers seems, at first blush, rather unlikely. Isn't the classical Western right wing traditionally anti-Semitic? Time and again, observers are surprised that certain regimes, well known for their anti-Semitism, seem to have close and comfortable relations with Israel. South Africa, the military regime in Argentina, the regime in Paraguay—how can Israel get along so well with such anti-Semites?

Obviously those who pose such a question have not thought through the meaning of anti-Semitism in our time. Israel is quite acceptable to traditional anti-Semites, because of its image and its historical role. Many contemporary anti-Semites have made the startling discovery that, paradoxically, Israelis are not Jews! So anti-Semitism can still be directed at Jews, while Israel and Israelis are admired and emulated. Anybody can tell that Israelis are different from Jews—totally unlike Jews, as a matter of fact, embodying all the qualities and virtues Jews have never been known for: military ability, cold-blooded abilities as oppressors, ruthless pragmatism in carrying the White Man's Burden. Charles de Gaulle expressed his amazement that Jews could be "both good farmers and good soldiers" (Golan, 1982, p. 73). For two thousand years Jews have been neither, but Israelis have excelled at both. What the anti-Semite doesn't like is the stereotypical Jew—passive, intellectual, liberal, and gentle. What the modern right-winger loves is the Israeli—tall, tough, armed with an Uzi, and killing dark-skinned natives in a triumph over the forces of Third World radicalism. That is how Argentine generals, Paraguayan colonels, and Afrikaner brigadiers have come to love Israelis. The romance between Zionism and the right in the United States is based on this change of image, from the Diaspora Jew, who is despised and mocked, to the Israeli, who is admired and emulated.

Even in the 1950s, Israel was seen by French right-wingers as the instrument to stop radicalism. Jacques Soustelle, a leading French right-wing ideologue, supported a formal alliance. "For Soustelle, only the existence of Israel prevented Syrian volunteers from marching into Algeria. He suggested that a tripartite alliance between France, Israel and the world Jewish community would enable 'Jewish influences' to be brought to bear in support of pro–*Algérie Française* policies" (Crosbie, 1974, p. 99)—a preview of similar designs later concocted by right-wing leaders around the world.

At the 1961 trial of the French generals who had attempted a coup against De Gaulle over the Algerian question, General André Zeller testified that the officers expected support from Portugal, South Africa, South America, and perhaps Israel (Crosbie, 1974); even then, Israel was being mentioned in the same breath as other right-wing centers. Indeed, the coup leaders and their sympathizers such as Soustelle and generals Jouhaud, Salan, and Challe were known as Israel's friends in France. After his release from prison in 1967, General Maurice Challe was hired by the Israeli government-owned shipping concern Zim (Crosbie, 1974). After the end of the Algerian War in 1962, the Mossad's contacts with French secret services "tended to be with . . . those opposed to De Gaulle for what they believed to be his sellout of French interests in the Algerian War of Independence" (Steven, 1980, p. 200).

Israel has similar admirers in Germany, such as Franz-Josef Strauss. Another was the influential German publisher Axel Springer (who died in 1985). In addition to his German publishing empire, which controls most newspapers in West Germany, Springer owned right-wing organs all over Europe. He was among those German right-wingers who, despite their Nazi past, saw Israel as an ally; he was rewarded for his vocal support with many honors, including an honorary doctorate from the Hebrew University.

Israel offers a model of success in facing up to the Third World and proving it vulnerable and weak. Israel is defiantly and victoriously offering this model for export. Beyond the fraternity of professional military men, the fraternal feeling seems to be felt by all those fighting against radical movements—searching, chasing, and destroying guerrillas and terrorists wherever they are. Israel is admired for its success in stopping radical movements in the Middle East, for pushing the dangers of "Communist expansionism" further away. In South Africa in 1976, Louis Le Grange, then deputy minister of the interior (he later became justice minister under P. W. Botha), said that the Israelis would have been able to put down the Soweto riots more effectively than the South Africans, because they "shoot quicker than we do . . . they act far more vigorously than we do" (Kuttner, 1976, p. 2).

When "international terrorism" is discussed in the West, Israel is often cited as the best example of standing up to it by military means. "No nation has had more experience with terrorism than Israel, and no nation has made a greater contribution to our understanding of the problem and the best way to confront it. Israel's contribution goes beyond the theoretical. Israel has won major battles in the war against terrorism in actions across its borders, in other continents, and in the land of Israel itself." So said U.S. secretary of state George P. Shultz in 1984 (Gwertzman, 1985, p. 22), which helps explain the special role Israel has been playing in the Third World.

A representative American conservative sees Israel as a model for counterinsurgency: "This countering of the Palestinian threat . . . is a textbook example of how a . . . nation should fashion its own secret services. And, frankly, it does as good a job of advising other . . . countries on this topic as does the United States" (Shackley, 1981, p. 44). In contrast to the Vietnam syndrome, representing U.S. defeat and fatigue after a long war, in 1976 Israel produced the commando rescue at Entebbe, showing confidence, resourcefulness, and the ability to defeat the Third World easily and decisively.

What Israel offers the embattled West, and not just South Africa, is the victory of the few over the many. The numerical superiority of the Third World is obvious in the Middle East and in Southern Africa, and it is never far from the minds of First World strategists. Israel offers proof that with advanced technology the masses can be effectively controlled. The battle cry of Israelis (and of other right-wingers around the globe) is "The West can win!" It can win, that is, against the onslaught of radical movements in the Third World, be it Southern Africa, the Middle East, or Central America. And it can win if it adopts the Israeli strategy of unilaterial military actions against any radical movement, anywhere.

For right-wingers in the United States, "Israel symbolized the will to win and the . . . virtue of unilateralism in foreign and military policy" (Mintz, 1985, p. 113). American prophets of neoconservatism, on the ascendant since the 1970s, have long since adopted Israel as their model; support for this "strategic asset" has become a neoconservative tenet, just like support for other right-wing regimes around the world. The new "down with the Third World" rhetoric developing in the United States since the 1970s was tied to Israel, and its champions such as Daniel Patrick Moynihan and Jeane Kirkpatrick have regarded Israel as an ally and an inspiration.

Meanwhile, of course, Israel has lost the support of liberal and left groups. But "those aspects of Israel's foreign and military policies which alienate left-wing sympathy attract rightist support. Many non-Jewish conservatives see in Israel's successful military resistance to the Arab world, and its defiance of United Nations resolutions, an example of the way in which a nation which has self-pride—and which is not 'corrupted by the virus of internationalism and pacifism'—can defend its national self-interests. Some see, in the Israeli defeat of the Arabs, the one example of an American ally which has decisively defeated Communist allies in battle" (Lipset, 1969, p. 34).

A representative Israeli view of the Third World and of U.S. policies there was offered by Ezer Weizman, when he was Israeli defense minister in 1979. At a diplomatic cocktail party in Washington, Weizman—known for his bluntness as well as his liberalism—got into an argument with Harold Saunders, then U.S. assistant secretary of state. Saunders criticized Israeli policies in Lebanon, and predicted that Lebanon would turn out to be Israel's Vietnam. Weizman shot back, "Don't tell us what to do. You lost everywhere. You lost Angola, Iran, Ethiopia. . . . You are showing weakness. Take Cuba, for example" (Deming, 1979, p. 34). The implication is quite clear: Americans are too soft to handle the Third World. Israelis know how to do it. They are tough and determined. Eliyahu Ben-Elissar, Likud member of the Knesset since 1977 and former Mossad operative, said, "I wish the Americans had listened to our advice on Ethiopia and Iran. Because they didn't, both were lost to the West" (Barabash, 1982, p. 15). Israeli leaders customarily imply that American policies in the Third World have failed because they reflect hesitancy, loss of nerve, "softness." Against this American "softness" they represent Israeli ruthlessness and callousness. The Decline of the West thus becomes a theme that unites American right-wingers and all the pariah states—Augusto Pinochet said that the United States was in no position to give him advice, because "they have never won a war" (Christian, 1986, p. 3); U.S. timidity is a common theme of the World Anti-Communist League (Anderson and Anderson, 1986).

In one area, ardent admiration for Israel flares up to burning envy —the area of Israel's relations with the United States, its unique position in U.S. public opinion and U.S. media. What does Taiwan want to be? Israel, of course, an ally trusted and praised. What does South Africa want to be? Israel, of course, a trusted ally whose colonialist practices are defended as "liberal" in the United States. Israel has the enviable status of the most-favored client state, almost a favorite son of the United States, with continuing and unlimited support, and it has the media image of "the only democracy in the Middle East." Wouldn't South Africa, South Korea, or Taiwan love to have that status? Cooperating with Israel, for quite a few Third World regimes, is a way of improving their image in the United States—another reason for right-wing international cooperation.

And Israel cashes in on the advantage. "Israeli officials claim that some of the advantages that Israel will receive out of the Memorandum of Understanding on Strategic Cooperation will be an increased role in the Third World. Leaders of pro-Western countries in the Third World, and particularly those with unpopular, authoritarian regimes, whose image in Washington is negative, are interested, according to these officials, in using the Israeli 'U.S. connection.' They hope apparently that Israel could help them through its influence and its lobby in Washington, to obtain from the U.S. political, military, and economic aid" (Hadar, 1981).

From far and wide, Third World leaders have turned to Israel when they have wanted to improve their image in the United States. King Hussein of Jordan turned to Israel back in 1963 for help with the U.S. government (Zak, 1985). He was followed by a long list of leaders—the shah of Iran, Mobutu of Zaire, and the leaders of South Africa, among others.

And even mighty Japan, the economic giant of the 1980s, attempted to use Israeli connections to improve its standing with the U.S. Congress and public. According one observer, Japan's invitation to Foreign Minister Yitzhak Shamir to visit in September 1985 "has its roots in a peculiar Japanese understanding of how the American Congress works. Israeli officials believe that Tokyo's invitation to

Shamir was partly in the hope that the gesture would impress Congress, which is irritated with Japan over trade issues. . . . The Japanese simply assume that pro-Israel constituencies in the United States would either be impressed enough . . . or powerful enough to shape broader congressional attitudes toward Japan" (Alter, 1985, p. 17).

8

Israelis and Natives

s all this "out of character" for Israel? Before we can answer, we have to take a long look at the character and history of political Zionism since its inception.

Zionism was created in the late nineteenth century, against the backdrop of two unrelated phenomena that changed the face of the world: the triumph of nationalism in Europe and the parallel, but contrary, triumph of European colonialism overseas.

Zionism as a political ideal centers around the aspiration for a Jewish political sovereignty. It was born in the context of European nationalism. Zionism as a practical political objective "unquestionably fit into the great movement of European expansion in the nineteenth and twentieth centuries, the great European imperialist groundswell. There is no reason whatsoever to be surprised or even indignant at this. Except for a section (only a section) of the European socialist parties and a few rare revolutionary and liberal elements, colonization at the time was essentially taken to mean the spreading of progress, civilization, and well-being" (Rodinson, 1973, p. 42). Thus Zionism is, paradoxically, both a movement for liberation and independence, and a colonialist movement. It can be analyzed in terms both of what it has done for Jews, and what is has

225

done for (or against) others (see Cohen, 1970, 1976; Rodinson, 1973, 1982; and Waines, 1971).

Its efforts to bring the dream of the Jewish state to reality involved the Zionist movement in two related political strategies: first, an alliance with major world powers, and second, the dispossession of the native population of Palestine. When political Zionism started developing seriously, its first priority, under Theodor Herzl and his successors, was to gain legitimacy and support in the First World. The first world Zionist congress convened in 1897; twenty years later the movement won the recognition and support of Great Britain, the dominant foreign power in the Middle East, in the form of the Balfour Declaration of November 2, 1917. In another thirty years, on November 29, 1947, Zionism won its broadest support with the U.N. Partition Resolution, calling for a Jewish state in Palestine. The state came into official being on May 14, 1948, and in June 1967 became the dominant force in the region, seemingly destined to rule forever over its backward and humiliated Arab neighbors.

Zionism and Imperialism

The Zionist movement always sought to ally itself with the imperial power in control of the Middle East, be it Turkey or Britain (Halpern, 1961). This was the whole point of the Zionist political strategy of Herzl, who said in 1896, "If his majesty the Sultan were to give us Palestine, we would undertake to regulate Turkey's finances. For Europe, we would constitute a bulwark against Asia down there, we would be the advance post of civilization against barbarism" (Rodinson, 1973, p. 43). The design of offering Zionism as a useful ally in the Middle East was expressed again by Max Nordau in 1905: "The Turkish government may feel itself compelled to defend its reign in Palestine, in Syria, against its subjects by armed force. . . . In such a position, Turkey might become convinced that it may be important for her to have, in Palestine and Syria, a strong and well-organized people which, with all respect to the rights of the inhabitants living there, will resist any attack on the authority of the Sultan and defend this authority with all its might" (Avnery, 1968, p. 51).

The policy was to form an alliance with the major power in the Middle East; the problem was only to determine which power was dominant. The Ottoman Empire, an ally of Germany in World War I, was dismantled after the war, so Turkey was out of the running. Britain dominated, and the strategic value of Palestine for the empire was assumed by all Zionist leaders. Thus, Moshe Sharett wrote in 1935, "The development of air traffic has made Palestine indispensable for the British Empire; no connection with India, the Persian Gulf and Iraq is possible without it. Haifa, built with Jewish money, has become more important to them, and if they need Aqaba we'll build it up" (Flapan, 1979, p. 157).

Vladimir Jabotinsky, the leader of right-wing Zionism before World War II, was quite blunt about the alliance between Zionism and imperialism. His words, written in the 1920s and 1930s, sound as if they were spoken by Israeli leaders in the 1980s. Zionism has the "unshakable resolve to keep the whole Mediterranean in European hands. . . . The independence of Syria, for instance, is clearly and hopelessly out of the question. . . . It would . . . be understood by France, Italy, and Britain alike as a most fateful attempt against the security of their colonial empires. . . . In every East-West conflict, we will always be on the side of the West, for the West has represented a more superior culture than the East over the last thousand years, after the destruction of the Baghdad Caliphate by the Mongols . . . and we today are the most prominent and loyal bearers of the culture. . . . Our interest lies in expanding the British empire even further than intended by the British themselves. . . . We can never support the Arab movement which is at present opposed to us, and we are heartily pleased at every mishap to this movement, not only in neighbouring Transjordan and Syria but also in Morocco" (Brenner, 1984, pp. 75–77).

The decline of the West was a major threat to the success of Zionism, and Jabotinsky was concerned about it as early as 1931: "England is no longer inspired by her old lust for building and leading. And what we ask of the English is, indeed, this lust and resolution, the capacity for more courageous, and more creative action. . . . England is becoming continental! Not long ago the prestige of the English ruler of the 'colored' colonies stood very high. Hindus, Arabs, Malays were conscious of his superiority and obeyed, not unprotestingly, yet completely. The whole scheme of training of the future rulers was built on the principle 'carry yourself so that the inferior will feel your unobtainable superiority in every motion.' But a decline of imperialist instinct is felt in Englishmen. . . . This lessening of the taste for imperialist scope is revealed in various ways—in the indifference with which the emancipation of Egypt was received, in the lack of concern at the prospect of the loss of India and Ireland. This does not mean that all is lost. In five or ten years all this may change. England may still reeducate her proconsuls. The imperial appetite may flame up anew, because this is a very powerful and gifted people" (Brenner, 1984, p. 77).

But England was exhausted after World War II, and its empire was coming unglued. "Ben-Gurion . . . believed that an alliance between the Zionist movement and a great power was the *sine qua non* for its success. Ben-Gurion foresaw the decline of Great Britain as the decisive factor in the Middle East, and the emergence of the United States as a global superpower, and eventually switched the alignment of the Zionist movement from Great Britain to the United States" (Flapan, 1979, p. 131). So Israel was launched on its statehood with strong Western allies.

Those who express surprise at Israel's policies in the Third World usually don't know much about Zionism and its history. Some would suggest that this pattern of Israeli involvement reflects the rise of right-wing Zionism, which came to power in Israel in 1977. According to this thesis, what we have observed is a temporary aberration, reflecting the victory of right-wing forces in domestic Israeli politics, and the leadership of such individuals as Menahem Begin and Ariel Sharon. As soon as Labor is in control again, policies will change, and there will be nothing more to explain.

Even a cursory look at the facts shows that this explanation is false. The pattern of involvement we have been discussing began while Labor was firmly in power in Israel. The right-wing Likud bloc came into power only in 1977, when most of the specific relationships with Third World regimes discussed here were quite well developed. It was a Labor government that was allied with France in the 1950s and supported Portuguese colonialism in Africa in the 1960s. Labor governments cemented the alliance with South Africa and with Somoza. And these Labor governments usually included Mapam, a party that is considered by many to be socialist and progressive, and until recently called itself Marxist. Mapam was in the government when Vorster visited Jerusalem, and its ministers had first-hand knowledge of what the alliance with South Africa means.

Furthermore, in the fall of 1984, Shimon Peres, a Laborite, became the prime minister of Israel, under a national-unity government with the Likud. If a return to power by Labor makes a difference, this difference was not noticed anywhere in the Third World, where the emissaries of Israel were still doing what they had done before. But the government, of course, was a government of national unity, and indeed one basis for unity was a perfect consensus on policies in the Third World. While the Labor Party was in opposition between 1977 and 1984, it never criticized the government on this issue. The Labor Party continued its own ties with the ruling party in South Africa even while in opposition, and also continued its support for the South Africa–Israel alliance—which was, after all, the creation of successive Labor governments.

The idea that Israel's world war is a temporary right-wing aberration is based on the myth of the golden past of Zionism. According to this myth, Zionism was once a progressive and humanistic movement, and only in recent years (since 1977, or perhaps 1967) has it changed, becoming a reactionary, colonialist one. A corollary of this idea, often expressed in Israel and within the Zionist movement, is the longing for the good old days of Zionist purity and progressive idealism.

But Zionism has clear, inescapable ideological implications in terms of dealing with the Third World. Zionism meant the creation of Jewish sovereignty in Palestine through settlement and political domination. Thus by definition it entails an attack on the indigenous population, and a confrontation with the Third World.

Israel's confrontation with the Third World did not start in Central America or South Africa, and it did not start ten years ago. It started a hundred years ago, with the beginnings of Zionist colonization in Palestine. The confrontation with the Third World did not start in Manila or Managua. It started in the Middle East. How can Israelis escape from their immediate reality, and act differently in the rest of the world from the way they act in the Middle East?

To illustrate the basic attitude of Israeli leaders toward the Third

World, we need to look at one of the lesser sidelights of Israeli foreign relations. It was one of the ideas that grew out of the French-Israeli alliance, and it originated with the thirty-five-year-old director-general of the Israeli Defense Ministry in 1959, Shimon Peres, the man responsible for running the alliance on the Israeli side. He made friends with many French leaders, among them Jacques Soustelle, the right-wing champion of French colonialism in Algeria and elsewhere. In 1959, Soustelle was a member of de Gaulle's cabinet, in charge of overseas territories.

One of them is Guiana, a French colony in South America. By French law, it is considered an overseas district of metropolitan France—a part of the mainland somehow separated from it by several thousand miles of ocean. How did Peres become interested in Guiana? "It all began during the visit of a French delegation to Israel at the beginning of 1959. One of the members of the delegation was the representative of French Guiana, France's colony in South America. In his boundless enthusiasm for what he was seeing in Israel, he remarked to Peres: 'Listen, if we were tied to Israel, instead of France, we'd be in a different situation.' Peres later mentioned this to Soustelle, adding: 'Do you really need Guiana? We could do wonders there!' If Soustelle could do without Guiana, why would Peres want it? He envisioned an area of 90,000 square kilometers, rich in natural resources, with a total population of some 30,000 people, and could not bear the thought of such waste. But there was also another, more important reason for Peres' attraction to Guiana. It was associated with the EEC, and Peres hoped that through it Israel would be able to make inroads into the European community. Another reason was that Guiana was rich in cypress trees, from whose wood orange crates were made, and oranges were Israel's leading export. Peres therefore suggested to Soustelle that Israel lease Guiana from France for a period of thirty to forty years, or, alternatively, establish a joint development company with France. Who would do the developing? A few thousand Jews, who would be sent there to establish a Jewish society linked to Israel—something like a branch of the Jewish state" (Golan, 1982, p. 77).

To check on the feasibility of the Peres plan, a seven-man Israeli delegation went to Guiana, and returned with a report and a film.

When the film was shown to the Israeli cabinet, its members reacted with horror, one of them referring to the idea as "colonialism," and nothing ever came of it. Today it is mentioned only in biographies of Peres, who became prime minister of Israel in 1984.

This strange exemplary tale of modern colonialism reflects a certain way of seeing the world and of seeing people in the world. In a sense, the Peres Guiana plan is a replay of the Zionist plan in Palestine. It is identical with nineteenth-century colonization schemes for Africa and South America. From the Zionist point of view, Palestine in the late nineteenth century was an empty wasteland, waiting to be "developed" and changed. The country—along with the natives, if there were any—was simply a natural resource to be exploited, an element of nature. The natives of Guiana were not part of the Peres plan. They were not even mentioned. Likewise, the natives of Palestine had no place in the Zionist vision. Their existence, and their rights, were simply not part of the equation. It is this worldview that Peres was extending in South America, in his vision for the future of Guiana. It is the same worldview that Israeli leaders extend to the Third World of today.

Mercenaries, Official and Otherwise

The most telling piece of evidence in all of this is the actual participation of Israelis in the struggles of the Third World—as mercenaries with the blessing of their government, or as official military advisers. This is the real involvement, when Israelis take sides and fight alongside their hosts. Being there and facing the liberation movements of the world is immediate, unlike the sale of military hardware or the transfer of technology. It does take some identification to fight somebody else's war.

Israeli mercenaries have become notorious; according to some estimates there are over a thousand such freelancers trading in blood and money, usually working for regimes that do not have popular support. Why have Israelis become so prominent among mercenaries? Most soldiers of fortune today come from Britain, the United States, West Germany, and Israel. In terms of population, Israel is the nation most overrepresented in the marketplace of mercenaries. Why did

Israelis win this world record? There may be two reasons. First, many Israelis do have military expertise. Second, they share the worldview and morality of other mercenaries.

Letting private citizens operate as freelance mercenaries is a good way for Israel to intervene without getting officially involved. Retired Israeli officers, using contacts acquired while in uniform, have been selling their services to several regimes, not without the knowledge and support of the government. We can see a pattern in the private involvement of former Israeli military and government officials in Third World regimes. After retiring from their official positions, these individuals turn up in the Philippines, Haiti, or Ciskei, operating as private businessmen, offering both civilian and military services.

In most normal societies, mercenaries are a low form of life, despised and scorned, the dregs of their societies and their military establishments. But Israeli mercenaries are unique; they come from among the finest of Israel's military. One cannot find former American generals or colonels making their living as mercenaries. The Israelis who operate as mercenaries in the Third World are the cream of the crop, part of the old-boy network of the Israeli elite, part of a success ideal presented in the media. The fact is that Israeli mercenaries, wherever they are in the Third World, do represent their society, and do fulfill a national mission. They receive their assignment through connections developed officially and formally, while they are still in government service.

Let us imagine the flesh-and-blood individuals involved in these events. Let us give them names, which are likely to be the right ones in some cases, such as Danny, Ronny, Gideon. Let us imagine Danny and Gideon in Guatemala, the Philippines, or Namibia. What is going through their minds when they are involved in the defense of the "free world," helping local dictators, whom they barely know and barely trust, to survive? Are they pleased with what they are doing? Presumably there is a meeting of minds that makes cooperation possible. What is it based on? What do they share? The individuals involved are nice guys, the best and the brightest. They are devoted, cool, and brave. They are tough and resilient. They can fight and they can inspire.

A profile of an Israeli mercenary in the Philippines was presented in the magazine *Monitin* (Shahak-Bufman, 1986). Yitzhak Bahar is one of those who train local private armies, a vegetarian with the looks of a movie star and a book of poetry to his credit. He describes his job as a "professional shooting instructor in Third World countries," which is certainly accurate. His poetry includes moving portrayals of life in the Philippines: poverty, prostitution, hopelessness, and "blood merchants." "I am too small to change the world / I am not the creator," he writes. Bahar does not want to admit that he is involved in changing the world, or rather preventing it from changing.

An individual will not readily carry out a policy if it does not agree with his worldview. Israeli mercenaries were not recruited on dark street corners and smoke-filled bars. They arrived at their destinations through a system that has much to do with the Israeli state, and most of them are emissaries of the state, not real soldiers of fortune. There is a connection and a similarity between oppression in one particular situation and oppressions in other situations, geographically and culturally remote. How does an Israeli officer feel in Namibia, or while training South Africans in counterinsurgency? The answer is "right at home."

The Israeli perspective, which is shared by South Africans, is that of the settler-colonialist, a determined fighter who knows that war is his way of life. The identification of Israelis with Europeans fighting against the natives is natural: this is exactly their lot in this world. A colonialist worldview serves as the basis for whatever dealings Israel has with the Third World. This colonialist way of thinking, which views the natives as an element of nature to be controlled or exploited at will, raw material to be shaped by powerful masters, was normal and accepted in Europe of the nineteenth century. It can still be found among many Israelis because of Israel's history and present realities.

Israeli Politics and the Third World

So far we have mainly considered the actions and policies of the Israeli government. What about Israeli citizens? How does their view of the world relate to what their government is doing? Does the government truly represent the people in this case? How is the Israeli government able to do all of these things?

In Israel today, there is no opposition to speak of when it comes to Israel's global strategic role. There is no human-rights lobby to oppose military involvement in Guatemala, Haiti, or South Africa. There are no angry editorials or pickets when leaders of repressive Third World regimes come on official visits. The 1982 signing of a treaty of cultural cooperation and exchange with Haiti aroused no interest whatsoever. When Israeli military advisers are training UNITA forces in Walvis Bay, the Knesset has nothing to say about such matters, which in any case are defined as classified military business. The "Peace Now" marchers would not dream of demonstrating against Israeli involvement in Guatemala, Haiti, or the Philippines. As far as the Israeli public is concerned, this is a non-issue.

The extent of Israeli intervention in the Third World War is well known in Israel, but it has not become an issue for public debate. Very few individuals have tried to draw attention to this issue; since they all come from the small group of Israeli progressives who support equal rights for the Palestinians, they do not have much of a following. A few nonconformists—journalists such as Yuri Avneri, Haim Baram, Yoav Karny, Amnon Kapeliouk; Knesset members Matityahu Peled and Muhamad Miari—these were the only voices raised in the wilderness. The response was less than lukewarm: there was simply no response at all.

Israeli intervention in Central America has been particularly well publicized. Has that prompted any opposition in Israel to the government's policies? No—the truth is that in Israel there is no significant opposition on foreign-policy issues, and this is no exception. "Occasionally, opposition members from the Zionist Left and the Communists have criticized governmental policy. . . . However, Labor Alignment was not willing to sponsor an individual motion by one of its members calling for a cessation of sales" (Kaufman, 1984, p. 43)

Knesset member Dov Zakin, of Mapam, the left-Zionist party, sought in March 1982 to propose a bill that would forbid arms sales to dictatorial regimes. In his presentation before the Knesset caucus of the Labor Alignment, of which Mapam was then a partner, Zakin specifically mentioned South Africa, El Salvador, Nicaragua (under Somoza), and Guatemala. His proposed bill received no support at the caucus, and was never presented to the Knesset (*Al Hamishmar,* 1982).

The Progressive List for Peace, a new Israel-Palestinian party that won two seats in the 1984 elections, has actively tried to raise questions of Third World involvements in the Knesset—not surprising from a group that has had contacts with the PLO and calls for establishing a Palestinian state. The attempts failed, though, for lack of support from any other party. On October 24, 1984, MK Muhamad Miari proposed an urgent plenary discussion of the proposed visit by the South African foreign minister. On November 14, he proposed a discussion of Israeli aid to the contras. On November 4, 1985, and again on November 11, MK Matityahu Peled proposed a discussion of Israeli contacts with South Africa. On November 18 he proposed discussion of military sales to South Africa. All these motions were turned down without discussion or support. On December 4, Peled presented a motion for debate on the broader question of "Israeli aid to repressive regimes in the Third World," including Ethiopia, Iran, Guatemala, and South Africa. The motion was easily defeated.

Do the Knesset and the government represent the will of the majority of Israeli citizens? Yes—the reason only a few voices are heard opposing Israeli involvements in the Third World is that very few Israelis are opposed. If policies in South Africa or Central America were unrepresentative, the government would hear about it. Israeli citizens do have ways of expressing their disapproval: they can demonstrate, or at least write letters to the editor. They can do a lot more.

Israeli public reactions must be examined in the context of Israeli political culture. And this culture is radically different from Western political culture. A society built on Zionism is bound to have a political culture that is different from the Western democracies, because Israel is not a Western democracy. To understand Israeli behavior we must understand the Israeli worldview, a view built on past experiences and future wishes. Israelis are rightly concerned about the mortality of their nation. They are obsessed with their own survival, and no one can blame them for this. That obsession is their starting point for any consideration of the outside world. The only issue is whether something improves Israel's chances to survive.

This becomes clear when we observe Israeli reactions to the crisis of apartheid. While the rest of the world followed the anti-apartheid struggle closely, and in the West, public demonstrations and calls for divestment were the order of the day, none of this could be observed in Israel. If its citizens were opposed to apartheid and at one with those fighting to end it, most of them kept it a secret, and did it quite well.

When we observe that Israelis are bedfellows of Duvalier in Haiti and Pinochet in Chile, we ask ourselves in amazement how they feel, how they can get involved—but we are using the wrong frame of reference and comparison. We are implicitly comparing them to Western Europeans or Americans of similar ages and backgrounds, and we assume that certain values and ideals are shared among most citizens of Western democracies—among which we include Israel. But while these ideals may be shared by most Western publics, they are definitely not held by most Israelis. Israelis simply do not share the Western liberal ideology, taken for granted in most Western media. Once we realize this, the presence of Israelis in Haiti, Chile, or Ciskei is no longer amazing, and requires little explanation.

The idea of liberation for Third World groups threatens the very essence of Zionism. Concepts of human rights are too dangerous for the Israeli political system. Any serious examination of Israeli policies in the Third World must inevitably lead to a radical critique of Zionism and its political aims. This explains why such an examination is not likely to be undertaken in Israel, or to gain a following there.

Discussing the question from a purely moral point of view raises the prospect (or danger) of a wider discussion of moral issues, leading to some basic questions about the moral justification of Zionism. And those must be avoided at all costs. Pursuing them will lead to the complete undermining of Zionism. If you become sensitized to injustice, you will be forced to change your behavior and the power arrangements around you. This is too dangerous. The injustice done to the Palestinians is so clear and so striking that it cannot be openly discussed, and any discussion of what Israel has been doing in the Third World is certain to lead to an examination of the rights of Palestinians. If you start talking about equality, liberation, and self-determination, you will soon encounter a problem: you must then consider these ideals in the relationship between Israel and the Palestinians. Small wonder, then, that Israel is opposed to liberation movements in the Third World.

Few would wonder why white South Africans usually don't support such movements. Political discourse in Israel is similarly limited by the need to avoid discussion based on basic moral principles. Such discussion, even if it starts with a seemingly remote and morally simple question, such as apartheid, will end up dealing with the basic question of the morality of Zionism. If you start asking questions about the morality of events and acts in Haiti or Ciskei, you will end up asking questions about the morality of actions in the Galilee. Thus, any discussion of moral principles in public life is avoided; decisions and attitudes are based instead on realpolitik. Thus, helping to maintain the existing order in Haiti or Ciskei reinforces the desirable order from Zionism's point of view. If the whole system is seen as unjust, all those who take part in it must be accomplices, so any discussion of moral issues is simply to be avoided.

What Israelis pride themselves on, and indeed make a cult of, is their "refreshing" lack of hypocrisy and their readiness to tell it like it is: "Everybody is out for himself in this world and nobody really cares about us, so we have to be selfish, like the rest of the world." "That's the way the world is." "You have got to be tough to survive." "Everybody else is a hypocrite!" These are the claims often heard from Israelis who are asked about Israeli activities in the Third World. They are quick to denounce the rest of the world as hypocritical when issues of human rights and universal justice are discussed. In that they are quite similar to white South Africans.

The cynicism of Israeli political discourse, which shocks many observers, is expressed through the absence of any moral considerations in discussion of policy. The arguments for or against any given step are always purely pragmatic: "We can gain a political advantage." "It may improve our standing with the United States." "We can make money." These are the only arguments heard. If anybody tries to introduce moral considerations, the standard Israeli responses are, "If we don't do it, somebody else will," "Why should we worry about the rest of the world?" or "Don't be a baby. That's how the world operates."

It is true that in many other countries moral arguments are often used dishonestly and hypocritically, but in Israel they are simply unvoiced and unheard. There is something to be said in favor of hypocrisy and evasiveness—their presence at least indicates an uneasiness, and a concern about moral issues. If you need to pay lip service to moral considerations, it shows that your conscience is bothering you, or at the very least that you are concerned about the reactions of others.

Israeli Experience
and the Third World

A significant part of the Israeli self-image is an ideal of toughness, which is contrasted with the softness of the Diaspora Jews. The creation of a separate new Israeli identity was accompanied by many expressions of contempt for any form of weakness or moral sensitivity. How could Israelis identify with the weak and the dispossessed? Whose side can they be on? What does one get from identifying with the weak, the poor, and the oppressed?

How can people with the Holocaust and endless persecution in their history do all of this? This question, though commonly asked, shows a great deal of ignorance about the history of Zionism and Israel today. First, while it is true that Zionism was created in response to anti-Semitism and the persecution of Jews, it was started long before the Holocaust. Second, for most Israelis today, the Holocaust is something that happened two generations ago in Europe, and not part of their experience or even their parents'. Most Israelis today were born in Israel, and the majority of their parents are non-European. Holocaust survivors are a distinct minority. Existence determines consciousness, and the existence, the immediate experience, of most Israelis does not include the Holocaust. What it does include is the life of settler-colonialists and the constant war against the natives. The Jewish history of persecution and oppression is remote. The war against the Palestinians is close and permanent. If Israelis know about oppression, it is mostly from the oppressor's end of the gunsight.

The Israeli ethos, like the dominant American one, is one of identifying with the winners, and showing no feeling for the losers. Never identify with the weak, because you don't want to be like them. This seems to be the guiding spirit of Israeli life. If there is one thing Israelis don't want to be it is losers. The most powerful condemnation is reserved for those who dare to be losers, for those who end up being the victims of the powerful and the wily.

Seeing the Israelis as former or present victims is totally unfounded in reality. The key to understanding the Israeli military advisers in South Africa, the Philippines, and Guatemala, is realizing that they have never been victims and they apparently don't understand what being a victim means. On the other hand, they know quite well what it means to be oppressors, because that is what they have been all their lives. An Israeli-born officer who is thirty-five years old has not been a victim under any circumstances. The only reality he knows is that of being dominant, in control, on top of other people.

So Israelis have two reasons for not identifying with victims: first, victimhood isn't within their experience; second, it is contrary to the ideal of being tough. If we admire toughness and success, there is nothing to admire in the masses of the Third World. Israelis view the people of the Third World with contempt—contempt because they are mostly peasants, weak, and oppressed. There is no pity in this contempt, no compassion for the victims. The people of the Third World are the victims, the weak, and the helpless. They find no sympathy in Israel.

When Israelis look at the people of the Third World, they see the Arabs of Gaza. Israeli travelers, coming back from trips to Asia, Africa, or Latin America, compare the poverty and squalor they have seen to the poorest and ugliest area of the occupied territories: Gaza. This name is heard over and over again in their descriptions. Gaza serves Tel-Aviv as a convenient source of cheap labor. In 1986, the Gaza population stood at 525,000, and the density at 2,150 per square kilometer (in Israel it is 186). The Gaza population will reach 900,000 in fifteen years, while their living space is expected to shrink, because Israel has expropriated a third of the narrow strip. Most able-bodied Gazans, starting sometimes at age eight, work in Israel, at wages which are 40 percent below average Israeli pay. They pay income tax and social security tax—without being entitled to any benefits, since they are defined as nonresidents. Gaza is Tel-Aviv's Soweto.

The Third World is Gaza, and Gaza is the Third World. In the Israeli consciousness Gaza has become the symbol of helplessness and squalor, but there is no sympathy for the denizens of Gaza, for they are the enemy. There is no need to travel to Latin America in order to experience the problems of the Third World. The Third World, for

Israelis, is not an abstraction or a distant rumor. They live with it and they fight against it every day, right at home.

Any attempt to understand the Israeli view of the world has to start with the Israeli view of the Palestinians, because the Israeli view of the Third World is an extension of the Israeli view of the Arabs. Israel is in constant confrontation with the Arab Middle East, and therefore with the whole Third World, just as the Zionist movement that created it has always been in confrontation with the Arabs of the Middle East, and Palestine in particular. The war with the Third World, in which Israel is so actively involved, is often a war over the rights of natives in their homelands—the rights of natives in South Africa, in Namibia, in Guatemala. And these are all tied, naturally, to the rights of the natives of Palestine, whose existence and identity have been denied for so long. Within Israel itself, the struggle between the First World and the Third World is reproduced through an internal political system that preserves the privileges of Jews and denies equal political power to Arabs.

There is a basic fear in the First World—a fear of the masses of the Third World—the hungry, the poor, the oppressed—who are going to rise one day and demand their share in the world's wealth. These masses have only numbers on their side, and that is the basic source of fear. These huge numbers may be too much to stop when the day comes. Israelis, on their own smaller scale, are afraid of the Arab masses, the Arab millions who they fear will rise and engulf them one day. This fear is expressed time and again in Israel. When Israelis look at the Third World they see an extension of the Middle East masses, and they are worried.

What has marked the experience of being an Israeli is fighting—constantly, without any hope for eventual peace. War becomes not only a way of life, but a way of viewing life. There can be no other outcome to settler colonialism. It leads to a worldview that can only be described as cutthroat: seeing the social world of relations between people and between peoples as a jungle in which only the fittest survive. The foundation of the Israeli worldview is a large dose of what is often called social Darwinism, a vision of a world divided into the rulers and the ruled, the dominators and the others.

With whom could we expect the Israelis to identify? With the black-liberation groups of Rhodesia? With the Sandinistas fighting against Somoza? With Mao's Long March? With the African National Congress? It would take a great deal of ignorance, naiveté, or deliberate deception to assume that. Israelis do not often think about events that do not touch them directly, but when they do, they are likely to identify with the conservative, oppressive forces.

Epilogue

Many readers like books to have happy endings. This one can't.

Our journey around the Third World has led us to an unpleasant but unavoidable conclusion. Vorster's visit to Jerusalem was not an odd aberration but a symptom, a sign of significant underlying forces, and following the coincidences and connections has led us to something we really needed to know about Zionism and its place in history. We have to conclude that Israel's involvement in the Third World War is no accident and no detour.

The events described here can be fully known only when secret files are opened. Some documents will come to light only when the Israeli government declassifies them after a thirty-year period. So we can see this book as a first draft and an agenda for future historians working with more sources. Many years from now, it will become clear that this book has erred on the side of caution, that Israeli complicity in Third World repression was much greater than currently appreciated.

Israel's activities in the Third World are significant reflections of the basic nature of Zionism and the state of Israel, and of the resulting Israeli society and worldview.

From Manila in the Philippines to Tegucigalpa in Honduras to Windhoek in Namibia, Israel's emissaries have been involved in a continuous war, which is truly a world war. And what enemy is Israel fighting? It is the population of the Third World, which cannot be allowed to win its revolution.

The only thing that guarantees the continuing rule of the Third World oligarchies is the suppression of any spark of independence or power among their peoples. Israeli advisers have much to offer in the technology of death and oppression, and that is why they are so much in demand. There is another reason for this demand: There are not many mercenaries in the world today, and not many governments want to find themselves in bed with the Afrikaner racists of South Africa or with Baby Doc Duvalier or with the generals in Latin America whose names so often change, but whose regimes do not. The state of Israel finds itself in such beds with every new dawn; they are, apparently, its natural place of repose. Half a century ago, Joseph Conrad described it in "Heart of Darkness" as "the conquest of the earth, which mostly means the taking of it away from those who have a different complexion or slightly flatter noses than ourselves." Israel has been taking part in that conquest. It is becoming uglier and dirtier all the time, as the natives grow more and more resistant.

The reality we have discovered is surprising only if we assume that Zionism is basically a progressive movement. My assessment of the situation is radical, because it proposes that the problem begins not with Begin, Sharon, or Peres, but with Zionism itself. Zionism is a whole that is greater than the sum of its individual leaders. The problem has very little to do with personalities and everything to do with basic principles.

There are those who, when they see Israeli jets and advisers in South Africa, start wailing and gnashing their teeth, wondering what has happened to the "humanistic Zionism" of yore. My answer is that nothing has happened: Zionism never was very humanistic in the first place. There are those, especially in the United States, who are shocked by the facts presented here. They believe that Israelis are enlightened, progressive, and humanistic; how can such paragons be engaged in all these terrible things? Israel's defenders claim that its support for reactionary regimes in the Third World occurs *despite* Zionist ideals. But is it not possible that it occurs *because of* those ideals? Our conclusion must be not only that Israelis are no more enlightened, progressive, and humanistic than anyone else, but also that there is something about Israel's history and Israelis' experience that makes them especially suitable for what they have been doing in the Third World. That something is Zionist ideology and practice.

Israel is, of course, ready to accept support from any quarter, and would be happy to have it from sources less malodorous than those it has had to rely on in recent years. But the search for support, though it may be lame, is never blind. The conscious effort to create bonds requires attention to the winds of change in the world, and these winds are seen as ominous for Israel. The decolonization and the radicalization of the Third World are viewed as dangers, and rightly so. Objectively, Israel should be worried about these trends. I recall once hearing the late historian J. L. Talmon being interviewed on Israeli state radio. "The tragedy of Zionism," he said, "is that it started in the age of decolonization, and not earlier." This is indeed the predicament. How can Zionism survive in a world that has doomed colonialist enterprises to extinction? Had it started earlier, its course would have run smoother.

The Palestinian national movement has to be seen as one national liberation movement among many in a postcolonial Third World. Thus we can understand why the very idea of a "national liberation movement" has become anathema in both Israel and the United States. The emergence of the natives of Palestine as a political force and their resistance to Zionist colonization has become a growing challenge to Zionism just as it was achieving its first goal of political support and legitimacy. This challenge has been a part of a more general global development: the historical stage of decolonization. Since World War II the process has become a permanent war between the First World and the Third, raging on several fronts at the same time, sometimes flaring up, sometimes cooling down. The Middle East is one front that has been rather hot for many years. The complexities and ambiguities of the situation in the Middle East can and should be analyzed in the context of this continuing global war.

The relations between Israel and South Africa illustrate the similarities between fronts in the global war. There is an intimate alliance between the two regimes; in areas such as weapons development, it has become a complete merging of the two systems. The two countries are today the two bastions of the First World within the Third, symbols of settler colonialism—symbols recognized throughout the Third World.

The real question is one of sheer survival. Can the state of Israel, the great creation and the great achievement of political Zionism, survive while the historical forces threatening it become stronger and stronger? If it can survive, at what physical and human cost will it be? Any Israeli evaluation starts with the realization that Israel exists in the shadow of annihilation. And the answer, from Israel's point of view, is to increase its activity in the global war, against any kind of radical or anticolonialist movement. The future of Israel is so uncertain, given the growing power of its enemies, that it cannot be choosy in the means it selects for survival. It is clear that Israel will not survive without the continuing domination of the First World, so Israel is committed to maintaining that domination.

After all, what kind of world is more friendly to Israel's survival? A world where Pinochet and García Meza rule South America, or a world where radical movements have wrested control from the oligarchies? The answer is obvious: Only the former will ensure Israel's survival in the long run. It is not only that radical movements in the Third World pose a danger to Israel; it is that conservative movements everywhere promise friendship and trust, and deliver on those promises. To secure survival, everything possible is done and alliances are formed with regimes facing the same predicament.

Yet history has not been kind: Israel already has a list of extinct former allies, such as the shah of Iran, the Somozas of Nicaragua, Sálazar in Portugal, Smith in Rhodesia. By aligning itself with regimes doomed to extinction, Israel may reinforce its own feelings of doom and despair, and, moreover, may end up once again on the losing side.

The storm is fast approaching. As in the story of Job, a great wind is coming from the wilderness, ready to smite the four corners of the house. This is the nightmare Israeli leaders have when they contemplate the rise of the Third World. And nobody can claim that Israel will have an easy time of it in a world where South Africa has been replaced by the independent Republic of Azania. One can easily imagine how Azania will view Israel, and how it will treat apartheid's most enthusiastic ally.

Israel's global involvement is by this time a necessity, not a luxury. Israel's survival is tied to global processes and global structures. The rise of the Third World is the real threat to Israel's future, because in a world where liberation movements win, Israel's future looks bleak.

What, for instance, will happen in Zaire—to Israel's interests and investments, to Mobutu's mercenaries and machinery—when Mobutu is deposed? The Uzis sold by Israel will change hands, as part of an inevitable process—they always pass from those who bought them to those who win the battles against the oppressive buyers. Every case of an Uzi or a Galil changing hands from oppressor to oppressed is another tick of the historical time bomb, another letter written on the wall for Israel.

The world has become a more threatening place for Israel, despite the failure of the surrounding Arab countries to unite, despite the historic achievement of peace with Egypt. In the world of the late 1980s, while the United States has become Israel's horn of plenty, Israel's true friends may be found only among fellow members of the pariah club. Only those who fully share one's troubles can be trusted as friends—as true of nations as of people. South Africa's circumstances are most similar to Israel's; Taiwan's are only slightly less so. But Israel enjoys more international legitimacy than these others: its claims to legitimacy are recognized not only by other pariah nations, not only by the United States and its allies, but also by the Soviet Union and its allies. This is something that is often overlooked, and it may be enough of an advantage for Israel to be able to survive.

As of 1987, Israel's international situation, and its survivability, don't look bad at all. The radical Third World is mostly in retreat and disarray; in the best case it is stagnating. Reactionary regimes seem to be doing quite well, including many of Israel's friends. Nevertheless, Israel's leaders are justifiably worried.

Israel's prognosis looks good only as long as the Arab world, and the rest of the Third World, remains divided and weak. Any change in this picture bodes ill. Any victory of a national liberation movement, or of a revolutionary one, is a dangerous precedent and a dangerous inspiration for the Palestinians. The liberation movement in South Africa is one of those bad examples that have to be eliminated at any cost.

"Whose side are you on?" asks the world. "Are you just standing on the sidelines, or are you involved in the fight?" Nobody can claim to be just an innocent bystander, least of all the Israelis. We have seen that they are very much implicated in the global struggle, and cannot claim either clean hands or a clean conscience. They are engaged; they know what they are doing. Possibly the most significant phenomenon we have uncovered here is the camaraderie between Israelis and their allies, the blood-brotherhood between Israelis, South Africans, Chileans, and Taiwanese—a new class of Third World warriors. Whose side are you on? Do you really have a choice?

Israelis have answered that they don't. Confident right-wingers answer that history is on the side of the strong and the powerful. They say that the West is winning its war against the natives, and that the case of the Middle East proves it.

But there is another answer, a less confident but compelling one, that the Third World is, possibly very slowly, gaining strength, and that in the case of the Middle East, one should remember the earlier invaders who were eventually defeated by the indigenous population. The Battle of Hittin in 1187 is never far from the minds of anybody in the Middle East. This was the decisive battle in which Saladin defeated the Crusaders. Hittin is now in Israel, not far from Tiberias. There are no roadside markers to remind drivers of this historic event, to point out the nearby battlefield, still covered with forbidding black basalt. Israelis don't like to think about it, because they cannot ignore the likelihood of another Battle of Hittin.

So we can understand what Israel is doing in various remote corners of the world when we contemplate the Middle East itself and consider what Israel is doing there. Given the past and the present of Zionism in the Middle East, what else could one expect? What Israel is doing in the Third World is simply to export the Middle East experience of Zionism. This product doesn't need much adaptation to suit the export market, because the Middle East is part of the Third World, and what Israel does in such remote corners of the world as Chile and the Philippines is a direct outgrowth of what it has done at home.

What Israel has been exporting to the Third World is not just a technology of domination, but a worldview that undergirds that technology. In every situation of oppression and domination, the logic of the oppressed is pitted against the logic of the oppressor. What Israel has been exporting is the logic of the oppressor, the way of seeing the world that is tied to successful domination. What is exported is not just technology, armaments, and experience, not just expertise, but a certain frame of mind, a feeling that the Third World can be controlled and dominated, that radical movements in the Third World can be stopped, that modern Crusaders still have a future.

References

Abendroth, K. "When Learning Beats Politics." *Citizen,* September 27, 1979.

Adams, J. *The Unnatural Alliance.* London: Quartet Books, 1984.

AFP *(Agence France-Press).* "Des Israéliens Entrainent les Rebelles du MNR, Selon un Officier Mozambicain." January 1, 1984.

Africa Now. "U.S. Aids Israeli Arms for Africa." October 1983.

Africa Research Group. "David and Goliath in Africa." *Leviathan,* 1, no. 5 (September 1969).

AfricAsia. "New Israeli Advisers in Chad." February 1984.

Alfon, D. "Israel–South Africa: Business (Almost) as Usual." *Kotoret Rashit,* June 25, 1986 [Hebrew].

Al Hamishmar. "A Law to Stop Israeli Arms Sales to Dictatorial Regimes." March 7, 1982 [Hebrew].

———. "Shemtov and Sarid Congratulate Duarte on His Brave Initiative." October 19, 1984 [Hebrew].

Allon, G. "The Israeli Confidant of President Mobutu." *Haaretz,* January 30, 1984 [Hebrew].

Allon, I. "Murder by Natural Science." *Haolam Hazeh,* January 22, 1986 [Hebrew].

Alter, J. "Japan, Israel, and Congress." *Newsweek,* September 9, 1985.

Americas Watch Committee, *Rule by Fear: Paraguay After Thirty Years Under Stroessner.* New York, January 1985.

Anderson, H. "The CIA Blows an Asset." *Newsweek,* September 3, 1984.

Anderson, J. "3 Nations to Begin Cruise Missile Project." *Washington Post,* December 8, 1980.

Anderson, S., and Anderson, J. L. *Inside the League.* New York: Dodd, Mead, 1986.

Arkin, D. "Ciskei President: 'No Enemy Can Conquer Israel.' " *Maariv,* February 11, 1983 [Hebrew].

Arkin, M. "Why the SA–Israel Axis Thrives." *Sunday Times,* March 1, 1981.

References

Aronson, G. "Mixed Blessing: The Arms Industry Boom in Less-developed Lands." *Washington Post,* July 1, 1985.

Avineri, S. "Speaking Out on Apartheid." *Jerusalem Post,* August 2, 1985.

Avnery, Y. *Israel Without Zionists.* New York: Macmillan, 1968.

Avriel, E. "Israel's Beginnings in Africa." M. Curtis and S. A. Gitelson (eds.), *Israel in the Third World.* New Brunswick, N.J.: Transaction Books, 1976.

Babcock, C. R. "The U.S. and Israel Are Closer than Ever." *Washington Post,* August 18, 1986.

Bachar, A. "Come Grow with Us Under South Africa's Wings." *Yediot Aharonot.* May 27, 1983 [Hebrew].

Bachar, I. "Police Suspect: Classified Anti-terror Material Was Leaked." *Maariv,* November 18, 1984 [Hebrew].

Bahbah, B. "Israelis and Central America." *Chicago Tribune,* June 21, 1983.

Bailey, M. "The Blooming of Operation Flower." *Observer,* February 2, 1986.

Bamahane. "Uzi Becomes Ruzi in Rhodesia." May 25, 1977 [Hebrew].

Bamerhav. "Racism and the Kibbutz." February 1983 [Hebrew].

Barabash, B. "The Mouse That Roared." *Hair,* October 8, 1982 [Hebrew].

Barak, Z. "Israel Persuades Its Friends in Congress to Support Military Aid to Zaire." *Yediot Aharonot,* March 8, 1983a [Hebrew].

———. "U.S. Customs Confiscate Thousands of Rifles from Israel." *Yediot Aharonot,* December 23, 1983b [Hebrew].

———. "U.S. Demands Israeli Aid to Destabilize the Regime in Nicaragua." *Yediot Aharonot,* April 22, 1984 [Hebrew].

Baram, H. "Levy and the Murderers." *Haolam Hazeh,* May 5, 1982a [Hebrew].

———. "Indonesia: A Caricature Called Elections." *Haolam Hazeh,* May 19, 1982b [Hebrew].

———. "The Death Export of Yanush Ben-Gal." *Haolam Hazeh,* August 10, 1983 [Hebrew].

Barel, Z. "New York Times: 'Israel, Saudi Arabia and China Finance Afghan Guerrillas.' " *Haaretz,* November 29, 1984 [Hebrew].

Barnet, R. J. *Intervention and Revolution.* Cleveland and New York: World Publishing, 1968.

Bar-Zohar, M. *Ben-Gurion: A Political Biography.* Tel-Aviv: Am Oved, 1977 [Hebrew].

Bayne, E. A. *Four Ways of Politics.* New York: American Universities Field Staff, 1965.

Beaton, L. "Must the Bomb Spread? The Case of India, Egypt and Israel." *Jewish Observer and Middle East Report,* January 14, 1966.

Beaton, L., and Maddox, J. *The Spread of Nuclear Weapons.* New York: Praeger, 1962.

Becker, G. "Israel Will Operate Among World Jews to Help Liberia's Economy." *Yediot Aharonot,* January 25, 1984 [Hebrew].

———. "Israel Pushes U.S. to Increase Aid to Zaire." *Yediot Aharonot,* August 9, 1985a [Hebrew].

———. "Deals with China Underground Again." *Yediot Aharonot,* November 15, 1985b [Hebrew].

Beckett, I. F. W. "The Rhodesian Army: Counter-insurgency 1972–1979." In I. F. W. Beckett and J. Pimlott (eds.), *Armed Forces and Modern Counter-Insurgency.* London: Croom Helm, 1985.

Beckett, I. F. W., and Pimlott, J. Introduction. In I. F. W. Beckett and J. Pimlott, (eds.), *Armed Forces and Modern Counter-Insurgency.* London: Croom Helm, 1985.

Behr, E. A. "CIA Reportedly Gave Israel Millions While It Was Paying Jordan's Hussein." *Wall Street Journal,* February 22, 1977.

Ben-Gurion, D. *The War Diaries of David Ben-Gurion.* Tel-Aviv: Defense Ministry, 1984 [Hebrew].

Benziman, U. "U.S. to Set Up a Fund to Finance Israeli Aid in Central America." *Haaretz,* April 20, 1984a [Hebrew].

———. "Kimche Discussed Joint Aid to Central America in U.S." *Haaretz,* April 27, 1984b [Hebrew].

———. *Sharon: An Israeli Caesar.* New York: Adama Books, 1986.

Beshir, M. O. *The Southern Sudan: From Conflict to Peace.* New York: Barnes & Noble, 1975.

Bialer, U. "The Iranian Connection in Israel's Foreign Policy—1948–1951." *Middle East Journal,* 39 (1985), pp. 292–315.

Biddle, W. "$14 Million for Guerrillas: What Could It Buy?" *New York Times,* April 17, 1985a.

———. "Salvador Official Said to Have Told of Napalm Use." *New York Times,* September 27, 1985b.

Bird, D. "Israel Won't Act Against Pretoria." *New York Times,* September 27, 1985.

Black, G. "Israeli Connection: Not Just Guns for Guatemala." *NACLA Report on the Americas,* 17, no. 1 (1983), pp. 43–45.

Blitzer, W. "Israeli, U.S. Foes Meddle in Central America." *Jewish Week,* June 24, 1983.

References

————. "U.S., Israeli Plan Joint Third World Aid Projects." *Jerusalem Post,* May 6, 1984a.

————. "Defence Pact with U.S. on the Horizon." *Jerusalem Post,* May 27, 1984b.

————. "Towards Military Ties with U.S." *Jerusalem Post,* June 3, 1984c.

Bloch, J. "Israel's New Openings in Africa." *Middle East,* January 1985.

Bloch, J., and Fitzgerald, P. *British Intelligence and Covert Action.* London: Junction Books, 1983.

Bloch, J., and Weir, A. "The Adventures of the Brothers Kimche." *Middle East,* April 1982.

Blumenkrantz, Z. "Israelis Still Leaving for South African Tours." *Haaretz,* September 2, 1985a [Hebrew].

————. "Chile and Israel Decide to Increase Tourism Cooperation." *Haaretz,* September 4, 1985b [Hebrew].

————. "An Engraving Exhibit of Artists from Chile to Open in Bat-Yam." *Haaretz,* September 19, 1985c [Hebrew].

Brecher, M. *The Foreign Policy System of Israel.* New Haven: Yale University Press, 1972.

————. *Decisions in Israel's Foreign Policy.* London: Oxford University Press, 1974.

Brenner, L. *The Iron Wall.* London: Zed Press, 1984.

Breytenbach, B. *The True Confessions of an Albino Terrorist.* London: Faber and Faber, 1984.

Brilliant, J. "Lesotho Minister Complains: 'Israel Aids S. African Phony Black States.' " *Jerusalem Post,* September 19, 1984.

Brisset, C. "Un Rapport de l'UNICEF: Quinze Millions d'Enfants Morts en 1983." *Le Monde,* December 19, 1983.

Brittain, V. "Ghana Government Claims to Have Thwarted New Coup." *Observer,* April 15, 1983.

Buckley, T. *Violent Neighbors.* New York: Times Books, 1984.

Bunce, P. L. "The Growth of South Africa's Defense Industry and Its Israeli Connection." *Royal United Services Institute,* June 1984.

Business Week. "Israel: The Growing Trade Link with South Africa." May 22, 1978.

Buthelezi, M. G. "My Israeli Experience." Address to a dinner of the South Africa Zionist Federation, Johannesburg, September 5, 1985.

Butterfield, F. "Taiwan Forces Reportedly Buy Israeli Missiles." *New York Times,* April 6, 1977.

Cantarow, E. "The Secret War in East Timor." *Mother Jones,* May 1979.

Cashman, G. F. "Showing the Third World the Way." *Jerusalem Post Magazine,* September 26, 1984.

Cashmore, E. *Rastaman.* London: Allen and Unwin, 1979.

Cervenka, Z., and Rogers, B. *The Nuclear Axis.* New York: Times Books, 1978.

Chee, C. H. "Singapore." In Z. H. Ahmad and H. Crouch (eds.), *Military-Civilian Relations in South-East Asia.* Singapore: Oxford University Press, 1985.

Chomsky, N. *Turning the Tide.* Boston: South End Press, 1986.

Christian, S. *Nicaragua: Revolution in the Family.* New York: Random House, 1985.

———. " 'All the People Are with Me,' Chilean Leader Says." *New York Times,* September 13, 1986.

Churba, J. *The American Retreat.* Chicago: Regnery Gateway, 1984.

CIA (Central Intelligence Agency). *Israel: Foreign Intelligence and Security Services.* Washington, D.C., March 1979.

Clapham, C. *Third World Politics: An Introduction.* London: Croom Helm, 1985.

Cody, E. "Sharon to Discuss Arms Sales in Honduras." *Washington Post,* December 7, 1982.

———. "Salvador, Israel Set Closer Ties." *Washington Post,* August 17, 1983.

Cohen, A. *Israel and the Arab World.* New York: Funk and Wagnalls, 1970.

———. *Israel and the Arab World.* Boston: Beacon, 1976.

———. "The Civil War in Nicaragua." *Al Hamishmar,* July 20, 1979 [Hebrew].

Connell, D. "Protecting South Africa's Fledgling Grass-roots Democracy." *Christian Science Monitor,* April 9, 1986.

Conrad, J. "Heart of Darkness." In *Youth and Two Other Stories.* Garden City, N.Y.: Doubleday, Page, 1925.

Cooley, J. K. "Ten More Nations May Have Nuclear Arms on the Drawing Board—if Not in Hand." *Christian Science Monitor,* June 6, 1985.

Coone, T. "Israel's Dangerous Exports." *New Statesman,* May 9, 1980.

Cowell, A. "Four Rebel Units Sign Anti-Soviet Pact." *New York Times,* June 6, 1985.

Crosbie, E. *The Tacit Alliance.* Princeton: Princeton University Press, 1974.

Crossette, B. "Sri Lanka Buys Arms to Fight Rebels." *New York Times,* May 20, 1985.

References

Cuevas, F. "Nicaragua: Israeli Role 'Worrisome.' " *Philadelphia Inquirer,* December 9, 1982.

Dabat, A., and Lorenzano, A. *Argentina: The Malvinas and the End of Military Rule.* London: Verso Editions, 1984.

Daly, R. R. *Selous Scouts: Top Secret War.* Alberton, South Africa: Calagos, 1982.

Dan, U. "SWAPO, Afrikaner, Bush-War." *Monitin,* January 1982 [Hebrew].

Dankner, A. "Our Man over There." *Haaretz,* February 26, 1982 [Hebrew].

Davar. "8,300 Tourists from Israel to South Africa in 1980." April 28, 1981 [Hebrew].

Dayan, M. *Milestones.* Tel-Aviv: Idanim, 1976 [Hebrew].

Debusmann, B. "After Embassy Flap, a Look at Israel's Latin Arms Role." *Philadelphia Inquirer* (Reuters), April 24, 1984.

Decalo, S. "Afro-Israel Technical Cooperation: Patterns of Setbacks and Successes." In M. Curtis and S. A. Gitelson (eds.), *Israel in the Third World.* New Brunswick, N.J.: Transaction Books, 1976

Deming, A. "Family Quarrels." *Newsweek,* October 1, 1979.

de Villiers, L. *Secret Information.* Cape Town: Tafelberg, 1980.

Dickey, C. "Salvadoran Colonel Turning Rebels' Tactics Against Them." *Washington Post,* June 21, 1982.

————. *With the Contras: A Reporter in the Wilds of Nicaragua.* New York: Simon and Shuster, 1985.

Diederich, B. *Somoza and the Legacy of U.S. Involvement in Central America.* New York: Dutton, 1981.

Dillon, J., and Anderson, J. L. "Who's Behind the Aid to the Contras." *Nation,* October 6, 1984.

Dingeman, J. "Covert Operations in Central and Southern Africa." In Western Massachusetts Association of Concerned African Scholars (ed.), *U.S. Military Involvement in Southern Africa.* Boston: South End Press, 1979.

Dishon, A. "Israelis Investing Huge Sums in S.A." *Yediot Aharonot,* June 18, 1984a [Hebrew].

————. "10 Israeli Investors Starting Plants in South Africa." *Yediot Aharonot,* June 21, 1984b [Hebrew].

————. "Bophuthatswana Wall to Wall." *Yediot Aharonot,* June 24, 1984c [Hebrew].

Dodenhoff, G. H. "The Congo: A Case Study of Mercenary Employment." *Naval War College Review,* 21 (1969), pp. 44–70.

Dori, I. "Hasty Trip by Dov Tavori to South Africa Creates a Storm." *Hair,* June 5, 1981a [Hebrew].

———. "A Mission to South Africa Paralyzes Sports in Ramat-Gan." *Hair,* September 25, 1981b [Hebrew].

Duek, N. "A Man's Way." *Yediot Aharonot,* May 16, 1986 [Hebrew].

Dunkerley, J. *The Long War.* London: Junction Books, 1982.

Economist. "The Israeli Connection." November 5, 1977.

———. "New Scramble for Africa." September 19, 1981.

Edelist, R. "Very Close." *Monitin,* February 1986 [Hebrew].

Egozi, A. "Haiti Buys Anti-aircraft Guns from Israel." *Yediot Aharonot,* December 7, 1984 [Hebrew].

———. "Israelis for Hire." *Yediot Aharonot,* April 5, 1985 [Hebrew].

Eldar, A. "A Senior Official from Sri Lanka Met with Kimche in Jerusalem." *Haaretz,* August 21, 1984a [Hebrew].

———. "Israel South Africa Connections Today at the Rabin-Botha Meeting." *Haaretz,* November 6, 1984b [Hebrew].

———. "The Blunt Visit by Botha." *Haaretz,* November 9, 1984c [Hebrew].

———. "Foreign Public Relations." *Haaretz,* November 8, 1985 [Hebrew].

Eliason, M. "Israel Seeks to Fix Broken Ties with Black African Countries." Associated Press, August 20, 1983.

Enfoprensa. "De Manera Espontánea EU, Israel y Argentina han Proporcionado Ayuda Militar a Guatemala." September 7, 1984.

Erez, Y. "How We Saved the U.S. Money." *Maariv Weekend Magazine,* February 17, 1984 [Hebrew].

Eshed, H. *Who Gave the Order?* Jerusalem: Idanim, 1979 [Hebrew].

Evans, R., and Novak, R. "The CIA Secret Subsidy to Israel." *Washington Post,* February 24, 1977.

———. "Israel's Zaire Connection." *Washington Post,* March 4, 1983.

Eytan, E. "Mobutu Expects Israeli Support, Aided by World and U.S. Jewry." *Yediot Aharonot,* June 7, 1982 [Hebrew].

———. "Israel Sold Arms to Iran—Including 50 Ground-to-Ground Missiles." *Yediot Aharonot,* July 13, 1983a [Hebrew].

———. "Israelis Who Sold Arms to Iran Published the Receipts in a French Weekly." *Yediot Aharonot,* July 27, 1983b [Hebrew].

———. "Under the Embargo, Arms Were Smuggled from France to Israel in Diplomatic Pouches." *Yediot Aharonot,* June 12, 1986 [Hebrew].

Eytan, W. *The First Ten Years: A Diplomatic History of Israel.* London: Weidenfeld and Nicolson, 1958.

Faro, D. "Israel Doing U.S. Dirty Work." *Guardian,* October 19, 1983.

Farrell, W. E. "South African Link to Israel Grows." *New York Times,* August 18, 1976.

Feron, J. "Israelis Honor Atom Scientist." *New York Times,* May 14, 1966.

References

Fishman, A. "What Did We Do Wrong?" *Al Hamishmar,* March 26, 1985a [Hebrew].

———. "Made in Israel." *Al Hamishmar,* June 25, 1985b [Hebrew].

Flapan, S. *Zionism and the Palestinians.* London: Croom Helm, 1979.

Foy, C. "The Grim Reality Behind South Africa's Ruthless Terror Team." *New African,* October 1982.

Franck, T. M. *Nation Against Nation.* New York: Oxford University Press, 1985.

Frankel, P. H. *Pretoria's Praetorians.* New York: Cambridge University Press, 1984.

Frenkel, S. "Any Ism You May Like." *Haolam Hazeh,* February 20, 1980 [Hebrew].

———. "The Secret Visit." *Haolam Hazeh,* March 2, 1983a [Hebrew].

———. "Thou Shalt Sell Arms." *Haolam Hazeh,* August 31, 1983b [Hebrew].

Fried, J. L., Gettelman, M. E., Levenson, D. T., and Peckenham, N. *Guatemala in Rebellion.* New York: Grove Press, 1983.

Friedman, M. "Let the Protesters Themselves Divest." *New York Times,* May 16, 1986.

Friedman, T. L. "Israel and China Quietly Forge Trade Links." *New York Times,* July 22, 1985a.

———. "Zulu Leader Sets Primary Demands." *New York Times,* August 14, 1985b.

Gann, L. H., and Duignan, P. *Why South Africa Will Survive.* New York: St. Martin's, 1981.

Gelb, L. H. "Israel Said to Step Up Latin Role, Offering Arms Seized in Lebanon." *New York Times,* December 17, 1982.

Geldenhuys, D. *The Diplomacy of Isolation.* Johannesburg: Macmillan South Africa, 1984.

Getegno, I. "To Dance with the Gold Miners." *Yediot Aharonot,* December 30, 1981 [Hebrew].

Ghilan, M. "Too Far to the Other Side." *Israel and Palestine Political Report,* October 1984.

Gillette, R. "Uranium Enrichment: Rumors of Israeli Progress with Lasers." *Science,* March 22, 1974.

Girandet, E. "For Many Kenyans, the Road to Riches Is Paved with Politics." *Christian Science Monitor,* March 24, 1986.

Gitelson, S. A. "Israel's African Setback in Perspective." In M. Curtis and S. A. Gitelson (eds.), *Israel in the Third World.* New Brunswick, N.J.: Transaction Books, 1976.

Golan, A. "Filipino President's Wife Came to Israel's Mission—and Charmed Everybody." *Yediot Aharonot,* December 11, 1981 [Hebrew].

Golan, M. "The Answer to Hypocrisy is Hypocrisy." *Haaretz,* November 9, 1977 [Hebrew].

———. *Shimon Peres: A Biography.* New York: St. Martin's, 1982.

Golan, T. "L'Express: 'Israel Removed Advisers from Chad.'" *Maariv,* February 12, 1984 [Hebrew].

Goldfield, S., Hunter, J., and Glickman, P. "Israeli Arms Pipeline Bolsters Rightists." *In These Times,* April 13, 1983. pp. 5–6.

Goodman, H. "A Mutual Dependence." *Jerusalem Post,* May 25, 1984a.

———. "Behind the Emerging Pact with the U.S." *Jerusalem Post,* June 3, 1984b.

Goodsell, J. N. "Bolivia Coup Perils S. American Trend Toward Civilian Rule." *Christian Science Monitor,* July 22, 1980.

Goshko, J. M. "U.S., Israel Discuss Increasing Aid to Third World Countries." *Washington Post,* April 27, 1984a.

———. "Peres Says U.S. Gains by Aiding Israel." *Washington Post,* October 14, 1984b.

Graham, V. "Counter-insurgency Training in Sri Lanka." Associated Press, August 24, 1984.

Granot, O. "U.S.A. Will Integrate Israel in Development of 'Third World.'" *Maariv,* November 16, 1984 [Hebrew].

Green, S. *Taking Sides.* New York: Morrow, 1984.

Gregor, A. J., and Chang, M. H. *The Iron Triangle: A U.S. Security Policy for Northeast Asia.* Palo Alto, Calif.: Hoover Institution Press, 1984.

Greve, F. "Israel Could Fill the Gap if U.S. Latin Aid Funds Cut." *Miami Herald,* May 27, 1984.

Grose, P. *A Changing Israel.* New York: Vintage 1985.

Gurtov, M., and Maghroori, R. *Roots of Failure: United States Policy in the Third World.* Westport, Conn.: Greenwood, 1984.

Gwertzman, B. "Reticence and Foreign Policy." *New York Times,* October 8, 1985.

———. "Singapore Solicited on Contras." *New York Times,* January 23, 1987.

Haaretz. "Botha Will Meet with Rabin." November 7, 1984 [Hebrew].

Hadar, L. "Imelda Marcos: 'Israel Isn't Isolated in the Third World.'" *Al Hamishmar,* December 29, 1981 [Hebrew].

———. "The Beginization of Reagan." *Al Hamishmar,* October 31, 1983 [Hebrew].

References

Halevi, N., and Klinov-Malul, R. *The Economic Development of Israel.* New York: Praeger, 1968.

Hall, R. "Angola Worried by Israelis Next Door." *Observer,* January 23, 1983.

Halliday, F. *Iran: Dictatorship and Development.* New York: Penguin, 1979.

Halliday, F., and Molyneux, M. *The Ethiopian Revolution.* London: Verso Editions, 1981.

Halpern, B. *The Idea of a Jewish State.* Cambridge: Harvard University Press, 1961.

Hamizrahi, Y. "South African Commandoes Raid a 'Congress' Base in Mozambique." *Haaretz,* February 1, 1981 [Hebrew].

Handwerker, H. "Trade with South America." *Haaretz,* January 18, 1983 [Hebrew].

———. "Hundreds in an Anti-apartheid Demonstration in Tel-Aviv." *Haaretz,* November 14, 1985 [Hebrew].

Handwerker, H., and Levy, Y. "Suspect that Two Former Anti-Terror Officers Gave Away Secret Material." *Haaretz,* November 18, 1984 [Hebrew].

Haolam Hazeh. "A Cohen in a Cemetery." September 18, 1957 [Hebrew].

———. "An Israeli Mercenary in Rhodesia." December 26, 1978 [Hebrew].

———. "A Thousand Kisses." April 14, 1982a [Hebrew].

———. "An Israeli Secret Police for the Dictator." December 8, 1982b [Hebrew].

———. "Patriotic Lie." October 26, 1983 [Hebrew].

———. "Hefetz to Stay Here." April 4, 1984 [Hebrew].

———. "Israeli Physicians in South Africa." May 12, 1985a [Hebrew].

———. "Psychiatrists to South Africa." November 27, 1985b [Hebrew].

———. "Israel and the Dictators." February 12, 1986 [Hebrew].

Harel, I. *When Man Rose Against Man: A Reevaluation of the "Lavon Affair."* Jerusalem: Keter, 1982 [Hebrew].

Harkabi, Y. *Nuclear War and Nuclear Peace.* Jerusalem: Israeli Program for Scientific Translations, 1966.

Harsch, J. C. "King Hassan Gets Points, President Reagan Gets None." *Christian Science Monitor,* July 25, 1986.

Heckleman, A. J. *American Volunteers and Israel's War of Independence.* New York: Ktav, 1974.

Hermann, K. "Klaus Barbie: A Killer's Career." *Covert Action Information Bulletin,* no. 25 (Winter 1986).

Hermoni, Y. "An Oval Kibbutz." *Yahad,* May 30, 1986 [Hebrew].

Herzog, H. "Time for Initiatives." *Haaretz,* December 7, 1973 [Hebrew].

Hirschfeld, Y. "Israel's Gulf Option." *Migvan,* June 1985 [Hebrew].

Hoagland, J. "The Waning Era of Haile Selassie." *Washington Post,* May 28, 1972a.

———. *South Africa: Civilizations in Conflict.* Boston: Houghton Mifflin, 1972b.

Hoche, C. "Côte-d'Ivoire: La Fin d'un Miracle." *L'Express,* July 6, 1984.

Hoffman, F. S. "Israel Seen Arming Central America." *Washington Post,* September 30, 1975.

Hoge, W. "Nicaragua Official Warns U.S. on Arms." *New York Times,* August 12, 1979.

———. "Bolivia Regime Looks to Its Friends to Help Foil U.S." *New York Times,* August 6, 1980.

Honey, M. "Israel Dabbles in a Distant War." *Sunday Times,* August 28, 1983.

Hornung, M. "Motorola Ponders Return to S. Africa via Israeli Unit." *Crain's Chicago Business,* January 6, 1986.

Hunter, J. Interview with Francisco Guerra y Guerra. *Israeli Foreign Affairs,* January 1985.

Huntington, S. P. "After Containment: The Future of the Military Establishment." *Annals,* 406 (March 1973), pp. 1–16.

Indian Ocean Newsletter. "Somalia: Siad Barre Courts Mutual Enemies." June 1, 1985.

International Defense and Aid Fund. *The Apartheid War Machine.* London: IDAF, 1980.

Isacowitz, R. "Twinning with a Tyrant." *Jerusalem Post Magazine,* November 9, 1984.

———. "What Price Freedom?" *Jerusalem Post Magazine.* March 8, 1985a.

———. "Germany, Israel to Expand Joint Third World Projects." *Jerusalem Post,* June 15, 1985b.

———. "Israelis Tied to Ciskei Corruption." *Jerusalem Post,* July 31, 1985c.

Isacowitz, R., and Richardson, D. "Aid for South African Blacks Is Likely." *Jerusalem Post,* August 24, 1985.

Israeli, T. "Israelis Love Sought Africa." *Davar,* January 25, 1987 [Hebrew].

Israeli Foreign Affairs. "Sigifredo Ochoa: Israel's Salvadoran Protégé." April 1985a.

———. "Israel Woos Turkey." June 1985b.

———. "Sharon Met Contras in 1982." October 1985c.

Jameson, K. P. "The South American Mix: The Market and the Military." *Coexistence,* 21 (1984). pp. 247–57.

Jerusalem Post. "Honduras to Open Embassy Here." August 24, 1985.

References

Jeune Afrique. "L'étape de Nairobi." December 15, 1982.

Jewish Chronicle. "South Africa 'Close Ties' Denied by Jerusalem." May 7, 1971.

Jones, A. S. *"Washington Times* and its Conservative Niche." *New York Times,* May 26, 1985.

Joseph, B. *Besieged Bedfellows: Israel and the Land of Apartheid.* Westport, Conn.: Greenwood, 1987.

Jouve, E. *Le Tiers-Monde dans la Vie Internationale.* Paris: Berger-Bevrault, 1983.

Kaplan, I., et al. *Area Handbook for Ethiopia.* Washington, D.C.: Government Printing Office, 1971.

Karliner, J. "U.S. Proxy in Latin America?" *Latinamerica Press,* August 4, 1983.

Karny, Y. "Embracing Apartheid in Public." *Davar,* August 31, 1981a [Hebrew].

———. "Remove the Shame." *Yediot Aharonot,* November 26, 1981b [Hebrew].

———. "Mobutu Asked Shamir for Jewish Capital from the U.S." *Yediot Aharonot,* December 1, 1982a [Hebrew].

———. "Israel Is Damaging Its Interests with Its Current Role in Zaire." *Yediot Aharonot,* December 9, 1982b [Hebrew].

———. "Mozambique Believes Israelis Are Training the Underground Fighters." *Yediot Aharonot,* February 22, 1983a [Hebrew].

———. "Dr. Shekel and Mr. Apartheid." *Yediot Aharonot,* March 13, 1983b [Hebrew].

———. "Houphouët-Boigny Following Mobutu?" *Yediot Aharonot,* July 18, 1983c [Hebrew].

———. "The Rise and Fall of the General Who Admired Arik Sharon." *Yediot Aharonot,* April 3, 1984a [Hebrew].

———. "The Price of an Embassy in Jerusalem." *Yediot Aharonot,* April 18, 1984b [Hebrew].

———. "Israelis Helping Nicaragua Rebels." *Haaretz,* August 8, 1985a [Hebrew].

———. "The New President in Guatemala to Investigate Israeli Activity." *Haaretz,* December 10, 1985b [Hebrew].

———. "In the Land of Organized Violence." *Haaretz,* February 7, 1986 [Hebrew].

Kartin, A. "Post-Retirement Advisers." *Hadashot,* May 30, 1984a [Hebrew].

———. "The Arms Map." *Hadashot,* June 8, 1984b [Hebrew].

Kaufman, E. "Israel's Foreign Policy Implementation in Latin America." In

M. Curtis and S. A. Gitelson (eds.), *Israel in the Third World*. New Brunswick, N.J.: Transaction Books, 1976.

———. "The View from Jerusalem." *Washington Quarterly,* Fall 1984.

Kaufman, E., Shapiro, J., and Barromi, J. *Israeli–Latin American Relations*. New Brunswick, N.J.: Transaction Books, 1979.

Kelly, J. "Fears of War Along the Border." *Time,* December 6, 1982.

Kenan, A. "The Dilemma of Israel's Future." *Nation,* December 4, 1982.

———. "Welcome, Prime Minister." *Yediot Aharonot,* October 14, 1984 [Hebrew].

Kessary, G. "Pesah Ben-Or: Business in the Dark." *Maariv,* December 13, 1985 [Hebrew].

Kesse, Z. "A Balance of Powers." *Haaretz,* July 8, 1983 [Hebrew].

Kfir, I. "Mobutu Took Sharon Fishing." *Maariv,* January 19, 1983a [Hebrew].

———. "Mobutu Will Pay for the Division Israel Is Building in Zaire." *Maariv,* June 10, 1983b [Hebrew].

Kinzer, S. "Nicaragua Plans Ties with Peking. *New York Times,* November 17, 1985.

Klare, M. T. *American Arms Supermarket.* Austin: University of Texas Press, 1984.

Klich, I. "The New Carve-up." *South,* April 1982a.

———. "Caribbean Boomerang Returns to Sender." *Guardian* (London), August 27, 1982b.

Klieman, A. *Israeli Arms Sales: Perspectives and Prospects.* Tel-Aviv: Tel-Aviv University, Jaffe Center for Strategic Studies, February 1984.

———. *Israel's Global Reach: Arms Sales as Diplomacy.* Washington, D.C.: Pergamon-Brassey's, 1985.

Koeppel, B. "The Indonesia Reagan Won't Recognize." *Christian Science Monitor,* April 30, 1986.

Krivine, D. "Sri Lanka Braving Hostility to Israel." *Jerusalem Post,* June 1, 1984.

Krivine, D., and Maoz, S. "Economic Pact with South Africa." *Jerusalem Post,* December 20, 1980.

Kuttner, J. "South African Minister Says Eichmann Was a Jew." *Jerusalem Post,* September 7, 1976.

Kwitny, J. "Where Mobutu's Millions Go." *Nation,* May 19, 1984a, pp. 601, 606–610.

———. *Endless Enemies: The Making of an Unfriendly World.* New York: Congdon and Weed, 1984b.

References

LaFeber, W. *Inevitable Revolutions: The United States and Central America.* New York: Norton, 1983.

Landau, D. "Vorster Announces Schemes for Cooperation." *Jerusalem Post,* April 13, 1976.

Langellier, J.-P. "La Visite du Chef de la Diplomatie Sud-Africaine Illustre les Relations Étroites entre les Deux Pays." *Le Monde,* November 6, 1984.

Langley, L. D. *Central America: The Real Stakes.* New York: Crown, 1985.

Lathem, N. "Israeli Spies Aiding in Four CIA Operations." *New York Post,* October 4, 1983.

Latin America Regional Reports: Mexico and Central America RM-83-04. "Transforming the Indian Highlands." May 6, 1983.

Laufer, L. *Israel and the Developing Countries: New Approaches to Cooperation.* New York: Twentieth Century Fund, 1967.

Ledeen, M., and Lewis, W. *Debacle: The American Failure in Iran.* New York: Vintage, 1982.

Lefever, E. W. *Nuclear Arms in the Third World.* Washington, D.C.: Brookings Institution, 1979.

Legum, C. "International Rivalries in the Southern Africa Conflict." In G. M. Carter and P. O'Meara (eds.), *Southern Africa: The Continuing Crisis* (2nd ed.). Bloomington: Indiana University Press, 1982.

Lelyveld, J. *Move Your Shadow.* New York: Times Books, 1985.

Lemieux, J. "Le Rôle d'Israel en Amérique Centrale." *Le Monde Diplomatique,* October 1984.

Leonard, R. *South Africa at War.* Westport, Conn.: Lawrence Hill, 1983.

Levin, B. "Israel's Spies in the U.S." *Newsweek,* September 3, 1979.

Levin, E. "Most Trade with South Africa Held by the Koor Group of Companies." *Haaretz,* February 16, 1981 [Hebrew].

———. "Rassco Negotiating Building 500 Apartments in Haiti." *Haaretz,* December 28, 1983 [Hebrew].

———. "Ciskei, Another Israeli Speculation." *Koteret Rashit,* February 13, 1985 [Hebrew].

Levine, B. "Israel and Bolivia." *Israel & Palestine Political Report,* October 1984.

Levite, T. "I Had Tea with the Russian Spy." *Maariv,* June 14, 1984 [Hebrew].

Lewis, F. "Despair in Guatemala." *New York Times,* October 2, 1981.

Lichtman, M. "Israeli Arms Exports—Good or Bad for the Jews?" *Monitin,* July 1983 [Hebrew].

Lindsay, J. J. "The President Is on Sound Ground." *Newsweek,* January 14, 1985.

Lipkin, D. "The Israelis Come to Ciskei." *Maariv,* June 29, 1984 [Hebrew].

Lipset, S. M. " 'The Socialism of Fools': The Left, the Jews and Israel." *Encounter,* 32, no. 6 (1969), pp. 24–35.

Love, J. *The U.S. Anti-Apartheid Movement.* New York: Praeger, 1985.

Lubrani, U. "Allon in the Shah's Palace." *Davar,* April 20, 1980, pp. 3–4 [Hebrew].

Lusane, C. "Israeli Arms in Central America." *Covert Action,* Winter 1984, pp. 34–37.

Maariv. "Israel and South Africa Support Bolivia." November 11, 1980.

———. "A 'Summit Meeting' in Pretoria." October 31, 1983.

———. "A New Brigade in Zaire Trained by Israelis." January 15, 1986 [Hebrew].

McCartney, J. "Others Said to Supply 'Contras.' " *Philadelphia Inquirer,* May 31, 1984.

McDonald, G. C., et al. *Area Handbook for the Democratic Republic of the Congo (Congo Kinshasa).* Washington, D.C.: Government Printing Office, 1971.

McMahan, J. *Reagan and the World.* London: Pluto Press, 1984.

McManus, D. "Sandinista Foes Turn Toward Israel for Aid." *Los Angeles Times,* April 16, 1984.

Mann, R. "Arms and Rumors from East, West Sweep Ethiopia." *Washington Post,* August 12, 1977.

Mann, R. "Shamir Proposal to Shultz of Cooperation in Aid to Central America." *Maariv,* October 22, 1982 [Hebrew].

———. "Chief Buthelezi's Visit May Soften Criticism About Israel–South Africa Relations." *Maariv,* August 12, 1985 [Hebrew].

Maoz, S. "Strategic Bargain." *Jerusalem Post,* April 4, 1986.

Marcum, J. A. *The Angola Revolution, Vol. II.* Cambridge: MIT Press, 1978.

Marcus, Y. "Sharon's End." *Haaretz,* October 1, 1982 [Hebrew].

Marder, M., and Oberdorfer, D. "How the Powers Combined to Halt an A-Bomb Test." *Philadelphia Inquirer,* September 4, 1977.

Margalit, D. "Eban Is the Chief." *Haaretz,* August 16, 1985 [Hebrew].

Marshall, R. "The Palestinization of Central America." *Israel and Palestine Political Report,* May 1984.

Martin, P. "Israel's War Machine Out of Control?" *Globe and Mail,* March 30, 1985.

Medzini, M. "Reflections on Israel's Asian Policy." In M. Curtis and S. A.

Gitelson (eds.), *Israel and the Third World*. New Brunswick, N.J.: Transaction Books, 1976.

Melman, Y. "Worry About Soviet Spy in S.A. Transmitting Israeli Military Secrets to the USSR." *Haaretz,* January 20, 1983a [Hebrew].

———. "Israel to Supply Skyhawk Planes to Indonesia." *Haaretz,* July 1, 1983b [Hebrew].

———. "S.A. Officer Transmitted to USSR Information About His Military Ties with Israel." *Haaretz,* September 15, 1983c [Hebrew].

———. "Israel Will Continue All Contacts with South Africa." *Davar,* January 18, 1987 [Hebrew].

Mendes-Flohr, P. *A Land of Two Peoples.* New York: Oxford University Press, 1983.

Merari, A. *PLO: Core of World Terror.* Jerusalem: Carta, 1983.

Metrowich, F. R. *South Africa's New Frontiers.* Sandton City, South Africa: Valiant Publishers, 1977.

Meyer, R. "Is It Hard to Understand Botha?" (Letter). *Haaretz,* November 12, 1985.

Meyer, S. M. "A Statistical-risk Model for Forecasting Nuclear Proliferation." In D. L. Birto, M. D. Intriligator, and A. E. Wicks (eds.), *Strategies for Managing Nuclear Proliferation.* Lexington, Mass.: Lexington Books, 1983.

———. *The Dynamics of Nuclear Proliferation.* Chicago: University of Chicago, 1984.

Middleton, D. " 'South Africa Needs More Arms,' Israeli Says." *New York Times,* December 14, 1981.

Miller, J. "Three Nations Widening Nuclear Contacts." *New York Times,* June 28, 1981.

Mintz, F. P. *The Liberty Lobby and the American Right.* Westport, Conn.: Greenwood, 1985.

Molina, R. "Toward Understanding the Political Situation." In S. Jonas, E. McCaughan, and E. S. Martinez (eds.), *Guatemala: Tyranny on Trial.* San Francisco: Synthesis Publications, 1984.

Le Monde. "Le Procès du Mercenaire Rolf Steiner." August 11, 1971a.

———. "Seuls les Israéliens Aident Effectivement les Rebelles Sud-Soudenais." August 12, 1971b.

Moorcraft, P. L. *Africa's Super Power.* Johannesburg: Sygma-Collins, 1981.

Morgan, S. "Israel Selling Fighter Jets, Tanks to Honduras?" *Christian Science Monitor,* December 14, 1982.

Morris, J. "South African's Tel Aviv Stop." *Christian Science Monitor,* September 7, 1977.

————. "Begin Airs Secret Israeli Aid to Kurds as Reminder for Iraqis." *Christian Science Monitor,* October 8, 1980.

Mortimer, R. A. *The Third World Coalition in International Politics.* Boulder, Colo.: Westview Press, 1984.

Moss, R. "When the UN Go Too Far." *Daily Telegraph,* November 5, 1977.

Mufson, S. "Can Pretoria Evade Sanctions? Let us Count the Ways . . ." *Business Week,* September 1, 1986.

Mullen. W. "BBC: 'Firm in Skokie Sold Rhodesia Helicopters.' " *Chicago Tribune,* June 12, 1979.

Murphy, C. "Israeli's Visit Bolsters Ties with South Africa." *Washington Post,* February 8, 1978.

Nakdimon, S. "Raful: We Should Tell the Arabs, 'Are You Having a Hard Time Living with Us?—You Have 22 States.' " *Yediot Aharonot,* August 7, 1983 [Hebrew].

Nation. "Terror Tactics." May 31, 1986.

Neff, W. *Warriors for Jerusalem.* New York: Simon and Shuster, 1984.

Newman, A., and Gouterman, M. "Immigration and Racism: Ethiopian Jews." *Israel and Palestine Political Report,* January 1985.

Newsweek. "The Secret South African–Moroccan Affair." August 20, 1984.

New York Times. "No Curbs Are Seen in Israel's Trade." May 21, 1977.

————. "Leftist Says Salvadoran Troops Are Being Trained by the Israelis." October 10, 1979.

Nyang, S. S. "Palestinians and Human Rights: A Study of African Opinions and Attitudes to the Palestinian Question." Paper presented to the Second United Nations Seminar on the Question of Palestine, 1980.

Nzuwah, M. *The OAU on Southern Africa.* Brunswick, Ohio: King's Court, 1981.

O'Toole, T. "South African Spying Seen as Painful Blow to West." *Washington Post,* June 11, 1984.

Ottaway, D. B. "Savimbi Warns Oil Firms in Angola." *Washington Post,* February 4, 1986.

Parry, R. "President Linked to Secret Aid." *Washington Post,* October 8, 1985.

Peckenham, N. "Bullets and Beans." *Multinational Monitor,* April 1984.

Peled, M. "Israel and the Arms Market." *Haaretz,* August 4, 1985a [Hebrew].

Perera, V. "Uzi Diplomacy." *Mother Jones,* July 1985a, pp. 40–48.

————. "Guatemala: An Israeli Dream Turned Nightmare." *Haaretz,* November 25, 1985b [Hebrew].

References

Peres, S. "The Minister and the Real Danger." *Yediot Aharonot,* September 28, 1979 [Hebrew].

Peres, Z. "20,000 Emigrants in South Africa." *Davar,* December 15, 1981 [Hebrew].

Peri, Y. "The Rise and Fall of Israel's National Consensus." *New Outlook,* May 1983.

————. "Israeli Colonialism in Latin America." *Davar,* July 19, 1985 [Hebrew].

Perlmutter, A. *Politics and the Military in Israel.* London: Frank Cass, 1978.

Perlmutter, A.; Handel, M.; and Bar-Joseph, U. *Two Minutes over Baghdad.* London: Valentine, Mitchell, 1982.

Poindexter, J. Memorandum for the President. The White House, January 17, 1986.

Porat, A. "The Game in Bophuthatswana Ended in 'Explosion.' " *Maariv,* June 9, 1981 [Hebrew].

Pringle, P., and Spigelman, J. *The Nuclear Barons.* New York: Holt, Rinehart and Winston, 1981.

Prister, R. "Beyond India." *Haaretz,* December 20, 1985 [Hebrew].

Pry, P. *Israel's Nuclear Arsenal.* Boulder, Colo.: Westview Press, 1984.

Quinn-Judge, P. "Israel Sells Arms to Asia Discreetly, Even Secretly." *Christian Science Monitor,* December 27, 1982.

————. "The Philippines Brace for a Power Vacuum." *Christian Science Monitor,* February 26, 1985.

Raanan, N. "For Soweto's Children, Perhaps." *Hotam,* February 24, 1984 [Hebrew].

Rand Daily Mail. "Nujoma Accuses Israelis of Training Unita." June 23, 1981.

————. "Israeli Desert Research Expert in SA." October 3, 1984.

Rapoport, L. "Out of the Shadows." *Jerusalem Post,* March 8, 1986.

Reich, B. *Israel: Land of Tradition and Conflict.* Boulder, Colo.: Westview Press, 1985.

Reid, T. R. "House Subcommittee Report Links Rev. Moon to the KCIA." *Washington Post,* August 5, 1977.

Reif, R. "9,000-Year-Old Objects to Be at Israel Museum." *New York Times,* March 21, 1985.

Reppa, R. B., Sr. *Israel and Iran.* New York: Praeger, 1974.

Rettie, J. "Arms and Equipment from Israel Help Fight Against Guerrillas." *Daily Telegraph,* December 29, 1981.

Reuters News Agency. "A U.S. Delegation to Zaire President." March 1, 1983.

————. "Sharon: 'We Sold Arms to Iran So That It Will Beat Iraq.' " May 15, 1984.

————. "Bombing at Israeli Embassy in Singapore." March 19, 1985.

Rhoodie, E. *The Paper Curtain.* Johannesburg: Voportrekkerperse, 1969.

Riding, A. "Nicaragua Says Argentina Will Quit Region." *New York Times,* December 19, 1982.

Rivard, R. "The Little Village in Between." *Newsweek,* January 21, 1985.

Rivkin, A. "Israel and the Afro-American World." *Foreign Affairs,* 37 (1959), pp. 486–95.

————. *Africa and the West: Elements of Free-World Policy.* New York: Praeger, 1962.

Rivlin, B., and Fomerand, J. "Changing Third World Perspectives and Policies Toward Israel." In M. Curtis and S. A. Gitelman (eds.), *Israel in the Third World.* New Brunswick, N.J.: Transaction Books, 1976.

Rodinson, M. *Israel: A Colonial-Settler State.* New York: Monad Press, 1973.

————.*Israel and the Arabs.* New York: Penguin, 1982.

Ronel, E. "Bleeding Hearts in Ciskei." *Al Hamishmar,* April 8, 1985 [Hebrew].

Rosen, E. "Lonely Wolves in the Arms Jungle." *Maariv,* August 12, 1982 [Hebrew].

Rothmyer, K. "Mapping Out Moon's Media Empire. *Columbia Journalism Review,* November-December 1984, pp. 23–71.

Rubenberg, C. A. *Israel and the American National Interest.* Urbana: University of Illinois Press, 1986.

Russell, P. L. *El Salvador in Crisis.* Austin, Tex.: Colorado River Press, 1984.

Sachar, H. M. *Egypt and Israel.* New York: Marek, 1981.

Sagir, D. "Flumin in Ciskei." *Haaretz,* May 12, 1985 [Hebrew].

————. "Swaziland: Long Live the New King." *Haaretz,* May 22, 1986 [Hebrew].

Sale, R. T. "SAVAK: A Feared and Pervasive Force." *Washington Post,* May 9, 1977.

Salpeter, E. "The Bastion and the Terror." *Haaretz,* May 16, 1980a [Hebrew].

————. "The Inevitable Parallels." *Haaretz,* May 18, 1980b [Hebrew].

————. "Mobutu Says Israel—and Means the United States." *Haaretz,* June 11, 1982 [Hebrew].

————. "Is My Enemy's Enemy My Friend?" *Haaretz,* April 6, 1984 [Hebrew].

————. "South Africa as an Inspiration." *Haaretz,* March 2, 1986 [Hebrew].

References

Samet, G. "Business as Usual." *Haaretz,* March 3, 1981 [Hebrew].

———. "On the Weakness Path." *Haaretz,* June 17, 1983a [Hebrew].

———. "Where the United States Needs Israel." *Haaretz,* November 6, 1983b [Hebrew].

Samet, S. "Freddy's Escapades." *Haaretz,* January 30, 1986 [Hebrew].

Schenker, H. "Haggai Erlich: Facing the Ethiopian Tragedy." *New Outlook,* February-March 1985.

Schiff, Z. "Iran Involvement." *Haaretz,* February 12, 1982 [Hebrew].

———. "A President Under the Auspices of the Galil Rifle." *Haaretz,* June 27, 1983a [Hebrew].

———. "Israeli Tracks." *Haaretz,* June 29, 1983b [Hebrew].

Schmidt, S. W. *El Salvador: America's Next Vietnam?* Salisbury, N.C.: Documentary Publications, 1983.

Schumacher, E. "Argentina Buying New Arms." *New York Times,* June 6, 1982.

Schwab, P. *Haile Selassie I: Ethiopia's Lion of Judah.* Chicago: Nelson-Hall, 1979.

Schweitzer, A. "Moshe Dayan: Between Leadership and Loneliness." *Haaretz,* December 12, 1958 [Hebrew].

———. "The Hidden Ally." *Haaretz,* June 11, 1984 [Hebrew].

———. "Why South Africa?" *Haaretz,* August 6, 1985a [Hebrew].

———. "Two Faces of Alienation." *Haaretz,* September 23, 1985b [Hebrew].

Sciolino, E. "Documents Detail Israeli Missile Deal with the Shah." *New York Times,* April 1, 1986a.

———. "Report Shows U.S. Was Outvoted in the U.N. Through Most of 1985." *New York Times,* July 4, 1986b.

Segal, M. "Public Faces." *Jerusalem Post,* November 30, 1984.

Segev, S. *The Iranian Triangle.* Tel-Aviv: Maariv, 1981 [Hebrew].

———. "Israel's Representatives are Quarreling in Zaire." *Maariv,* December 23, 1983 [Hebrew].

———. "The Israeli Ambassador Went Underground." *Maariv,* February 17, 1984 [Hebrew].

Segev, T. "Indonesia, Malaysia, Morocco: The Secret Customer." *Koteret Rashit,* April 4, 1984 [Hebrew].

Shackley, T. *The Third Option: An American View of Counterinsurgency Operations.* New York. Reader's Digest Press, 1981.

Shahak-Bufman, N. "Yitzhak Bahar: Israel's Defense Exports." *Monitin,* January 26, 1986 [Hebrew].

Sharett, M. *Personal Diary.* Tel-Aviv: Maariv, 1978 [Hebrew].

Sharif, R. "Latin America and the Arab-Israeli Conflict." *Journal of Palestine Studies,* 7, no. 1 (1977), pp. 98–122.

Sharon, A. "Iran-Israel-U.S." *Maariv,* November 28, 1986 [Hebrew].

Shaw, T. M., and Leppan, E. "South Africa: White Power and the Regional Military-Industrial Complex." In O. Aluko and T. M. Shaw (eds.), *Southern Africa in the 1980s.* London: Allen and Unwin, 1985.

Shemi, D. "The Senior Ones Stay in the Military; They Have Nowhere to Go." *Haolam Hazeh,* June 11, 1986 [Hebrew].

Shepherd, N. "Israel's Uneasy Connections in Africa." *New York Times,* February 27, 1977.

Shimshi, Z. "The Good Robber." *Haaretz,* October 31, 1985 [Hebrew].

Shipler, D. K. "After Iran, Israel Seeks a Role as Strategic U.S. Staging Area." *New York Times,* February 3, 1980.

———. "Israel Sees Soviet Gain as U.S. Shuns Iran." *New York Times,* May 29, 1982.

———. "Israel Is Quietly Expanding Links with Nations Throughout Africa." *New York Times,* August 21, 1983.

———. "Israel's Denials It Knew of Diversion of Arms-sale Profits to Contras Are Questioned by U.S. Officials." *New York Times,* December 5, 1986.

Shohat, O. "A Paper Trap." *Haaretz,* April 19, 1985 [Hebrew].

SIAG (Guatemalan Information and Analysis Service). "The Guatemalan Connection." Weekly Letter no. 32, September 14, 1984.

Siegel, J. "Shamir Meets Turkish MPs." *Jerusalem Post,* September 21, 1984.

Silver, E. "Israel Renews African Links." *Observer,* December 6, 1981.

Simon, B. CBS Television News, February 16, 1983.

Simon, J.-M. *"Civil Patrols in Guatemala."* New York: Americas Watch, 1986.

SIPRI (Stockholm International Peace Research Institute). *SIPRI Yearbook 1975.* Cambridge: MIT Press, 1975.

———. *World Armaments and Disarmament, SIPRI Yearbook 1978.* London: Taylor and Francis, 1978.

———. *SIPRI Yearbook 1981.* London: Taylor and Francis, 1981.

Slater, L. *The Pledge.* New York: Simon and Shuster, 1970.

Slucki, S. "A Torture Ship at the Statue of Liberty." *Al Hamishmar,* July 11, 1986 [Hebrew].

Smith, G. "The Legacy of Monroe's Doctrine." *New York Times Magazine,* September 9, 1984.

References

Smith, T. "An Arab Campaign Is Damaging Israel's Standing in Black Africa." *New York Times,* January 12, 1973.

Smith, T. "Shared View on Mideast." *New York Times,* November 14, 1983.

Smol. "Israel and Latin America: The Second Lebanon War." June 1984 [Hebrew].

Smolowe, J. "The Ethnic Fires Burn Again." *Newsweek,* August 27, 1984.

Somoza, A. *Nicaragua Betrayed.* Belmont, Mass.: Western Islands, 1980.

South Africa Digest. "Mutual Goodwill Strengthened." April 30, 1976.

South Africa, Republic of. *South Africa 1984, Official Yearbook of the Republic of South Africa.* Johannesburg, 1984.

Spector, L. S. *Nuclear Proliferation Today.* New York: Vintage, 1984.

———. "Proliferation: The Silent Spread." *Foreign Policy,* Spring 1985a, pp. 53–78.

———. *The New Nuclear Nations.* New York: Vintage, 1985b.

Star. "Vorster on Israeli-SA Pact: 'Alliance of Twelve in Sight.' " April 24, 1976.

Sterling, C. *The Terror Network.* New York: Holt, Rinehart and Winston, 1981.

Steven, S. *The Spymasters of Israel.* New York: Macmillan, 1980.

Steward, A. *The World, the West, and Pretoria.* New York: McKay, 1977.

Stone, P. H. "Muldergate on Madison Avenue." *Nation,* April 14, 1979.

Strauch, E. "Ministers from El Salvador to Meet Begin Today." *Yediot Aharonot,* August 3, 1983 [Hebrew].

Streek, B. "Israel and Taiwan Woo SA Homelands." *Guardian,* October 15, 1983.

Stressler, N. "Israel Ranks Second in South Africa Investments." *Haaretz,* June 20, 1984 [Hebrew].

Subasinghe, D. R. "Rest of Third World Can Profit from Sri Lanka's Example." *Wall Street Journal,* August 22, 1983.

Sulzberger, C. L. "Strange Nonalliance." *New York Times,* April 30, 1971.

Tamarkin, M. "Israeli-South African Relations and the Strategy of Israeli Foreign Policy. *Skira Hodshit,* December 1980 [Hebrew].

Taubman, P. "Israel Said to Ship Arms to Argentina." *New York Times,* May 27, 1982.

———. "Israel Said to Aid Latin Aims of U.S." *New York Times,* July 21, 1983.

———. "Nicaragua Rebels Reported to Raise Millions in Gifts." *New York Times,* September 9, 1985a.

———. "Letting Citizens Give Rebels Aid Was U.S. Policy." *New York Times,* September 11, 1985b.

Tavori, A. "The South African Hypocrisy Connection." *Davar,* April 1, 1986 [Hebrew].

Taylor, D. "Israel–South Africa Nuclear Link Exposed." *Middle East,* April 1981.

Temkin, A. "Israel Got $38 Billion in Grants." *Jerusalem Post,* October 5, 1985.

Terrill, W. A. "South Africa Arms Sales and the Strengthening of Apartheid." *Africa Today,* 31, no. 2 (1984), pp. 3–14.

Thompson, W. S. *Ghana's Foreign Policy 1957–1966.* Princeton: Princeton University Press, 1969.

Time. "An Israeli Connection?" May 7, 1984a.

———. "Bomblets Away." August 27, 1984b.

Toase, F. "The South African Army: The Campaign in South West Africa–Namibia Since 1966." In I. F. Beckett and J. Pimlott (eds.), *Armed Forces and Modern Counter-Insurgency.* New York: St. Martin's, 1985.

Toriello, C. T. "On the Role of the United States and Israel." In S. Jonas, E. McCaughan, and E. S. Martinez (eds.), *Guatemala: Tyranny on Trial.* San Francisco: Synthesis Publications, 1984.

Tzur, Y. "Israeli Aids Pinochet in Producing Planes and Cluster-bombs." *Al Hamishmar,* June 10, 1984.

Ungar, S. J. "South Africa's Lobbyists." *New York Times Magazine,* October 13, 1985.

United Nations Centre Against Apartheid, Special Report. "Relations Between Israel and South Africa." No. 5-77. February 1977.

———. General Assembly Supplement no. 22A (A/34/22/Add.1). New York, 1980.

UPI (United Press International). "Israel Hoping to Double Its Arms Sales." August 17, 1981.

———. "South Africa Puts Wall on Zimbabwe Border." March 20, 1985.

USGAO (United States General Accounting Office). *U.S. Assistance to the State of Israel.* Washington, D.C., June 24, 1983.

U.S. House of Representatives, Committee on International Relations. *Investigation of Korean-American Relations.* Appendixes to the Report (vol. 2). Washington, D.C.: Government Printing Office, 1978.

Uys, S. "The Upswelling of Black Anger That Must Now Bring Apartheid to Its Apocalypse." *Guardian,* May 23, 1986.

Vincour, J. "A Republic of Fear." *New York Times Magazine,* September 23, 1984.

Waines, D. *The Unholy War: Israel and Palestine 1897–1971.* Montreal: Chateau Books, 1971.

References

Walter, J. "Kalashnikov's Brother." *Maariv,* May 4, 1984 [Hebrew].

Walters, R. *South Africa and the Bomb: Responsibility and Deterrence.* Trenton, N.J.: Africa World Press, 1986.

Waltz, K. N. "The Spread of Nuclear Weapons: More May Be Better." In J. A. Schear (ed.), *Nuclear Weapons Proliferation and Nuclear Risk.* New York: St. Martin's, 1984.

Watson, R. "The Friends of Mr. Botha." *Newsweek,* September 2, 1985.

Weil, M. "Reagan Meets Zulu Leader." *Washington Post.* February 5, 1985.

Weinraub, B. "U.S. Is Considering Having Asians Aid Nicaraguan Rebels." *New York Times,* March 6, 1985.

Weir, A., and Bloch, J. "Mossad's Secret Rivals." *Middle East,* December 1981.

Weisfelder, R. "Lesotho: Changing Patterns of Dependence." In G. M. Carter and P. O'Meara (eds.), *Southern Africa: The Continuing Crisis* (2nd ed.). Bloomington: Indiana University Press, 1982.

Weisman, S. R. "India Shows Impatience with Sri Lanka Talks." *New York Times,* December 27, 1985.

Wills, R. J. "Liberian Rejects U.S. Linkage of Aid and Rights." *New York Times,* December 23, 1985.

Wilmshurst, M. J. "Reforming the Non-proliferation System in the 1980s." In J. Simpson and A. G. McGrew (eds.), *The International Nuclear Non-Proliferation System.* London, 1984.

Wilson, G. C. "U.S. Is Fronting Israeli Sale of Jets to Indonesia." *Washington Post,* October 5, 1979.

Windhoek Advertiser. "Israel to Aid Namibia." April 22, 1985.

Winston, E. A. "Worth Five CIAs." *Newsweek,* January 2, 1985.

Winter, G. *Inside BOSS.* New York: Penguin, 1981.

Woodward, R. "CIA Sought Third-Country Contra Aid." *Washington Post,* May 19, 1984.

Woodward, R. L., Jr. *Central America: A Nation Divided.* New York: Oxford University Press, 1985.

Wright, C. "A Back Door to War." *New Statesman,* August 5, 1983.

Wrong, D. "After Afghanistan." *Dissent,* Spring 1980.

Yediot Aharonot. "Arafat's Picture Will Not Be Shown in Argentina." March 13, 1983a [Hebrew].

———. "Chad Rebels: Israeli Military Aiding Government." August 14, 1983b [Hebrew].

———. "Business as Usual in South Africa." November 20, 1984 [Hebrew].

———. "An Israeli Company to Build 3000 Apartments in Ciskei." May 13, 1985 [Hebrew].

Yefet, Z. "Israeli Entrepreneurs in Ciskei." *Haaretz,* May 9, 1986 [Hebrew].

Yehezkeli, Z. "The 'Unknown' Basketball Team That Played in South Africa —from Hapoel Beit-Zait." *Yediot Aharonot,* May 24, 1983 [Hebrew].

Yemma, J. "Israeli Guns for Worldwide Arms Market." *Christian Science Monitor,* December 27, 1982.

Young, C., and Turner, T. *The Rise and Decline of the Zairian State.* Madison: University of Wisconsin Press, 1985.

Zak, M. "Aid to the Kurds—Without a Defense Treaty." *Maariv,* October 1, 1980 [Hebrew].

——. "Talking to Hussein." *Jerusalem Post,* May 4, 1985.

——. "Following the Summit." *Maariv,* July 25, 1986 [Hebrew].

Zayad, K. "Uzan Reveals: The Rabin Government Signed Many Agreements with Morocco." *Al Hamishmar,* May 25, 1984 [Hebrew].

Zeiger, Y. "The Danger of Economic Recovery." *Maariv,* October 23, 1984a [Hebrew].

——. "The Americans Buy Us at Bargain Prices." *Hadashot,* October 31, 1984b [Hebrew].

Zelnick, C. R. "U.S.-Israeli Relations after the Pollard Affair." *Christian Science Monitor,* December 27, 1985.

Index

Abdullah ibn Hussein, King, 4
Addis Ababa Agreement on Southern
    Sudan (1972), 48
Afghanistan, 178
    Israeli involvement in, 32–33, 204
Afitra company, 139
Afrati, Amikam, 66
Africa:
    decolonization of, 38, 64
    Israeli involvement in:
        CIA, cooperation with, 40–41
        civilian-aid program, 39
        conservative regimes, focus on, 74–75
        diplomatic decline, 41, 42, 43–44
        diplomatic status in 1987, 73–74
        France, cooperation with, 40, 43
        liberation movements, 44
        military training program, 39
        newly independent countries, 39
        pattern of, 73
        West as benefactor of, 40, 72
    Taiwan's agricultural programs, 214
    see also specific countries
African National Congress (ANC), 113,
    122, 128, 170
Agency for International Development
    (AID), 204
Agosti, Brig. Gen. Orlando, 101
Agro-Carmel company, 144
Aguilar, Joaquín Antonio, 87
Alfonsín, Raúl, 103
Algeria, 8, 39, 44
    war of independence, 44–45
Algerian National Liberation Front, 45
Alison, Gen. Gray, 70
Allende, Salvador, 98
Allon, Gen. Yigal, 10, 37, 90, 113

Aloni, Shulamit, 87
Alvárez Martínez, Gen. Gustavo, 89
Amin, Col. Idi, 61–62
Amnesty International, 31, 55
Anaya, Adm. Jorge Isaac, 101
ANC: *see* African National Congress
Angola, 43, 214
    Israeli involvement in, 64–65, 73, 204
    South Africa's war against, 65, 121, 123
ANSESAL death squads (El Salvador), 86
anti-Semitism:
    right-wing network and, 219
    South Africa–Israel alliance and, 161
Anyanya rebel movement (Sudan), 48
apartheid:
    crisis of the 1980s, Israeli reaction to,
        166–67
        "business as usual," 168
        Buthelezi, support for, 170–71
        condemnation of apartheid, 171–73
        political assessments, 167–68
        political support for South Africa, 173
        popular protests, 168–69
        public and covert policies, 168
        state of emergency, advice re, 173
        "test case" perspective, 170
    destruction of, Israeli fears re, 167, 169,
        174
    in Israel, 112, 239
    Israeli public opinion on, 235–36
    Israeli support for, 114–15, 145, 146–47
    Zionism, similarity to, 147
Aquino, Corazón, 31
Arab-Israeli War of 1948, 3–4
    Nicaragua's role in, 92
Arab-Israeli War of 1967, 41, 43
    South Africa's assessment of, 160–61

Index

Index

Index

India, 51, 195
  Israel, policy toward, 23–24
Indonesia, 31–32
Inkatha (Zulu movement), 170–71
Inonu, Ismet, 16
International Atomic Energy Agency
  (IAEA), 132
International Fellowship of Reconciliation,
  84
International Institute for Development
  Cooperation and Labor Studies
  (Israel), 39
International Middle East Alliance, 216
International Monetary Fund, 58, 61
International Security Council, 216–17
Iran, 198, 199
  Israel, relations with:
    diplomatic, 9–11
    Iran-Iraq war and, 12–15
    Islamic revolution and, 9, 12, 15–16
    military cooperation, 11–12, 13–14
    trade, 12
  Israeli strategy re, 14–16
  Kurdish rebellion and, 19
  as regional superpower, 195
  U.S. arms sales to, 13–14
  Yemeni civil war, 17, 18
Iran-contra affair, xiv, 14, 95–96, 204–5
Iran-Iraq war, 12–15
Iraq, 4, 5, 15
  Kurds in, 18, 19
Iscor (South African Iron and Steel Corp.),
  138–39
Iskoor Steel Services, 138–39
Israel:
  African liberation movements,
    contribution to, 44
  apartheid in, 112, 239
  censorship, journalists' methods for
    dealing with, 116–17
  defeats of allies, consequences of, 246–47
  Defense Ministry, 27, 81, 120, 130
  East Asia strategy, 22–24
  economy of, 28, 192–95
  Foreign Ministry, x, 90, 142
  foreign policy, levels of activity in, xiii
  foreign wars, involvement in, 183–84,
    231–33; see also mercenaries, Israeli
  founding of, 3–4
  human rights policy, 78
  international legitimacy of, 247
  isolation from the international
    community, 180

Labor governments, 228–29
"lost colonies," obsession with, 182
the masses, fear of, 240
Middle East settlement plan, 5
as militarized nation, 180–81
morality issues, avoidance of, 236–38
national unity government, 229
nuclear weapons development, 129–31
  opposition within Israel, 131
  specific needs of Israel, 134, 136
  survival strategy, role in, 182–83
  testing, 131
  see also nuclear program under South
    Africa–Israel alliance
as oppressor nation, 238–39, 248
Palestinians, reduction in number of, 4
as pariah country, 208–10, 213, 247
political cynicism in, 237–38
right-wing admiration of, 184, 218–22
survival strategy, 180–84, 245–46; see
  also Third World War
terrorism, handling of, 221
"tough" self-image of Israelis, 238
victims, popular attitudes toward, 239
war as way of life, 240
worldview, 233, 235–36, 240–41
  248
  U.S. worldview and, 205–7
Zionism as basis for supporting
  reactionary regimes, 244–45,
  248
see also kibbutzim; Mossad; periphery
  strategy; SHABAK; South
  Africa–Israel alliance; Israel
  subheadings throughout
Israel Chamber Ensemble, 154
Israel Discount Bank, 139
Israeli Aircraft Industries, 118, 122, 124
Israeli Defense Force (IDF), 119, 121, 196,
  218
Israeli Philharmonic Orchestra, 154
Israel National Council for Research and
  Development, 152
Israel–South Africa Chamber of
  Commerce, 139, 145
Israel–South Africa Friendship League,
  115
Italy, 35, 56, 82, 119
Ivory Coast, 68
  Israel, relations with, 39, 40, 42, 69, 72,
    73, 163
  South Africa, relations with, 69
Ivri, Gen. David, 89, 99

Index

Index

SHABAK (Israeli internal security), 30, 34, 35, 127
Shahal, Moshe, 172
Shamir, Yitzhak:
  Iran, 14–15
  Israel as U.S. military proxy, 203
  Ivory Coast, 69
  Japan visit, 223–24
  Kenya, 67
  Liberia, 70
  South Africa, 113, 169, 172
  Swaziland, 71
  Turkey, 17
  Zaire, 57, 58, 61
Sharett, Moshe, 20, 110, 227
Sharon, Ariel:
  Bantustans, 142
  Central African Republic, 71
  Chad, 68
  contras, 93
  Honduras, 89
  Iran, 12, 13, 14
  Israel as U.S. strategic asset, 195
  Israel as U.S. military proxy, 204
  Ivory Coast, 69
  Liberia, 70
  Namibia, 146
  South Africa, 118, 127, 156, 173
  Soviet expansionism, 196
  U.S.-Israeli strategic cooperation, 191
  U.S. military assistance, 197
  Zaire, 56, 60, 61
Sharon, Emanuel, 168
Shemtov, Victor, 87
Shilansky, Dov, 142
Shostak, Eliezer, 115
Shultz, George P., 203, 221
Sierra Leone, 42
Siles Zuazo, Hernán, 104
Singapore, 213
  Israel, relations with, 24–26
Sixishe, Desmond, 145
Smith, Ian, 62, 199
Smuts, Gen. Jan C., 109
social Darwinism, 240
Solarz, Stephen, 31, 47, 58
Somalia, 39, 74
Somoza Debayle, Anastasio, xi, xiii, 76, 90–91, 104, 199, 213
Somoza García, Anastasio, 90, 92
Soustelle, Jacques, 219–20, 230
South Africa:
  Angola, war against, 65, 121, 123

Argentina, relations with, 102, 212
arms industry, 119
Bantustan policy, 140–41
Bolivia, relations with, 105
Chile, relations with, 212
Guatemala, relations with, 82
intelligence organizations, 112, 126
Iran, arms shipments to, 13
isolation, 163–64
Israeli contribution to African liberation movements, 44
Ivory Coast, relations with, 69
Malawi, relations with, 72
"Middle Power" organizations, 211–12
Morocco, relations with, 217–18
Mozambique, war against, 65, 121
Namibia, control of, 38, 121, 145–46
neighboring countries, attacks on, 65, 121–22, 123
Nicaragua, relations with, 90
nuclear weapons development, 132–33; see also nuclear program under South Africa–Israel alliance
Paraguay, relations with, 103, 212
as pariah country, 208–10, 211–12, 213
as regional superpower, 195
sanctions and embargoes against, 110, 117–18, 138, 173–74
Somalia, relations with, 74
Sri Lanka, relations with, 35
Taiwan, relations with, 137, 145, 146, 160
Third World coalition, exclusion from, 177, 178
torture in prisons, 162–63
Zaire, relations with, 60
see also apartheid
South Africa–Israel alliance, 43, 245
  academic exchanges, 152–53
  ambassadors, exchange of, 112
  anti-Semitism and, 161
  athletic exchanges, 153–54
  Bantustans and, 140–45, 154
  chronology of, 111
  comparison with other relationships, 157–58
  condemnation of, international, 114, 159, 163
  conservative regimes, support for, 74, 163
  consulates, establishment of, 110
  cultural exchanges, 154

Index

Index

ABOUT THE AUTHOR

Benjamin Beit-Hallahmi was trained as a clinical psychologist and teaches at the University of Haifa. He has published extensively in academic psychology and his articles have appeared in numerous periodicals. He is currently working on a history of Zionism.